Uncertain Perceptions

Uncertain Perceptions

U.S. Cold War Crisis Decision Making

Robert B. McCalla

Ann Arbor

THE UNIVERSITY OF MICHIGAN PRESS

Copyright © by the University of Michigan 1992
All rights reserved
Published in the United States of America by
The University of Michigan Press
Manufactured in the United States of America

1995   1994   1993   1992   4   3   2   1

Library of Congress Cataloging-in-Publication Data

McCalla, Robert B., 1959–
    Uncertain perceptions : U.S. Cold War crisis decision making /
    Robert B. McCalla.
        p.   cm.
    Includes bibliographical references and index.
    ISBN 0-472-10228-1
    1. United States—Foreign relations—Soviet Union—Decision
making.   2. Soviet Union—Foreign relations—United States—Decision
making.   3. United States—Foreign relations—1945–1989—Decision
making.   4. Cold War—Decision making.   5. Social perception.
I. Title.
E183.8.S65M374   1992
327.73047—dc20   92-11867
                                                              CIP

Acknowledgments

This book is a substantially revised version of my Ph.D. dissertation. Robert Axelrod and Harold K. Jacobson, as co-chairs of my dissertation committee at the University of Michigan, provided much-appreciated guidance and support. Particular thanks are due to Robert Axelrod, who provided invaluable encouragement and support as advisor and teacher during my five years at Ann Arbor. Ellen J. Gordon assisted greatly in reading, and patiently rereading, many early drafts, a task taken up by my colleague David Tarr as the manuscript made the transition from dissertation to book. Cynthia P. Williams provided valuable assistance in reading the final drafts for those inevitable lapses in spelling and grammar that escaped the author, the editor, and the spell-checker. Darren Hawkins carefully proofread the entire manuscript. A final thanks goes to Randolph M. Siverson who, many years ago, told an eager high school student that he could, if he really wanted to, take his college course on "International Relations" to see if he really was interested in the subject matter. I have not been disappointed since.

Contents

Chapter

1. Introduction 1

2. Case Histories 31

3. The View from the Top: The Origins of Crises 67

4. "He can't do that to me!" 85

5. Crises and Their Origins 111

6. Crises and Their Termination 145

7. The Search for Acceptable Outcomes 171

8. Conclusions 189

Bibliography 207

Index 221

CHAPTER 1

Introduction

There is an ever-growing body of literature on crises that approaches the topic from a number of different perspectives. This interest in crises is not new, but the topic has received considerable attention in the past decade. Fear of nuclear war has driven much of this interest, as have new insights into the psychology of decision making. An additional element that has spurred new interest in crisis decision making has been the release of further information concerning American decision making during the Cuban Missile Crisis of 1962. These new details have called into question some of the conventional wisdom concerning crises, and this has led to new research on American foreign policy crises in particular, and crises in general. This research has shown the importance of perceptions and decision-making pathologies in the conduct and outcome of crises. The approach here will be to develop a model of perceptions and crisis decision making and apply it to a specific set of case studies drawn from the history of U.S.-Soviet relations in the post–World War II era. By adopting an approach that identifies misperceptions based on their origins, a new insight into the dynamics of crises will be gained. With the ending of the Cold War, the intensity of the East-West conflict has subsided, affording analysts the opportunity to examine in new light the most significant U.S.-Soviet post–World War II crises.

The role of perception and misperception in international relations is an important one, and during crises it takes on even more importance. The ways in which decision makers view events and change their minds about an opponent's behavior can have an important impact on the origin, duration, and termination of a crisis. The initial views that a decision maker has about events will be affected by new information made available to the decision maker in the course of the crisis. The degree of change in those views will also be affected by the source of those initial views. As more has become known about crises through the work of historians and political scientists, the importance of perceptions has become even clearer, and this study is an effort to add to our understanding of the role of misperceptions in crises.[1]

---

1. The research on crises is extensive, requiring that some selectivity be employed in listing references to the existing literature. Some of the most useful recent works that deal with

In order to look at the role of misperception in U.S. crisis decision making during the Cold War, five crises that involved the Soviet Union will be carefully examined to test five propositions that will be advanced in later chapters. To see in condensed form many of the concepts and arguments that will be advanced here, let us look at a "crisis" that occurred in the fall of 1979—the Cuban brigade crisis. In historical retrospect, the crisis is almost comical—yet it illustrates some important elements of crises that will be taken up here: the role of initial impressions, changing flows of information, and changing perceptions based on that information.

The Dynamics of Misperception: An Example

In the late summer and fall of 1979, the Carter administration faced what appeared to be a major crisis in U.S.-Soviet relations.[2] In July, U.S. intelligence sources began to notice signs of Soviet military activity in Cuba, and initial suspicions were that this might be a Soviet combat brigade. If true, this could have been a violation of the assurances given the United States by the Soviet Union, following the 1962 Cuban Missile Crisis, concerning the stationing of Soviet troops in Cuba. The information about these troops was circulated within the intelligence community, prompting a long debate about its significance. After some time, it was concluded that the so-called brigade did not pose a threat because of its small size and composition. Further investigation suggested that it was likely that the brigade had been in Cuba since 1976 and it quite possibly was descended from troops that had been stationed there during the 1962 crisis.[3]

---

crises as an international phenomenon include Michael Brecher and Jonathan Wilkenfeld, *Crisis, Conflict, and Instability* (Oxford: Pergamon, 1989); Michael Brecher, ed., *Studies in Crisis Behavior* (New Brunswick, N.J.: Transaction, 1979); Daniel Frei, ed., *Managing International Crises* (Beverly Hills, Calif.: Sage, 1982); and Michael Brecher and Patrick James, *Crisis and Change in World Politics* (Boulder, Colo.: Westview Press, 1986). These works have extensive bibliographies. Works that deal with crises as foreign policy problems include Richard Ned Lebow, *Between Peace and War: The Nature of International Crisis* (Baltimore: Johns Hopkins University Press, 1981); Gilbert R. Winham, ed., *New Issues in International Crisis Management* (Boulder, Colo.: Westview Press, 1988); and Jonathan M. Roberts, *Decision-Making during International Crises* (New York: St. Martin's Press, 1988). These have extensive bibliographies as well.

2. This account is drawn primarily from Raymond L. Garthoff, *Detente and Confrontation: American-Soviet Relations from Nixon to Reagan* (Washington, D.C.: Brookings, 1985), 828–48. See also Richard E. Neustadt and Ernest R. May, *Thinking in Time: The Uses of History for Decision-Makers* (New York: Free Press, 1986), 91–96; Fen Osler Hampson, "The Divided Decision-Maker: American Domestic Politics and the Cuban Crises," *International Security* 9, no. 3 (Winter 1984–85): 130–65; and Gloria Duffy, "Crisis Mangling and the Cuban Brigade," *International Security* 8, no. 1 (Summer 1983): 67–87.

3. Garthoff, *Detente and Confrontation*, 829, 839. See also Jimmy Carter, *Keeping Faith* (New York: Bantam, 1982), 262–65.

Even though the intelligence community had decided that these troops were of little concern, news of these deliberations eventually leaked to Congress and the press. Because of these leaks, pressure on the Carter administration to take action on the brigade grew. Public pressure increased significantly when Senator Frank Church of Idaho revealed the information about these forces on 30 August 1979. The timing of the revelation had little to do with Cuba or the Soviet Union, but more to do with the fact that Church was in the midst of a tough reelection campaign. One aspect of his campaign was to show that Church, who had met with Cuban leader Fidel Castro earlier that year, was indeed tough on national security issues—including the spread of communism in this hemisphere. In his news conference announcing this information, Church demanded that the Carter administration put a stop to Russian "penetration" of this hemisphere. Following this announcement, public pressure increased for President Carter to "do something" about the threat posed by the combat brigade. A storm of controversy arose with these revelations, with many taking at face value Church's accusations about the combat brigade in Cuba. Many took advantage of this issue to criticize the Carter administration and its commitment to being tough on the Soviets.

The initial response of the Carter administration was low-key. State Department spokesman Hodding Carter announced that the intelligence services had confirmed the existence of such a combat brigade and that the Soviet Union had been asked to explain. He gave little sense of urgency. Later, the tone of the administration's response changed, as Secretary of State Cyrus Vance announced that this was "a very serious matter" and that he would "not be satisfied with the maintenance of the status quo."[4] This was, however, not enough for administration critics, and pressure continued to increase. Speaking about the issue for the first time on 7 September, President Carter first tried to calm the waters by playing down the significance of the brigade. He noted that the brigade had been in Cuba for quite some time and suggested that it was of little military significance. Following this, in the same speech, he declared that the brigade was "a very serious matter and that this status quo is not acceptable."[5] Senator Henry Jackson, a constant critic of détente and the Soviet Union, seized on this opportunity to attack the Carter administration for its weakness on defense and for not challenging the Soviet Union. This attack became a rallying point for critics of the Soviet Union, the Strategic Arms Limitation Talks (SALT), Cuba, and détente and any others who had complaints about the Carter administration's foreign policy.

---

4. "Soviet Combat Troops in Cuba," U.S. Department of State statement, 31 August 1979, and "News Conference of September 5," *Department of State Bulletin* 79 (October 1979): 14–15, 63, quoted in Garthoff, *Detente and Confrontation*, 829.

5. "Soviet Combat Troops in Cuba," President Carter's remarks to reporters, 7 September 1979, *Public Papers of the Presidents of the United States: Jimmy Carter, 1979* (Washington, D.C.: GPO, 1979), 1602.

The public discussion and debate about the combat brigade continued for a number of weeks, with charges and countercharges of weakness and duplicity being traded by the administration and its critics. Surprisingly, the debate appeared to have had little serious consequence for relations with the Soviet Union. For the first two weeks, there was no discussion with the Soviet Union about the issue of the brigade nor were there any serious actions taken to communicate U.S. displeasure or concerns. It seemed as if many were ignoring the role played by the Soviets in this. That changed, however, when Senator Church announced that U.S.-Soviet relations were at stake as a result of the combat brigade and that he, as chairman of the Foreign Relations Committee, was postponing the SALT II hearings pending a satisfactory resolution of the issue. At this point, tensions within the government escalated, and there was increased pressure to bring this to a conclusion. This crisis in U.S.-Soviet relations was not resolved until the Soviet Union gave assurances that the brigade was there only in a training function and that there were no plans to change its status.[6] President Carter announced on 1 October 1979 that "[t]hese assurances have been given to me from the highest level of the Soviet Government" and that he had "concluded that the brigade issue is certainly no reason for a return to the cold war."[7] As time went on and further research was conducted, it became increasingly clear that the intelligence agencies of the United States had known about the presence of the Soviet troops for many years and had not deemed them to be a threat. Increased surveillance of the island confirmed that the forces were there only in a training function, and after a month of public debate and statements, the crisis died down. For some, this crisis was seen as just a political ploy, while for others there was serious concern about the brigade and the threat that it seemed to pose to the hemisphere. Coming as it did at a time of increased Soviet-Cuban adventurism in Africa and Soviet support for various extremist groups in Central America, many were quite willing to see this as a logical extension of the Soviet-Cuban threat. These concerns decreased, however, as more information about the brigade became available.

The debate about this brigade ended as abruptly as it had started and on as confused a level. There was no question about the existence of the Soviet troops: they were there on the island. The real question was what they were doing there. As more effort was put into examining the question, it became clear that the troops had been there for a number of years and that they were

---

6. This was for the most part a one-sided crisis. Garthoff notes that the first two weeks of the crisis occurred without the active involvement of the Soviet Union. *Detente and Confrontation*, 837. A crisis need not be two sided: all that is needed is for one side to feel there is a crisis. The definition of crisis used in this study will be discussed later.

7. Carter, "Address to the Nation on Soviet Combat Troops in Cuba and the Strategic Arms Limitation Treaty," *Public Papers of the Presidents*, 1804–5.

actually doing what they said they were doing: training Cuban soldiers. Given these facts, the following question arises: If the Soviet forces had been on the island since 1962, and U.S. intelligence services were aware of their presence and did not consider them a threat, why was there such a fuss? The answer is seemingly trite: these forces led to a crisis because someone *thought* they were a combat brigade and, as a result, thought they were a threat to national security.[8] It did not matter that the U.S. government had known about these forces for years or that it was subsequently confirmed that they did not have any combat role—there was still a crisis. What mattered was that someone felt there was a threat—despite the fact that none existed. The dynamics of this crisis illuminate clearly the outlines of the model to be presented later. New information became available to decision makers that suggested a particular conclusion: Soviet combat troops were in Cuba. Decision makers were faced with a choice: to accept that interpretation, reject it until further information became available, or accept a different interpretation and not look for additional information on the issue. For those who accepted this, this process was repeated as new information became available, with the new information being interpreted or measured against the existing point of view. As information became available that suggested that the Soviet troops were not combat troops, the decision makers were again faced with a choice: to continue to believe the old interpretation or accept the interpretation suggested by the new information. In this case, decision makers changed their interpretation to a more benign view (there was no combat brigade). In so doing, the crisis for the decision makers came to an end. This points to an important theme that will be developed at greater length: the role of perceptions and information flows in international relations and crises.

Perception

For players who were genuinely concerned about the combat brigade, perception played a crucial role. Certain decision makers in Washington came to a conclusion about Soviet actions and intentions based on information available to them—information that eventually turned out to be wrong—that suggested

---

8. From a more cynical point of view, one could argue that there was never any real fear of Soviet troops and that the so-called crisis was nothing more than political maneuvering that played on people's fears about Soviet involvement in Cuba. This certainly appears to have been the case for Senator Church, but the available evidence does suggest that in the initial weeks there was genuine concern among top-level decision makers in the Carter administration. Neustadt and May, *Thinking in Time*, 93–95. Hampson makes a much stronger argument that many of the administration's actions were designed to simply be self-serving, but this is more in reference to how American leaders responded to what they thought was a threat—not in the creation of a threat. "The Divided Decision-Maker," 156–63.

that Soviet actions were a threat to them. As Richard E. Neustadt and Ernest R. May write:

> The brigade became an issue only because Carter and his aides did not know the brigade had been there all along, hence supposed it indicative of some new move by the Russians, hence reacted with their own form of the sovereign's complaint, *He can't do that to me*. Since problems or concerns arise because of some real or apparent change in a situation previously ignored or tolerated, a brief scan backward ought to be standard practice. In this case it would have been discovered that there had been no change, therefore there was no problem, unless the Administration wanted to invent one.[9]

As more information about the situation became available to decision makers, their views or perceptions of events changed to accommodate the new information. Initially there was a mismatch between what various administration officials thought the Soviets were up to and what the Soviets were actually doing.[10] This gap in perceptions helped fuel the crisis. The crisis came to an end as more information became available, allowing leaders to begin to see that there was less of a gap between what the United States thought the Soviets were doing and what they were actually doing. Officials in Washington, on the basis of information made available to them during the course of the crisis, adjusted their initial perceptions of events until the updated image of the crisis and Soviet actions diminished their concerns. The theory and propositions presented later will attempt to explain this dynamic of shifting perceptions in crises and ask what role this type of gap in perceptions plays in crisis behavior. The model of information processing and decision making assumed here will be discussed further.

Because the role of perception in international relations is too large to address here, the scope of this inquiry will be limited.[11] The first restriction in

---

9. Neustadt and May, *Thinking in Time*, 96. The authors note that Soviet Ambassador Anatolii Dobrynin asked one of Secretary of State Vance's aides, "Do you expect me to get people in the Kremlin to *believe* this story?" Apparently, no one in the Kremlin did.

10. The assumption here is that the Soviets were actually doing what they said they were doing: nothing. As far as can be ascertained, the Soviet troops in Cuba were doing nothing more than training Cuban troops.

11. For an excellent early bibliography on perception in international relations, see Robert Jervis, *Perception and Misperception in International Politics* (Princeton: Princeton University Press, 1976), 425–31. See also Christer Jönsson, ed., *Cognitive Dynamics in International Politics* (New York: St. Martin's Press, 1982), and Philip E. Tetlock and Charles B. McGuire, Jr., "Cognitive Perspectives on Foreign Policy" in *Psychology and the Prevention of Nuclear War: A*

scope will be to look at the role of perception only during crisis behavior. The second restriction will be to look at crises involving the United States and the Soviet Union. There are good practical and theoretical reasons for these limitations.

The U.S.-Soviet relationship provides a fertile ground for discussing and testing hypotheses about the impact of perception on crises. The history of relations between the two countries has spanned almost seventy years, with varying levels of interactions and intensity. The relationship got off to a hostile start when the United States sent troops to help the White Russians fight the Bolsheviks at the end of World War I. During the 1920s and 1930s, the United States retreated into isolationism while the Soviet Union turned its attentions inward to deal with collectivization and industrialization. The two countries did not formally recognize each other until 1933, and it was not until World War II that there was any period of sustained interaction. The breakdown in relations following World War II brought a decrease in formal interactions that was to last until the mid-1950s as the Cold War reached its height. Following the Geneva Summit of 1956, there was an increase in the scope and number of contacts between the two countries. The 1960s saw a continued increase in contacts and interactions that was to continue, with minor variations, up to the present day. During the first Reagan administration, relations between the two countries continued the downward trend that had begun with the Soviet invasion of Afghanistan, but after Reagan's reelection and the ascension to power of Mikhail Gorbachev in the Soviet Union, relations began to improve once again. That the relationship has exhibited elements of both continuity and change makes it useful for study.

A second factor that makes the U.S.-Soviet relationship a useful one for this study is the number of crises and near-crises that have occurred between the two countries. Both sides have interacted with each other over a range of situations, including those hostile and confrontational, as well as nonhostile and cooperative. In addition, there are well-established groups in both governments that are familiar with the other, both through study and actual contact. Neither side is a complete mystery to the other. For the purposes of this study this is useful because it helps reduce the variation that might be introduced into a relationship between two countries that were relatively unknown to each other. It is certainly true that particular issues that arise between the two countries might be new and unfamiliar (at what might be called the *tactical level*), but the overall position of the two states (the *strategic level*) appears to be well-known by each. The ability of each side to

---

Book of Readings, ed. Ralph K. White (New York: New York University Press, 1986), 255–73, which also contains a useful bibliography.

predict the general thrust of each other's foreign and military policies seems to be relatively high at the strategic level while predicting smaller events or changes is more problematic.[12] Much of the analysis here deals with strategic-level issues and concerns, which reduces the likelihood of unexpected behavior being seen at the tactical level. As a result, the expectation is that the problem of unexpected behavior will be minimized.

Crises

Dealing with crises is not a new endeavor; in fact, one is struck by how much work has been done in recent years on the topic. A variety of approaches have been taken in a number of different contexts, both geographical and military. *Crisis* is a term that is used widely in the literature, as well as in daily life, and it can take on any number of different meanings. The important elements of crises that are relevant to this discussion need to be addressed.

One of the influential early definitions of a crisis is provided by Charles Hermann. In his view a crisis is:

> a situation that (1) threatens high priority goals of the decision-making unit, (2) restricts the amount of time available for response before the decision is transformed, and (3) surprises the members of the decision-making unit by its occurrence.[13]

Hermann notes that all three of these elements have been cited as being central to crisis behavior but they have rarely been studied together. Each of these three elements can cause distress to a decision maker, but it is the combination of all three that causes the greatest problems. This definition allows crises to be examined along three dimensions: threat (high/low), awareness (surprise/anticipated), and decision time (short/extended).[14] The underlying assumption of Hermann's definition is that decision-making behavior when all three of these elements are present will be qualitatively different than if only one or two are present. A different definition focuses on "sequences of inter-

---

12. See Walter Laqueur, *A World of Secrets: The Uses and Limits of Intelligence* (New York: Basic Books, 1985), for a discussion of some of the limits of predicting even general trends in military and political activities. There is an exception that could be made to this argument that should be noted. It has been argued that the time to expect surprise is when the stakes involved are high because that is the time when the potential return of using a source of surprise is the greatest. Robert Axelrod, "The Rational Timing of Surprise," *World Politics* 31, no. 2 (January 1979): 228–46.

13. Charles F. Hermann, "International Crisis as a Situational Variable," in *International Politics and Foreign Policy: A Reader in Research and Theory*, rev. ed., ed. James N. Rosenau (New York: Free Press, 1969), 414.

14. Hermann, "International Crisis as a Situational Variable," 414–16.

action" that remain at a level below war but nonetheless contain a probability of war.[15] One aspect of crisis that needs to be addressed is time—what role it plays and how central that role is to crises. The usage of the term *crisis* usually carries with it the notion that time is of the essence: something needs to be done quickly. Glenn H. Snyder and Paul Diesing make a point of arguing that time is not an essential element in a crisis, a point that is accepted here. In one of the cases to be discussed later (the Berlin blockade) the crisis went on, with varying intensity, for almost a year. What is important for the present discussion of crises is that the decision makers feel that there is pressure to do something about the situation. It is the perception of time constraints that adds to the feeling of crisis. In the cases to be considered here there were a number of instances where the actions of the United States or Soviet Union generated pressures on American leaders to act (such as ships moving toward a blockade line or the completion of missile installations during the Cuban Missile Crisis), but it is not necessary that there be limited time for an event to be considered a crisis. A more useful definition of crisis that encompasses the points made thus far is provided by Richard Ned Lebow:

1. Policy-makers perceive that the action or threatened action of another international actor seriously impairs concrete national interests, the country's bargaining reputation or their own ability to remain in power.
2. Policy-makers perceive that any actions on their part designed to counter this threat (capitulation aside) will raise a significant prospect of war.
3. Policy-makers perceive themselves to be under time constraints.[16]

An important element of a crisis is a conflict of interest or perception of a conflict of interest. Snyder and Diesing suggest that a crisis usually involves a conflict of interest that is deep and difficult to resolve, and there must be some sort of conflict behavior before it can be said that a crisis exists.[17] A minor but important point needs to be added to this discussion: decision makers have to believe that there has been some type of conflict behavior. There must be a perception of conflict. In the Cuban brigade example noted at the outset of this chapter, there were many in the United States who felt that the Soviet Union had made a hostile move by stationing combat troops in Cuba. This was not the case, as the troops had been there for a number of years and did not have

---

15. Glenn H. Snyder and Paul Diesing, *Conflict among Nations: Bargaining, Decision Making, and System Structure in International Crises* (Princeton: Princeton University Press, 1977), 6.

16. Lebow, *Between Peace and War*, 10–12.

17. Snyder and Diesing, *Conflict among Nations*, 7.

any combat role. Nevertheless, the fact that some American decision makers believed that there had been a hostile act made this a crisis situation for them.

A final aspect of crises is the question of risk. Without the element of risk, there can be no crisis:

> What deters such crises [as the Cuban Missile Crisis] and makes them infrequent is that they are genuinely dangerous. Whatever happens to the danger of deliberate premeditated war in such a crisis, the danger of inadvertent war appears to go up. This is why they are called "crises." The essence of the crisis is its unpredictability. The "crisis" that is confidently believed to involve no danger of things getting out of hand is no crisis.[18]

The approach here will take a small deviation to make explicit what is no doubt implicit in Thomas C. Schelling's formulation: a crisis requires the perception of a danger of war resulting from certain actions. Even if there was no real threat of war breaking out (perhaps the required forces were unavailable or the opponent's decision makers had no intention of going to war), it would still be considered a crisis if the relevant decision makers thought that war or other military hostilities might break out or that significant values or goals were threatened. The risk can be of war or conflict arising out of a crisis, or the risk can be that of some value or policy being undermined.[19] The point to be made here is straightforward: the perceptions of the actors involved in crises are crucial to the dynamics of a crisis as well as to our understanding of crises.

Recent work on crises has suggested a useful distinction between international crises and foreign policy crises.[20] These two types of crises have important conceptual and levels-of-analysis consequences that are worth considering. An international crisis can be examined in terms of its behavioral characteristics:

> An *international crisis* is a situational change characterized by an increase in the intensity of *disruptive interactions* between two or more adversaries, with a high probability of *military hostilities* in time of peace (and, during a war, an *adverse change* in the *military balance*). The higher-than-normal conflictual interactions destabilize the existing

---

18. Thomas C. Schelling, *Arms and Influence* (New Haven: Yale University Press, 1966), 96–97.

19. Snyder and Diesing, *Conflict among Nations*, 7. Roberts, *Decision-Making during International Crises*, 36–65, is a useful overview of the literature on the components of crises.

20. This distinction and the discussion that follows is drawn from Brecher and Wilkenfeld, *Crisis, Conflict, and Instability*, 5–6.

relationship of the adversaries and pose a *challenge* to the existing *structure* of an international system—global, dominant and/or subsystem.[21]

The Berlin blockade of 1948 occurred against the backdrop of an international crisis that had its roots in a dispute about the nature of four-power control in Berlin and Germany. A foreign policy crisis, which will be the focus here, is based on perceptual information:

> A *foreign policy crisis*, that is, a crisis viewed from the perspective of an individual state, is a situation with three necessary and sufficient conditions deriving from a change in a state's external or internal environment. All three are perceptions held by the highest level decision-makers of the actor concerned: *a threat to basic values*, along with the awareness of *finite time for response* to the external value threat, and a *high probability of involvement in military hostilities*.[22]

This definition is an updating of Hermann's definition and will form the basis of the definition of crisis used here. The crises to be considered here are foreign policy crises for the United States, and most occur in the context of broader international crises. The broader international crises will not be considered here; rather the focus will be on these crises as foreign policy crises.

Crises: Intended or Unintended?

The next questions to consider are whether or not crises can be unintentional and whether or not that makes much of a difference to this discussion. An intended crisis is one in which a challenge is issued by one actor with the intent of securing some concession from an opponent or provoking a crisis that will lead to some positive gain (or at least prevent some future loss). When Argentina invaded the Falkland Islands, its leaders were hoping that the British would decide that the cost of challenging the fait accompli of a surprise Argentinean occupation of the islands was greater than the cost of conceding to Argentina's demands.[23] Intended crises will occur when one actor believes there is an incompatibility between its preferences and those of its opponent that it can exploit. The type of crisis that is of most interest here is the one in which neither side can be said to have deliberately generated the

---

21. Brecher and Wilkenfeld, *Crisis, Conflict, and Instability*, 5. Emphasis in the original.

22. Brecher and Wilkenfeld, *Crisis, Conflict, and Instability*, 5. Emphasis in original. Roberts, *Decision-Making during International Crises*, 69–93, is a useful overview of the literature on international crises.

23. Max Hastings and Simon Jenkins, *The Battle for the Falklands* (New York: W. W. Norton, 1983), 48.

crisis. Lebow's "spinoff crisis" comes close to the idea of unintended crises that is being presented here.[24] In order to make clear the distinction that is being made, a discussion of different dimensions of intentionality and anticipation will be useful.

Unintended crises can be thought of as being unintended on two different dimensions: unintended as to their occurrence and unintended as to their magnitude. The second is more frequent than the first although each will be considered here. An unintended crisis occurs when a state takes an action that it does not believe will lead to a crisis, yet a crisis occurs anyway. The argument being put forward here suggests that these types of crises will be found to rest on misperception. The second part of the argument is that these misperceptions will frequently be situational misperceptions—misperceptions derived from the information available to decision makers. Unintended crises based on dispositional misperceptions—misperceptions that have their origins in the attitudes and biases of the decision makers—can occur, but it will be argued in the following that these will be less likely.

The Unintended Occurrence of Crises

An example of a situational misperception leading to a crisis can be found in the October 1973 Middle East War between Egypt and Syria, on the one side, and Israel. One interpretation is that the Soviets did not think that the United States would view with any great alarm the introduction of a small number of Soviet troops into the region to enforce the cease-fire between Egypt and Israel that had been worked out in Moscow by Henry Kissinger and Leonid Brezhnev.[25] On the American side, it has been argued that American leaders did not think that the Soviet Union would move its troops into the Middle East because the United States had made it very clear that it would not tolerate such actions. The result was that the United States responded with great alarm and forcefulness when it appeared that the Soviet Union was about to send troops to the Middle East to enforce the cease-fire and save the Egyptian Third Army from destruction. This strong American response forced the Soviets to reassess their views about the desirability of sending their own troops in the face of American opposition, leading them to (apparently) drop the idea.

Unintended crises based on dispositional misperceptions can also occur,

---

24. A spinoff crisis is one in which a confrontation with one state leads to an unintended confrontation with a second state. This will be discussed further in chap. 5.

25. Mohamed Heikal, *The Road to Ramadan* (London: Colling; New York: Quadrangle, 1975), 255. See also John L. Scherer, "Soviet and American Behavior during the Yom Kippur War," *World Affairs* 141, no. 1 (Summer 1978): 3–23. A plausible alternative interpretation is that the Soviets were well aware of the risks of such a confrontation and decided that they were worth running anyway in order to gain influence in the region.

but it is likely that they will be less frequent than ones resulting from situational misperception. The reason for this is that dispositional factors are more likely to play a role with respect to an assessment of the general nature of an opponent than with respect to the interpretation of particular pieces of information. Dispositional misperception is more likely to play a role at the level of assessing an opponent's motives rather than an opponent's particular actions. A person's views and biases will provide the backdrop against which specific pieces of information will be assessed. The argument here is that unintended crises come from a misreading of specific pieces of information rather than a misreading of the general goals and intentions of an opponent.

An example of dispositional misperceptions leading to a crisis is shown by Allen S. Whiting in *China Crosses the Yalu*.[26] In this case, the United States consistently misread the signals that the Chinese government was sending about the consequences of a military thrust far into North Korea. The U.S. leadership assumed that the main concern of the Chinese government was the sanctity of its borders and the safety of its power plants across the Yalu River. In one respect, American leaders were projecting their own views of what would concern the Chinese leadership. Acting on this belief, American representatives gave repeated assurances about the limits of the U.S. drive into North Korea, as well as assurances about the safety of the Chinese power plants. The Chinese leadership was more concerned about the survival of North Korea as a Communist regime than they were with power plants and the border issue. Because many in the U.S. government felt that they had been able to reassure the Chinese on what they felt was an important point to the Chinese, they were quite surprised when Chinese "volunteers" crossed the Yalu River in a counterattack on the forces of the United Nations. There was little information available to American leaders about Chinese concerns that would lead them to conclude that the power plants and border were the main issues; in fact, the information available was quite explicit about Chinese concerns about North Korea. For a variety of reasons, American leaders chose to ignore it.

The Unintended Magnitude of Crises

A second dimension of unintentional crises is magnitude. The size or extent of a crisis can exceed (or possibly be less than) what was expected. An example of this would be the North Korean attack on South Korea and the subsequent American response. One can argue that this led to an unintended crisis for the North Koreans. They most certainly intended to create a crisis situation with

---

26. Allen S. Whiting, *China Crosses the Yalu: The Decision to Enter the Korean War* (New York: Macmillan, 1960).

the South Koreans, hoping to force the downfall of the South Korean government, but it is unlikely that they actually intended for the Americans to
become involved. Seen from this perspective, the American intervention in
the war created an unintended crisis for the North Koreans. Lebow notes that
many of the brinkmanship cases that he studied involved serious miscalcula-
tions about the adversary and its willingness to fight back.[27] Because this type
of crisis (unintended with respect to magnitude) falls into the category of
intended crises, it will not be considered further here. The interest here is with
unintended crises and the misperceptions that give rise to them.

Unintended Crises without Misperception?

A final question arises: Could a crisis that was found to be unintentional also
be found not to rest on any misperceptions? The answer is yes, but the
argument is that they will be rare. It is hard to find an example, so a hypotheti-
cal case will have to suffice: State A takes an action relative to State B that A
believes to be nonconfrontational and that the government of State B also sees
as nonconfrontational. However, it could be the case that domestic considerations in State B, or pressures from allies, would pressure State B into
challenging State A's action. A possible example of this can be found in some
interpretations of the Cuban Missile Crisis. It has been argued by revisionist
critics of the Kennedy administration that there was no need for a nuclear
confrontation because the military balance had not been seriously affected by
the Soviet moves. The argument that is usually made is that Kennedy responded with an eye toward domestic political considerations rather than
national security considerations.[28] Although the early critics could not have
known, the transcripts of the first ExComm meetings held on 16 October lend
support to their claims. In the afternoon meeting Secretary of Defense Robert
McNamara repeatedly argued in a series of discussions with National Security
Advisor McGeorge Bundy and President Kennedy that the missiles were not a
military threat:

> Bundy: . . . What is the strategic impact on the position of the United
> States of MRBMs in *Cuba*? How gravely does this change the strategic
> balance?

27. Lebow, *Between Peace and War*, 270–71.

28. An early and influential argument made along these lines is Roger Hagan, "Triumph or
Tragedy," *Dissent* 10 (Winter 1963): 13–26, reprinted in Robert A. Divine, ed., *The Cuban
Missile Crisis* (Chicago: Quadrangle, 1971), 72–89. This is also the argument made by Anatolii
A. Gromyko in "The Caribbean Crisis 1: The U.S. Government's Preparation of the Caribbean
Crisis," and "The Caribbean Crisis 2: Diplomatic Efforts of the USSR to Eliminate the Crisis,"
Voprosy istorii nos. 7–8 (1971), reprinted in *Soviet Law and Government* 11, no. 1 (Summer

McNamara: Mac, I asked the Chiefs that this afternoon, in effect. And they said, substantially. My own personal view is, not at all.[29]

A few minutes later in the same discussion, Kennedy appeared to second that view by suggesting:

JFK: . . . You may say it doesn't make any difference if you get blown up by an ICBM flying from the Soviet Union or one that was ninety miles away. Geography doesn't mean that much.[30]

It was also McNamara who repeatedly suggested that this situation was a political problem, not a military one:

McNamara: . . . this, this is a domestic, political problem. The announcement—we didn't say we'd go in and not, and kill them, we said we'd *act*. Well, how will we act?
....

McNamara: Because, as I suggested, I don't believe it's primarily a military problem. It's primarily a, a domestic, political problem.[31]

There was of course opposition from many at the ExComm meetings to this point of view, but it does suggest how there might be a crisis created (the United States responding to the Soviet Union) when in fact there did not exist a crisis. As stated already, it is hard to come up with examples for this type of crisis.

It is now time to outline the level of analysis used here, as well as the use of the term *misperception* in this analysis.

The Individual as a Source of Explanation

The model of decision making to be presented later rests on an explicit assumption about the vantage point to be used in examining and explaining crisis behavior. The historian (or political scientist) will never be able to fully

---

1972): 3–53. See also Anatolii A. Gromyko, *Through Russian Eyes: President Kennedy's 1036 Days* (Washington, D.C.: International Library, 1973), 168–81, and Hampson, "The Divided Decision-Maker."

29. John F. Kennedy, "Cuban Missile Crisis Meetings, October 16, 1962," *Presidential Recordings Transcripts* (Boston: John F. Kennedy Library), part 2, 12. These transcripts are available by mail from the Kennedy Library, along with a cassette tape of excerpts. (Hereafter they will be identified as *Transcripts of 16 October 1962*.)

30. Kennedy, *Transcripts of 16 October 1962*, 13.

31. Kennedy, *Transcripts of 16 October 1962*, 46, 48.

wear the shoes of the decision maker in a crisis, but in order to understand or explain that decision maker's actions, that is what one must try to do. The urge to explain on the basis of hindsight or additional information that was not available to the decision maker must be avoided. Making full use of the information available to the analyst is useful for explanation of outcomes but not always for the explanation of behavior. It is behavior that is of interest here.

The question of the vantage point from which to explain behavior has its roots in the field of psychology and personal behavior. The question is, put simply, if one wishes to explain why a person (or decision maker) acted in a certain way, from whose viewpoint does one look, that of the actor or an objective observer? The answer is that one should look at the world from the point of view of the actor, not from the point of view of an observer. In trying to explain why a person takes an umbrella in the morning, it is irrelevant to the explanation of this behavior whether or not it rains that day or even if there was any objective (true) likelihood of rain. All that matters for that explanation is that the person thought there was a chance of rain. This notion has parallels in other fields that are instructive. In explaining deviant behavior, it does not matter whether or not there is any external justification for that behavior. All that matters is that the individual believes that there is a justification. This same approach to explanation or justification of behavior can also be found in law in the area of self-defense. In the case of a person who has been attacked and has in turn responded with violence in self-defense, the burden on the victim is not to prove that there did in fact exist an actual threat to his or her well-being, but only that there were reasonable grounds for believing that there was such a threat:

> What the jury may think of the reasonableness of the appearances of danger is not the criterion of self-defense. It is the impression or effect in the mind of the accused and his belief in the appearance of danger.[32]
>
> It is not essential that the aggressor actually be making an attempt to inflict injury . . . [there] could be a self-defense claim because the circumstances created a reasonable expectation of imminent danger.[33]

The actual reality of the attack will be important in explaining and understanding the outcomes of actions, but for the explanation of the behavior, the perceptions of the actor are sufficient.

In addition to attempting to consider how the world looked to a decision maker, it is also important to consider what choices the decision maker felt

---

32. Adams v. State, 84 S.W. 231, 234 (1904).
33. State v. Negrin, 681 P. 2d 1287, 1291 (1985).

were available. The approach here adopts a perspective frequently found in the rational choice literature:

> It is important to stress the subjective nature of the choice situation. The fact that options are objectively available to an agent [actor] cannot enter into the explanation of his behavior if he has no rational grounds for believing that they are available, nor can the fact that certain options will objectively lead to certain outcomes if he has no reason to think that they will.[34]

What matters to the explanation is how the actor sees the world. One of the most important points that Robert Jervis makes in *Perception and Misperception* is that in understanding why an actor took certain actions it is frequently irrelevant what the objective nature of the situation was.[35] This is so because it was the subjective nature of the situation that the actor was responding to. When explaining behavior, it is necessary to look to the perceptions of the individual. The emphasis on these points is deliberate and should be made perfectly clear.

This subtle distinction between explanation based on objective factors and explanation based on subjective factors is frequently forgotten or ignored in the study of international relations and, in particular, studies of failures in international relations. To illustrate the problem, consider this example found in Congressional hearings reviewing the Cuban Missile Crisis. In the weeks leading up to the crisis, there were many difficulties in getting accurate U-2 information about the Soviet activities in Cuba. This was the result of a delay between the order for a U-2 flight over Cuba and the actual flight.[36] The main reason for this delay was a prediction for bad weather over the missile sites, making photographic reconnaissance impossible. During hearings in February 1963 on the 1964 Department of Defense Appropriations Bill, Congressmen William E. Minshall (Ohio) and Gerald R. Ford, Jr. (Michigan) criticized Secretary of Defense McNamara for this delay in U-2 overflights because the weather over the island at the time turned out to have been clear:

McNamara: . . . Moreover, you will recall that this was also the hurricane season, and the weather in that part of the Caribbean is very bad. We had a number of flights canceled during that period.

---

34. Jon Elster, ed., *Rational Choice* (Oxford: Basil Blackwell, 1986), 4.

35. Jervis, *Perception and Misperception*, 28–29.

36. The literature on the Cuban Missile Crisis is quite large and will be detailed in chap. 2. The impact of weather delays is discussed specifically in Elie Abel, *The Missile Crisis* (New York: Bantam, 1968), and Arthur M. Schlesinger, Jr., *A Thousand Days: John F. Kennedy in the White House* (Boston: Houghton Mifflin Company, 1965).

> Minshall: I have the official weather report here. You had clear days in the vicinity of Havana. . . .The weather from September 25 through October 2, at least at 7 o'clock in the morning, was generally clear.

Following Minshall, Ford took up the same theme:

> Ford: The point I want to make is, you had this forewarning of something of some considerable interest in the San Cristobal area, according to the information testified here, and the weather was appropriate for U-2 flights over this area according to the Weather Bureau. If that is the case, why did we not do it?[37]

Ford and Minshall were criticizing McNamara on the basis of hindsight: they wanted to know why, when the weather turned out to have been clear, U-2 flights were not ordered. It is interesting to note that neither McNamara nor General Joseph Carroll (director of the Defense Intelligence Agency) answered that flights were scheduled on the basis of predicted weather conditions, not actual weather conditions. Congressmen Minshall and Ford were off the mark in criticizing McNamara on the basis of what the weather turned out to be. The relevant question is "Were the decisions appropriate given the situation at the time?" As Roger Hilsman notes:

> In the aftermath of the Cuban crisis, some critics noted a discrepancy in delays attributed to cloud cover and the actual weather conditions over Cuba during the period. But it was not *actual* weather that determined whether a flight should or should not go, but the *predicted* weather. If the predicted weather was for less than 50 per cent clouds, the flight would go. If the predicted weather was for more than 50 per cent, the flight was usually delayed.[38]

The congressmen were wrong to say that a mistaken decision was made. From the perspective of a decision maker who expects there to be clouds (whether or not there turn out to be clouds), this was a correct decision:

> The decision-makers behave according to their interpretation of the situation, not according to its "objective" character as viewed by some

---

37. U.S. Congress, House of Representatives, Committee on Appropriations, Subcommittee on Department of Defense Appropriations for 1964, 88th Cong., 1st sess., 1963, 69–70. This exchange is noted by Roberta Wohlstetter, "Cuba and Pearl Harbor: Hindsight and Foresight," *Foreign Affairs* 43, no. 4 (July 1965): 697.

38. Roger Hilsman, *To Move a Nation: The Politics of Foreign Policy in the Administration of John F. Kennedy* (Garden City, N.Y.: Doubleday, 1967), 181 n. 4. Emphasis in original.

theoretical omnipotent observer. Therefore, in attempting to explain how different kinds of situations influence the type of choice that is made, the analyst must interpret the situation as it is perceived by the decision-makers.[39]

The heart of the inquiry should have been the accuracy of the forecasts, not the decision to postpone the U-2 flights in the face of predicted cloudy weather.

Along with the previous assumption goes a complementary one: in order to understand why a particular foreign policy decision was made, one must look at who made the decision. As any detailed analysis of a foreign policy crisis will show, there are always different views and perspectives on a crisis, and it is dangerous to assume that different decision makers have the same goals and objectives. As will be seen in a number of the case studies considered in later chapters, the views of central decision makers were not always unified, and the explanation of the crisis shifts with each decision maker.[40] One of the most useful points made by Graham T. Allison in discussing his organizational model is that there will frequently be mismatches between "what Washington wanted to do" and what actually happened.[41] President Kennedy probably did not want to have the navy using depth charges to force Soviet submarines in the Caribbean to the surface, an aggressive practice during a very tense time.[42] Nevertheless, that is what happened. Attempting to explain this from the point of view of the preferences of President Kennedy will not lead to a satisfactory answer because Kennedy did not want such a thing to happen and was unaware of the practice.[43] If, however, one attempts to explain this action from the point of view of the navy commander on the spot, one comes up with a better explanation. From his point of view, the risk to his ships was probably of greater immediate concern than the question of a

---

39. Hermann, "International Crisis as a Situational Variable," 413.

40. For this argument, see Richard C. Snyder, H. W. Bruck, and Burton Sapin, eds., *Foreign Policy Decision Making: An Approach to the Study of International Politics* (Glencoe, Ill.: Free Press, 1962), 5.

41. Graham T. Allison, *Essence of Decision: Explaining the Cuban Missile Crisis* (Boston: Little, Brown and Company, 1971), 67–143.

42. Scott D. Sagan, "Nuclear Alerts and Crisis Management," *International Security* 9, no. 4 (Spring 1985): 118. Sagan discusses the difference between what the president and his advisors had in mind with respect to naval operations and what actually happened. McNamara did know about this practice of aggressive tactics to get the subs to the surface. James G. Blight and David A. Welch, *On the Brink: Americans and Soviets Reexamine the Cuban Missile Crisis* (New York: Hill and Wang, 1989), 61–64, provide a discussion of this, as well as a presentation of McNamara's views.

43. Raymond L. Garthoff, *Reflections on the Cuban Missile Crisis*, rev. ed. (Washington, D.C.: Brookings, 1989), 69.

possible Soviet response elsewhere in the world. From the point of view of President Kennedy, these concerns were probably reversed. Thus, in order to understand why those submarines were forced to surface, one must look at the person (or group) with whom the decision rested and analyze the question from that point of view. The existence of an outcome that would not have been preferred by the top decision makers should not be taken as evidence of a lapse in their collective senses. It just might be the case that the particular decision or outcome made perfect sense from the perspective of those who actually made the decision. This is important because a Soviet interpretation that this aggressive behavior was a deliberate policy of the United States would have been an incorrect assumption, yet that is probably what they did, for as Raymond L. Garthoff notes, "The aggressive American naval measures to neutralize the Soviet submarine 'threat' were undoubtedly read in Moscow as a serious sign of American resolve."[44]

In the analysis that follows, an attempt will be made to portray the world from the point of view of the actor as well as to portray how the world actually was. This separation is similar to the distinction made between a psychological environment—the decision maker's *image* of the setting in which decisions are carried out—and an operational environment—the *actual* setting in which they are carried out.[45] In attempting to portray the world as seen by the actor, no effort will be made to explain why the actor saw the world in that particular way. The literature on the factors that influence an actor's perception of the world is vast and not directly relevant here.[46] This analysis will accept the fact that there is frequently a mismatch between perception and reality and proceed from there to try to understand what characteristics of crises are likely to bring about this mismatch and understand what impact this mismatch can have on crisis behavior.

---

44. Garthoff, *Reflections on the Cuban Missile Crisis*, 69.

45. Harold Sprout and Margaret Sprout, "Environmental Factors in the Study of International Politics," in *International Politics and Foreign Policy: A Reader in Research and Theory*, rev. ed., ed. James N. Rosenau (New York: Free Press, 1969), 48–49. Emphasis in original.

46. Lebow, *Between Peace and War*, 148–228. For a review of the role of psychological factors in foreign policy, see Ole R. Holsti, "Foreign Policy Formation Viewed Cognitively," in *Structure of Decision: The Cognitive Maps of Political Elites*, ed. Robert Axelrod (Princeton: Princeton University Press, 1976), 18–54. A very useful review is that of Donald R. Kinder and Janet A. Weiss, "In Lieu of Rationality: Psychological Perspectives on Foreign Policy Decision Making," *Journal of Conflict Resolution* 22, no. 4 (December 1978): 707–35. See also Roberts, *Decision-Making during International Crises*, 125–134, for a discussion of decision making and perceptions in specific crises; Martha L. Cottam, *Foreign Policy Decision Making: The Influence of Cognition* (Boulder, Colo.: Westview Press, 1986); and Christer Jönsson, *Cognitive Dynamics and International Politics*. At a general level, Jervis, *Perception and Misperception*, is about the factors that work to create misperceptions of the world in which a decision maker operates.

Misperception

The term *misperception* is used frequently, both in academic literature and in daily life, with seemingly little confusion as to its meaning. Yet, like trying to provide a useful definition of many terms in the study of world politics (e.g., *resolve* or *power*), attempting to define misperception is difficult. In one of the most influential works in this area, *Perception and Misperception in International Politics*, Jervis does not provide a clear definition of misperception, a phenomena seen in other works too. Lebow notes the problems in attempting to use the term:

> Almost everybody recognizes that misperceptions occur, and that they significantly affect policy-making, but nobody has been able to provide a clear, empirically useful and generally accepted definition of the concept. Some scholars define distorted perception in reference to an objective "reality"; they compare the actor's perception of the "facts" of the situation. . . .
>
> An alternative approach to misperception relies on a comparison between the actor's perceptions of a situation and those of a third party. The third party is used as a "relative" referent, and no assumption is made that his perceptions are any more correct or accurate than those of the actor.[47]

The usage of the term does, however, suggest an implicit definition: a situation where an actor's view (perception) of reality is not accurate. An example of misperception was Joseph Stalin's belief that Adolf Hitler would not attack the Soviet Union in June 1941, a belief that turned out to be wrong.[48] There was a great deal of information available to Stalin, most of which suggested that Hitler would not attack in June. Another example of misperception was Admiral Husband E. Kimmel's (commander in chief of the Pacific Fleet) belief that the Japanese would not attack Pearl Harbor in the winter of 1941.[49]

---

47. Lebow, *Between Peace and War*, 90–91.

48. For a useful discussion of misperception and deception in the context of Hitler's attack on the Soviet Union, see Barton Whaley, *Codeword BARBAROSSA* (Cambridge: MIT Press, 1973).

49. Irving L. Janis and Leon Mann, *Decision Making: A Psychological Analysis of Conflict, Choice, and Commitment* (New York: Free Press, 1977), 120–29. Janis and Mann's discussion covers a variety of psychological issues involved in avoidance reasoning. Roberta Wohlstetter discusses the similar problem facing General Sharp and his beliefs about outside attacks in *Pearl Harbor: Warning and Decision* (Stanford: Stanford University Press, 1962), 74, quoted in Jervis, *Perception and Misperception*, 206.

The problem facing Admiral Kimmel was how to interpret the various pieces of intelligence about Japanese activities coming into his office. Even though officials in Washington had sent warnings to officials in Pearl Harbor about the Japanese threat, because the threat of sabotage was the primary concern of those at Pearl Harbor, the warning from Washington was interpreted in the context of sabotage. This inclination to interpret ambiguous information as suggesting sabotage was strengthened by the belief of many in the Pearl Harbor command that the Japanese would not attack the U.S. Navy frontally but only indirectly through sabotage. Admiral Kimmel's interpretation of incoming information was consistent with his belief that the Japanese would not attack. As Irving L. Janis and Leon Mann show, the work of psychologists on the question of cognitive dissonance has convincingly shown the extent to which people will alter their views of the world in order to keep their various beliefs in balance.

Situational and Dispositional Misperceptions

A closer examination of these two examples suggests a distinction between the different types of misperception mentioned that requires further discussion. Most works on misperception do not distinguish between any different types of misperception, and this creates analytical problems. Not all misperceptions are alike, and their differences can have an impact on the outcome of crises. These two new conceptions of misperception will help clarify the role of misperceptions in crises and in crises outcomes.

The problem facing Stalin led to what will be called a *situational misperception*—a situation where an actor's perception of events is a plausible one, based on the information available, yet that conclusion about reality turns out to be incorrect. The implicit assumption here is that other actors in the same situation, faced with the same information, would be very likely to come to the same (incorrect) conclusion. It is the information available that drives the actor toward a particular conclusion, and changes in the information will lead to changes in the conclusions. Optical illusions or false stage sets can be thought of as attempts to create situational misperceptions. One can clearly see the type of situation described here in the following analogy. A police officer is called to a crime scene, only to see someone fleeing. The officer gives chase and follows the suspect down a dark alley—only to see the suspect turn suddenly and reach under a heavy overcoat. For what? In a situation such as this, the officer might conclude that the suspect is reaching for a weapon and take defensive action. If it turns out that the suspect is only reaching for a wallet, this would be a situational misperception because the information available suggested a conclusion—which turned out to be wrong. Only when more information about the nature of what is being observed is provided can the individual conclude with confidence that the initial interpretation is not correct.

The second type of misperception is *dispositional misperception*. Here the misperceptions that an actor has of the world are the result of that actor's internal predisposition to see the world in a certain way or process certain types of information in a particular way. Here the assumption is that other actors, viewing the same information, would be less likely to arrive at the same conclusions. Admiral Kimmel in Pearl Harbor consistently avoided updating his assessment of the nature and likelihood of the Japanese threat of direct attack in light of new information. He did not want to believe that there was a threat and made sure that his view of the world remained consistent, even when information became available to him that challenged that view. To continue with the police officer analogy, we could conclude that dispositional misperceptions were at work if the police officer were to draw a gun and shoot if the suspect was black but only threaten to shoot if the suspect was white. In these cases, the specific information (a fleeing suspect reaching under an overcoat) is less important than the race of the suspect. In cases involving this type of misperception, more information is unlikely to affect the officer's view of what is happening. The distinction between these two types of misperception is an important one, and it will be dealt with in more detail in later chapters.

Crisis Behavior and Perception

One of the important points that needs to be made before going further is the importance of perception in crises. The explosion of interest in crises and perception in the past ten years is testimony to the growing interest in cognitive factors in foreign policy as well as evidence of the ever-growing body of research showing just such a connection.[50] This should not be surprising. There are a number of reasons for thinking that perceptions and misperceptions will play an important role in crisis decision making. Crises are different than the day-to-day interaction of states, and as such, perceptions take on extra importance during such times. Crises produce changes on many dimensions, both individual and organizational, which in turn will affect, and be affected by, perception.

The role of the individual and his or her beliefs in explaining the outcome

---

50. See Robert Jervis, "A Critique of Early Psychological Approaches to International Misperception," Philip E. Tetlock and Charles B. McGuire, Jr., "Cognitive Perspectives on Foreign Policy," and Ralph K. White, "Motivated Misperceptions," in *Psychology and the Prevention of Nuclear War: A Book of Readings*, ed. Ralph K. White (New York: New York University Press, 1986): 255–301, for useful overviews and bibliographies on the role of perceptions in crises.

of foreign policy behavior has been debated for quite some time. Part of the debate about the role of perceptions in crises centers around what is at base a levels-of-analysis question. By placing perceptions in a prominent place in the analysis of foreign policy behavior, the role of the individual in foreign policy-making is given central importance. This is not without controversy, as there are other strong influences and constraints on foreign policy-making:

—Foreign policy decisions are made within complex bureaucratic organizations that place severe constraints on the individual decision maker. . . .
—Foreign policy is the external manifestation of domestic institutions, ideologies, and other attributes of the polity. . . .
—Structural and other attributes of the international system shape and constrain policy choices.[51]

While these criticisms about the limits on individual foreign policymakers may be true in the general case of day-to-day foreign policy, Ole R. Holsti suggests that individual cognitive factors will play a significant role in just those types of circumstances that are characteristic of crises: nonroutine tasks, decisions made by top leaders who are relatively autonomous, situations where the information available is ambiguous, situations in which there is information overload (forcing the decision maker to use some type of information-processing strategy), and "unanticipated events in which initial reactions are likely to reflect cognitive 'sets.'"[52] These factors figure prominently in the crisis literature, and in one way or another all of these elements were found in the crises to be considered here.

There are further reasons for thinking that perception will play an important role in our understanding of crises. Crises are stressful events, both for the individual and the decision-making apparatus that has to deal with them. A constant theme in accounts of the crises studied here was the strain put on individuals, as well as the pressure put on regular decision-making processes. The stress generated by crises seems to affect decision making in two important ways: first, heightened levels of awareness on the part of decision makers and, second, changes in information processing and decision making. Let us address each of these in turn.

Decision makers facing a crisis are more likely to be cognizant of the fact that what they are doing will be an important factor in their opponents' thinking. Evidence from the cases studied here shows that decision makers

51. Ole R. Holsti, "Foreign Policy Decision Makers Viewed Psychologically: 'Cognitive Processes' Approaches," in *In Search of Global Patterns*, ed. James N. Rosenau (New York: Free Press, 1976), 125–26.
52. Holsti, "Foreign Policy Decision Makers Viewed Psychologically," 127.

frequently do take into account how their actions might be seen by their opponents.[53] In addition, the evidence suggests that decision makers take into account the possibility that the other side might be sending signals that require careful interpretation. This is not to say that decision makers correctly understand the signals they are sending or receiving—just that signals, and hence perceptions, do play a role and decision makers are aware of this.

A final element that will have a significant impact on decision makers is stress. It is important to note that analysts are undecided as to whether stress improves or interferes with human performance and problem solving.[54] Peter Suedfeld and Philip E. Tetlock note that stress tends to decrease the complexity of information processing:

> This impairment [in information processing] includes a lessened likelihood of accurately distinguishing between relevant and irrelevant information, reduced search for novel information, the suppression or ignoring of unpleasant inputs, and greater concentration of both incoming and outgoing communications to the ingroup. Long-term plans tend to be ignored in favor of stimulus-bound reactions, fine distinctions among items of information or among other participants in the crisis are abandoned, and responses and attitudes become increasingly stereotyped.[55]

Janis and Mann, reporting on their studies, as well as on those of others, suggest that high levels of stress do impair information processing and decision making. They found that the consequences of stress are both physical (increased heartbeat, higher blood pressure) and mental or psychological (faulty reasoning and incomplete use of information).[56] Holsti's study of World War I found support for the argument that stress causes decision makers

---

53. The best examples of this type of behavior in the cases studied here can be found during the Cuban Missile Crisis. In this instance, Kennedy and his advisors made a conscious effort to ask how their actions would look to Nikita Khrushchev. See Robert F. Kennedy, *Thirteen Days: A Memoir of the Cuban Missile Crisis* (New York: W. W. Norton, 1969), 102–6. Ole R. Holsti argues that this ability to put oneself into an opponent's shoes is a necessary, if not sufficient, condition, for successful management of crises. *Crisis, Escalation, War* (Montreal: McGill-Queen's University Press, 1972), 223.

54. Thomas C. Wiegele, "The Psychophysiology of Elite Stress in Five International Crises," *International Studies Quarterly* 22, no. 4 (December 1978): 467–511, provides an interesting, if not completely persuasive, test of a means of measuring stress on leaders during crises. Alan Dowty's examination of the role of stress in specific crises is more comprehensive and persuasive. *Middle East Crisis: U.S. Decision-Making in 1958, 1970, 1973* (Berkeley: University of California Press, 1984). Roberts also provides a useful overview of research on stress and decision makers' performance. *Decision-Making during International Crises*, 218–26.

55. Peter Suedfeld and Philip E. Tetlock, "Integrative Complexity of Communications in International Crises," *Journal of Conflict Resolution* 21, no. 1 (March 1977): 171.

56. Janis and Mann, *Decision Making*, 47–52.

to perceive fewer options for themselves and more for their opponents.[57] These various studies point out that communications become more stereotyped and leaders overestimate the hostility of an opponent and underestimate the threat they pose to the opponent.[58]

Conclusion

The role of perception and misperception is not a new topic in the study of foreign policy or interstate relations. What this research will show is that there is room for some types of misperceptions (those that have been defined here as situational misperceptions) to be corrected during the decision-making process. As the work of Jervis and others shows, images or perceptions of the world are very resistant to change, even in the face of new information. For Secretary of State John Foster Dulles there was little that the Soviet Union could do that could not be explained in a manner consistent with his world view that the Soviets were expansionist and aggressive. It was very unlikely that new information about the Soviets or their behavior would lead Dulles to change his view of their motives and preferences. This is one of the problems of dispositional misperceptions on the part of decision makers. When a crisis involves situational misperception, there is room for change in the face of new information. In these cases, the decision maker's view of the situation is strongly affected by external information, and as a result, new information can lead to a change in that view. Many of the cases studied for this project involve situations in which a decision maker's view of an opponent's preferences changed when new information about the opponent or the opponent's actions was made available. Unlike situations involving the types of misperception identified by Jervis, cases involving situational misperception can lead to shifts in perceptions as new information is introduced. The importance of these changing perceptions on the course of a crisis will be the primary theme of the following chapters.

This difference suggests some possibly important policy considerations that will be discussed more fully in the concluding chapter. The most important implication is that more information can make a difference. One of the more troublesome conclusions of previous studies of misperception is that attempts to provide decision makers with more information was likely to make little difference because the decision makers' images were resistant to

---

57. Holsti, *Crisis, Escalation, War*, 162–67.

58. These last two points are also made by Robert Jervis in "Hypotheses on Misperception," *World Politics* 20, no. 3 (April 1968): 454–79, and he gives further examples in *Perception and Misperception*. Hypothesis 8 ("tendency . . . to see other states as more hostile than they are") and Hypothesis 13 ("it is hard for an actor to believe that the other can see him as a menace") in "Hypotheses on Misperception," 460–61.

change. Jervis notes that images will only change when incoming information contrasts greatly with the prevailing view.[59] This problem suggests that additional, smaller pieces of information will not have an impact on a decision maker's perception of an opponent.

The analysis here will suggest that in cases involving situational misperceptions, changes in perceptions on both sides can result as further information is made available. One particular implication is that during crises it is important to continue to provide as much information as possible to the decision maker. Decision makers whose interpretations of their opponents' actions and motives rest on the information that is coming to them, rather than their own internal views, will be more likely to change their interpretations when the information changes. Because there will always be a chance that decision makers will operate in this fashion, it becomes important to provide more information. These and other implications will be taken up more fully in the concluding chapter.

Plan

The outline for the rest of this study is straightforward. The next chapter contains detailed descriptions of the case studies that will be covered here, presented in chronological order. The detail is necessary to obviate the need for extensive discussion in the theoretical chapters that follow. Chapters 3 through 7 advance five propositions that build upon each other toward a specific understanding of the role of different types of misperception in crisis behavior. These propositions deal with the origins, continuation, and termination of crises and suggest a new conception of misperceptions that furthers our understanding of crisis behavior. For each chapter, a proposition will be introduced, and the five crises will be examined to assess the validity of the proposition.

The Crises

The crises covered here span the years 1946 to 1973. They include the

- —Iranian crisis of March 1946
- —Berlin blockade and air lift (1948–1949)
- —Berlin Wall crisis (August 1961)
- —Cuban Missile Crisis (October 1962)
- —October 1973 Middle East War and alert

---

59. Jervis, "Hypotheses on Misperception," 465. This line of argument is taken up further in Jervis, *Perception and Misperception*, 143–54.

These specific crises were selected because of the prominent role of perceptions and misperceptions in each, as well as for their historical content. A
brief overview of U.S.-Soviet relations during World War II will be provided
to set the backdrop for the first case, the Iranian crisis of 1946, as the roots of
many of the misunderstandings and antagonisms of the later years can be
found in the interactions of the United States and the Soviet Union during the
war years. The Iranian crisis of 1946 was the first major crisis involving the
United States and the Soviet Union in the post–World War II era. This crisis
has been described by many as the beginning of the Cold War, and it is a
useful starting point for a discussion of U.S.-Soviet crises.[60] Many questions
were raised about Soviet behavior, and the information available to U.S.
leaders was sufficiently ambiguous to allow for a variety of interpretations.
Another element that makes this crisis interesting is that it occurred before the
Cold War had settled in, before U.S. attitudes about the Soviet Union had
solidified in the minds of American leaders. Of all the crises considered here,
this one is least influenced by Cold War thinking and thus makes an interesting
starting point.

The remaining four crises constitute the most serious confrontations
between the United States and the Soviet Union that involved the risk of
military conflict in the post–World War II era. The Berlin blockade crisis and
the Berlin Wall crisis confronted U.S. leaders with the same basic questions:
What were the Soviets up to? How far were they going to go in pursuing the
confrontation? And what should the U.S. response be? The main concern of
American leaders in both cases was whether Soviet actions were the beginning of a campaign designed to put pressure on the Western position or were
actually the first steps in a more significant, possibly military, effort to oust the
Western powers from Berlin in particular and Germany in general.

The Cuban Missile Crisis needs no introduction. Seen by many as a
classic example of a crisis, it is a suitable test case for the propositions
advanced here. In addition, the wealth of information now available about this
crisis provides fertile ground to test theories about U.S. crisis behavior.[61] The
final crisis to be considered is the October 1973 War crisis, which came at the
height of détente. Although the shortest crisis of those considered here, it
shares some of the same elements of the Iranian crisis in that it came during a
period of generally positive relations between the two countries and there was
uncertainty about what Soviet motives were in the crisis and what they hoped
to accomplish by their various actions. The October 1973 War crisis is the last
one to be considered as there have been no major U.S.-Soviet crises since

---

60. This point will be discussed further in chap. 2.

61. One, of course, must be sensitive to the question of how far one can generalize from
the Cuban Missile Crisis (or any crisis for that matter), and this concern will be addressed
specifically in chap. 8.

then. The crisis that opened this chapter, the Cuban brigade crisis, is not included because there is no evidence currently available that indicates that decision makers feared any sort of military consequences from this crisis.[62]

Each crisis provides useful material for discussing changing perceptions and crisis behavior. All of these crises have been dealt with before in a variety of formats and approaches (although the Iranian crisis has received considerably less attention than the others). What this work will do is suggest new approaches to explaining the observed behavior with an emphasis on misperceptions and their origins. It will conclude by arguing that new insight into these crises has been provided through the use of these new conceptions of misperception.

The focus of the study, as noted, is on American foreign policy decision making. An earlier effort made a more explicit attempt to include consideration of Soviet perspectives in the framework of this discussion of situational and dispositional misperceptions.[63] The success of that effort was hampered by the difficulties of ascertaining Soviet perspectives on American preferences as well as evidence that would allow a determination of the existence of situational or dispositional misperceptions. The available data made such an effort extremely difficult, and hopefully more information will become available in the future that will allow such work.[64] At various points, informed speculation about Soviet motives and assessments will be provided, but it will, within the limits of the data available, remain informed speculation. We now turn to a discussion of the crises themselves to set the historical background for the theoretical chapters to follow.

---

62. Of course, when official records are made available, this assessment might change. Of the cases to be considered, only the October 1973 War crisis has not yielded up much insider information beyond that available in Kissinger's memoirs. Hopefully with time, that will change.

63. Robert B. McCalla, "The Dynamics of Perception in U.S.-Soviet Crises" (Ph.D. diss., University of Michigan, 1987).

64. A notable exception to this is the Cuban Missile Crisis: there has been a large outpouring of information about it in past years. Unfortunately, there remain a number of questions about the validity of that information that will have to be sorted out before it all can be taken at face value. The outlines of the debate can be seen in Mark Kramer, "Remembering the Cuban Missile Crisis: Should We Swallow Oral History?" *International Security* 15, no. 1 (Summer 1990): 212–18.

CHAPTER 2

Case Histories

The cases presented here are, for the most part, well-known to both political scientists and historians of the U.S.-Soviet relationship. The general history of each of the cases, as well as any special aspects that are particularly relevant to the theory being presented, are discussed. These are by no means comprehensive accounts of these crises; rather they are summaries sufficiently detailed to convey the context and decisional environment that faced American decision makers at the time. For further information on each crisis, the reader is directed to the additional sources listed in the notes.

Iranian Crisis of 1946

The crisis that confronted the United States and the Soviet Union in March 1946 was the first major confrontation of the postwar era.[1] While it was less apparent at the time, this crisis was symbolic of the crises that would characterize the Cold War for the next forty years. Unfortunately, historians and political scientists have overlooked this crisis's importance, necessitating a somewhat longer discussion here.

On Wednesday, 13 March 1946, the *New York Times* carried a full-page (eight-column) headline that read:

HEAVY RUSSIAN COLUMNS MOVE WEST IN IRAN; TURKEY OR IRAQ MAY BE GOAL; U.S. SENDS NOTE, CONNALLY ASKS BIG 3 MEET AND TALK BLUNTLY

---

1. Two of the more useful histories of the Iranian crisis are Gary R. Hess, "The Iranian Crisis of 1945–46 and the Cold War," *Political Science Quarterly* 89, no. 1 (March 1974): 117–46, and Bruce Robellet Kuniholm, *The Origins of the Cold War in the Near East: Great Power Conflict and Diplomacy in Iran, Turkey, and Greece* (Princeton: Princeton University Press, 1980). Also useful are George Lenczowski, *Russia and the West in Iran, 1918–1948: A Study in Big-Power Rivalry* (New York: Greenwood Press, 1968), and Lewis V. Thomas and Richard N. Frye, *The United States and Turkey and Iran* (Cambridge: Harvard University Press, 1951). An official summary of American policy with respect to Iran prepared by the director of the Office of Near Eastern and African Affairs for the Secretary of State on 23 August 1945 is found in U.S. Department of State, *Foreign Relations of the United States*, 1945, 8:393–400. (Hereafter

The heading over the lead story read "RED ARMY POURS IN." The next day the headline (five-column) read:

STALIN SAYS CHURCHILL STIRS WAR AND FLOUTS ANGLO-RUSSIAN PACT; SOVIET TANKS APPROACH TEHERAN.

The paper reported "large movements of combat troops from the border of the Soviet Union through Western Iran to Turkey" as well as "tanks, armored cars and necessary fuel supplies" near Tehran. The *New York Times* also carried the news that the House Military Affairs Committee had been told by senior military leaders that "world conditions were so unsettled that Congress should extend the Selective Service Act" in order to be strong "amid the turmoil" existing in the world.[2] With these bold announcements, a crisis over Iran that had been simmering for months, one involving the United States, the Soviet Union, and Great Britain, burst onto the front pages.

Iran had been in the news frequently during the preceding months, portrayed as the focus of a controversy between the Soviet Union and Great Britain over their traditional spheres of influence in Iran.[3] The crisis that the United States found itself in in March 1946 had its origins in a long-standing competition between Great Britain and the Soviet Union, as well as in events during the early years of World War II. As a State Department summary prepared in August 1945 notes:

> During the entire course of Iran's modern history, its foreign relations have been influenced principally by Russia and Great Britain, which have been engaged in a continuous struggle for political and economic ascendancy in Iran. The steady increase in Germany's interest in Iran, beginning in the 1920s, introduced a complicating factor into Iranian affairs. The extension of German influence, and the failure of Reza Shah Pahlevi to reply satisfactorily to repeated Anglo-Soviet demands for the expulsion of German fifth-columnists, finally resulted in a coordinated invasion of Iran by Russian and British forces in August 1941.[4]

FRUS.) For a detailed history of Soviet involvement in Iran, see Miron Rezun, *The Soviet Union and Iran: Soviet Policy in Iran from the Beginnings of the Pahlavi Dynasty until the Soviet Invasion in 1941* (Geneva: Sijthoff and Noordhoff International Publishers, 1981).

2. *New York Times*, 13–14 March 1946.

3. *New York Times*, 1–14 February 1946. For a general discussion of British foreign policy in the Middle East, see Royal Institute of International Affairs, *British Interests in the Mediterranean and Middle East: A Report by a Chatham House Study Group* (London: Oxford International Press, 1958). On Anglo-American relations with respect to the Soviet Union during 1944–47, see Terry H. Anderson, *The United States, Great Britain, and the Cold War, 1944–1947* (Columbia: University of Missouri Press, 1981), 118–43.

4. *FRUS*, 1945, 8:393.

What had caused this most recent controversy to be seen as one involving American interests was the question of the withdrawal of Soviet troops from Iran. The Soviet Union had let pass a negotiated deadline of 2 March 1946 for the withdrawal of some thirty thousand troops from northern Iran. This refusal on the part of the Soviets to remove their troops caused a great deal of concern in Washington and other capitals. The continued presence of these troops in northern Iran was seen as a threat to the integrity of Iran and a challenge to the fledgling United Nations Organization (Hereafter United Nations), which had been forced to take up the divisive Iranian controversy as its first substantive issue.

The first major crisis since the end of World War II, a mere six months earlier, was now under way. As seen by American leaders, what was at issue was the withdrawal of those Soviet troops, the integrity of the United Nations, the U.S. position in Iran, and fears of U.S.-Soviet conflict. All of these factors would serve to generate concerns among American leaders that would not be alleviated until the Soviets announced on 26 March that their troops would be withdrawn in six weeks. This action was reinforced on 4 April when the Soviet Union and Iran announced the signing of an agreement regarding the withdrawal of all Soviet troops.

It was Soviet unwillingness to withdraw their troops from Iran and the resultant American unease that was the most direct cause of the Iranian crisis. As Secretary of State Dean Acheson later writes:

> The Iranian crisis of 1945–1946 revolved about two issues: whether the Soviet Union would withdraw its troops from northern Iran as it had agreed to do in 1942 and 1943, and whether it would succeed in creating out of the northern Iranian province of Azerbaijan an autonomous entity subject to Soviet control.[5]

The question of what the Soviet Union intended with respect to the United States would be a tougher question to answer.

The United States had become involved in Iran for two major reasons: the use of Iran as a route for the shipment of Lend-Lease materials to the Soviet Union during World War II and, second, a subsequent concern about Soviet interference in Iran.[6] With the Dardanelles under the control of the

---

5. Dean Acheson, *Present at the Creation: My Years in the State Department* (New York: W. W. Norton, 1969), 197.

6. A third concern is cited by revisionist historians: American desires for control over Iranian oil. See Daniel Yergin, *Shattered Peace: The Origins of the Cold War and the National Security State* (London: Andre Deutsch, 1977), 179–82, and William Appleman Williams, *The Tragedy of American Diplomacy*, 2d rev. ed. (New York: Dell, 1972), 224–25. Yergin argues that "Oil . . . was very much at the heart of the Iranian crisis, although American officials almost

Axis powers in the early part of World War II, the only two routes available for the shipment of large quantities of Lend-Lease materials to the Soviet Union were the North Atlantic route and the Pacific route, each of which had its disadvantages.[7] Because of the lack of other supply routes, the Allies decided to use the Persian Gulf route for getting supplies to the Soviet Union. By the end of the war, almost a quarter of all Lend-Lease shipments from the Western Hemisphere traveled to the Soviet Union via this route.[8]

The second reason for American involvement in, and concern about, Iran was the fears held by both Iranian and American leaders about the influence of the Soviet Union in Iran. American concerns about Soviet action in Iran fell into two categories: concern about Soviet desires to annex the northern portions of Iran (primarily Azerbaijan) and, second, concerns about growing Soviet influence in the rest of Iran.[9] In particular, American leaders were concerned about Soviet influence in securing economic and petroleum concessions as a means of expanding its influence. A memorandum prepared on 14 February 1944 by Harold Minor of the State Department's Division of Middle Eastern Affairs on "Soviet Exploitation of Iran" notes:

> There has been noticeable for some time a tendency on the part of the Soviet Government to negotiate with the Iranian Government agreements and contracts in which the scales are tipped *heavily* in Russian favor. This trend has developed to the point where it amounts to consistent Soviet exploitation of the Iranians. The agreements find Iranian acquiescence only because the Iranians fear the consequences of opposing the much-feared Russians.[10]

---

routinely denied it." 180. While this is arguably true with respect to the overall American approach to Iran, it appears to have been a lesser concern with respect to this particular crisis. The oil-producing area that the United States was concerned about was in the southern part of Iran while the area of Soviet military actions was in the northern part of Iran. The British had much larger oil interests in Iran and acted accordingly. On American interests, see Kuniholm, *The Origins of the Cold War in the Near East*, 178–209; Anthony Sampson, *The Seven Sisters* (New York: Bantam, 1975), 135–44; and Lenczowski, *Russia and the West in Iran*, 76–86, 216–23. American leaders were more concerned about American oil operations in Saudi Arabia, across the Persian Gulf, and the possible negative impact that Soviet influence in Iran could have there.

7. See Robert H. Jones, *The Roads to Russia: United States Lend-Lease to the Soviet Union* (Norman: University of Oklahoma Press, 1969), 84–85, for a discussion of the considerations of using the Persian Gulf route.

8. Twenty-three percent of this aid went via the Persian Gulf, 47 percent via the Soviet Far East, 22 percent via the North Atlantic, and 6 percent via the Black Sea and Soviet Arctic routes. T. H. Vail Motter, *The Persian Corridor and Aid to Russia* (Washington, D.C.: Office of the Chief of Military History, Department of the Army, 1952), app. A, 481.

9. The history of Soviet interest and activity in northern Iran is covered by Rezun, *The Soviet Union and Iran*, and Lenczowski, *Russia and the West in Iran*, 12–69, 193–253.

10. *FRUS*, 1944, 5:311. The memo details Soviet exploitation of Iran in trade, finance, and petroleum. Emphasis in original.

American concerns about the use of Soviet influence in internal Iranian politics to secure "unfair" oil concessions had been evident for quite some time before this memorandum was written.[11] In summary, the United States was concerned about the Soviets gaining influence in Iran and the impact on the region if they did so. The concern was not about oil concessions per se but about the ability of the Soviet Union to use them to influence internal Iranian politics.

In addition to their usefulness as a case study, the events of early 1946 are important in furthering our understanding of the subsequent Cold War and in helping to understand the history of U.S.-Soviet relations. This first postwar crisis involving the major powers was seen as a victory for the United States (and, indirectly, for the United Nations) and a defeat for the Soviet Union. This crisis was also the beginning of a significant shift in attitudes in the West, particularly in the United States, regarding the Soviet Union and the perceived ability of the major powers (the United States, United Kingdom, and Soviet Union) to continue to work together. Many have suggested that this crisis marked the beginning of the Cold War and led directly to the announcement of the Truman Doctrine a year later:

> In its response to the Iranian crisis of November 1945 to June 1946, the United States reoriented its postwar policy toward the Soviet Union, shifting in the terminology of the era, from "appeasement" to "getting tough."[12]

The effect of this crisis was to accelerate the change in perception that was just beginning to occur in the West about a former ally.[13] That change in perception was from one of seeing the Soviet Union as an ally to one where it was viewed with suspicion and outright hostility.

There are a few interesting differences between this crisis and the others to follow. The first concerns what might be called the *psychological environment* in which this crisis occurred. Because this crisis came so soon after the end of World War II, the attitudes that would later fuel the Cold War had not yet formed. The events of late 1945 and early 1946 occurred against a backdrop of friendly feelings towards the Soviet Union. As noted, the acute phase

---

11. See *FRUS*, including 1943, 4:625–28; 1944, 5:445–80; and 1945, 8:397–98, 581–83.

12. Hess, "The Iranian Crisis of 1945–46," 117. For a discussion of the shift in American policies and attitudes coming as a result of this crisis, see Thomas G. Paterson, *Soviet-American Confrontation: Postwar Reconstruction and the Origins of the Cold War* (Baltimore: Johns Hopkins University Press, 1973), 182–83; John Lewis Gaddis, *The United States and the Origins of the Cold War, 1941–1947* (New York: Columbia University Press, 1972), 312–15; and Yergin, *Shattered Peace*, 163–71.

13. Joseph L. Nogee and Robert H. Donaldson, *Soviet Foreign Policy since World War II* (New York: Pergamon, 1981), 63.

of this crisis (March 1946) occurred just six months after the end of the war against Japan and only ten months after the surrender of Germany. This affected events in two important ways. The first was that hopes and aspirations for cooperation between the major powers were still strong. The first meetings of the United Nations had just taken place, and there was discussion of hopes for a cooperative international order. The hope was strong among the public, as well as the leadership, that the world had somehow changed for the better as a result of the war. The comments of John Oneal summarize many of the comments made by others about this era and are worth quoting at length:

> It is likely to prove difficult after thirty years' experience of the Cold War to appreciate the optimistic enthusiasm of this time [late 1945–early 1946] and to reconstruct faithfully the image of the Soviet Union commonly held. The more the war against Germany had taken on the aura of a crusade, a *jihad*, against the evils of fascism the more likely it became that euphoria would manifest itself when the fighting and sacrifice were no longer required. The Atlantic Charter, the Charter of the United Nations Organization, Henry Wallace's prediction of a "century of the common man," and Wendell Willkie's "one world" theme all reflected the hopes of individuals who had endured privation and suffering but anticipated rewards commensurate with their efforts. Essential to this vision of the future was the belief that the cooperation among the great powers which had resulted in the victory in the war could be continued into the era of peace which was to follow. In this new international order, the security of all nations was to be guaranteed by collective action and not by the outmoded diplomatic and military practices of the past.[14]

These hopes for postwar peace and cooperation among the major powers were reflected in the attitudes of the general public. A Gallup Poll taken immediately following the Japanese surrender found that 54 percent of the American public felt that the Russians could be trusted to cooperate with the United States after the war while only 30 percent thought that they could not be trusted.[15] As Secretary of State James Byrnes later writes:

---

14. John R. Oneal, *Foreign Policy Making in Times of Crisis* (Columbus: Ohio State University Press, 1982), 68–69.

15. The question was "Do you think Russia can be trusted to cooperate with us after the war?" Sixteen percent had no opinion. These feelings changed significantly over time. A survey conducted at the end of January 1946 asked, "Do you believe that any nation would like to dominate the rest of the world?" Fifty-nine percent answered yes (27 percent said no), and of those answering yes, 26 percent named Russia as that country, followed by Britain (12 percent) and Germany (10 percent). Only 2 percent thought that the United States was out to dominate the world. George H. Gallup, *The Gallup Poll: Public Opinion 1935-1971*, vol. 1, *1935–1948* (New York: Random House, 1972), 523, 564.

But, if one can recall the attitude of the people of the United States towards the Soviets in the days immediately following the German surrender, he will agree that, as a result of our sufferings and sacrifices in a common cause, the Soviet Union then had in the United States a deposit of goodwill, as great, if not greater than that of any other country.[16]

This atmosphere of goodwill and trust toward the Soviet Union would make many people reluctant to accept the reality of confrontation with the Soviet Union when it came in early 1946.

An inseparable element of this atmosphere of hope and goodwill toward the Soviet Union was the United Nations. There were strong hopes that the United Nations would be able to create and enforce a postwar climate of peace. Many looked to the United Nations to help keep the peace and solve the many interstate disputes that were bound to arise. The states of the world, large and small, would work together to keep the peace. The Iranian crisis threatened that vision.

The Iranian issue was the first substantive issue to be placed before the United Nations. It was the sort of issue that the creators envisioned for the United Nations to solve, yet there was considerable opposition to putting the issue on the agenda. During a meeting with Stalin in December 1945, Secretary of State Byrnes had said that he was "seriously disturbed" at the prospect of the Iranian issue being raised at the first meeting of the United Nations and he hoped that Stalin would do all that he could to resolve the issue before it got that far.[17] In addition to pressuring the Soviets to solve the problem with Iran, the United States also put pressure on the Iranians not to raise the issue before the United Nations. The fear was that a serious dispute between three of the major powers (Great Britain, Soviet Union, United States) supporting the United Nations would have undesirable consequences for the future viability of the United Nations.[18]

This concern about the impact of a U.S.-Soviet-British dispute in the United Nations was felt by others as well. The first Secretary General of the United Nations, Trygve Lie, recalls that his feeling was:

---

16. James F. Byrnes, *Speaking Frankly* (New York: Harper and Brothers, 1947), 71. This reservoir of good will evaporated quickly. A Gallup Poll taken at the height of the March 1946 crisis (interviews taken 15–20 March) found 71 percent disapproving "of the policy Russia is following in world affairs." Seven percent approved, while 22 percent had no opinion. Gallup, *The Gallup Poll*, vol. 1, 567. For a discussion of changes in American public opinion regarding the Soviet Union during World War II, see Ralph B. Levering, *American Opinion and the Russian Alliance, 1939–1945* (Chapel Hill: University of North Carolina Press, 1976).

17. Byrnes, *Speaking Frankly*, 119–21.

18. *FRUS*, 1946, 7:292–97, 299–300. See also Kuniholm, *The Origins of the Cold War in the Near East*, 278–82, and Hess, "The Iranian Crisis of 1945–46," 132.

The [Security] Council had held its first meeting—a purely formal affair on January 17—and was not generally expected to do much else in London. But then the hard realities of world politics intruded. Like gusts of wind warning of future storms to come, they blew in the door of the new-built house of peace, before the workmen had finished. The first blow came from Iran (Persia).[19]

Lie's fear that the prospects for international peace and the success of the United Nations in promoting that goal would be derailed by this first major dispute was shared by leaders in Washington. Many did not want to believe that the era of cooperation between the big three was over and shared Lie's concerns:

It [the Iranian crisis] was a bad omen, and a chill descended upon my optimism. . . .if the atmosphere of this very first debate of the Security Council . . . was a sign of future events I feared that the prospects for further agreements on all the great issues to come might be much poorer than I had thought.[20]

President Harry S. Truman had a number of concerns about this crisis as well. In addition to his concern about Soviet expansionism, Truman was also concerned about the impact of Soviet behavior on the United Nations and the principle of upholding one's obligations:

What perturbed me most, however, was Russia's callous disregard of the rights of a small nation and of her own solemn promises. International co-operation was impossible if national obligations could be ignored and the U.N. bypassed as if it did not exist.[21]

This crisis came at the end of a war that had produced great hopes for peace and postwar cooperation among the major powers and before the Cold War, which would destroy those hopes. Many in America were disinclined to

19. Trygve Lie, *In the Cause of Peace: Seven Years with the United Nations* (New York: Macmillan, 1954), 28. Lie discusses the early meetings of the Security Council and the future impact of this first U.N. skirmish on the evolution of the Cold War. 74–106. See Leland M. Goodrich and Anne P. Simons, *The United Nations and the Maintenance of International Peace and Security* (Washington, D.C.: Brookings, 1955), 23–32, 45–52, for a discussion of postwar hopes revolving around the U.N. and the impact of the Iran crisis on these hopes.

20. Lie, *In The Cause of Peace*, 32. For a discussion of the Soviet approach to the U.N., see Alexander Dallin, *The Soviet Union at the United Nations: An Inquiry into Soviet Motives and Objectives* (New York: Praeger, 1962), 26–41.

21. Harry S. Truman, *Memoirs, Volume II: Years of Trial and Hope, 1946–1952* (Garden City, NY: Doubleday, 1956), 95.

believe that conflict with the Soviet Union was inevitable or that it was coming so soon after the cooperation of the Big 3 to end the war, and they were concerned that the United Nations might not be able to do the job many hoped it would.

In addition to the lack of the Cold War as a backdrop, a second distinctive element in this crisis, relative to the others we will consider, was the lack of any immediate military option for American leaders. The United States had never maintained large numbers of combat troops in Iran,[22] and all of them had been removed by 1 January 1946. The number of troops that the Soviets had in Iran was significantly larger, and geographical proximity made it possible for them to introduce even more. This meant that, in the short run, the United States was in no real position to militarily threaten the Soviet Union locally in Iran. This lack of useful military options left the United States without the means to back up its position with force in the event of a crisis with the Soviet Union. As Oneal notes, this left the United States in an undesirable position:

> There is another possible explanation for why American actions in mid-March did not match the determination expressed by both the president and secretary of state earlier in the month. It is simply that there were no easy options available for influencing the situation if the Soviet Union had in fact decided to resort to military action. After the withdrawal of British troops in late February, the Red Army of 60,000 men constituted the only foreign military force in the country; it was, therefore, well within Soviet capabilities for Stalin to present the United States and Great Britain with a fait accompli, if it were decided that the prize was worth the consequences.[23]

Unlike the later Berlin blockade crisis, the United States was not even in the position to flex its nuclear muscles by making conspicuous shows of force.[24]

---

22. The number of American troops in Iran was approximately thirty thousand, all of a noncombatant character. Lenczowski, *Russia and the West in Iran*, 273.

23. Oneal, *Foreign Policy Making in Times of Crisis*, 102.

24. During the Berlin blockade, the United States very conspicuously moved B-29 bombers to Britain to put additional pressure on the Soviets by suggesting the possibility of American attacks if Soviet pressure on Berlin was too strong. Avi Shlaim, *The United States and the Berlin Blockade, 1948 1949: A Study in Crisis Decision-Making* (Berkeley: University of California Press, 1983), 233–40, and Jean Edward Smith, ed., *The Papers of General Lucius D. Clay: Germany 1945–1949*, vol. 2 (Bloomington: Indiana University Press, 1974), 707–9, 739–40. (Hereafter *Clay Papers*.) Interestingly enough, the nuclear weapons associated with those bombers did not accompany them. McGeorge Bundy, *Danger and Survival: Choices about the Bomb in the First Fifty Years* (New York: Random House, 1988), 200. By March 1946, the American nuclear arsenal was very small. At the end of 1945, the United States had only two

This lack of opportunity for immediate conflict did not mean that American leaders were not concerned about the possibility of future military conflict with the Soviets on this issue; it only meant that there was little chance of such a conflict in the short run.

Berlin Blockade

There are few events that seem to symbolize the Cold War more than the Berlin blockade and airlift. The clash of wills between East and West was laid bare for all to see, making clear that the Cold War was in full force. Unlike the crisis in Iran in 1946, this crisis did not occur against a background of U.S.-Soviet cooperation: there was little hope at that point that U.S.-Soviet relations would improve any time soon.

The Berlin blockade and the subsequent airlift were actually a series of crises involving the United States, the Soviet Union, Great Britain, and France. These crises began in early 1948 and continued with varying intensity until May 1949. The history of the four-power occupation and confrontation in Berlin in the three years from the end of World War II to the beginning of the Berlin blockade and airlift is complex and not directly relevant to our discussion here. Nevertheless, a brief review of the background will be useful in providing the setting for this crisis.[25]

As World War II was drawing to a close, the Allied powers arrived at a number of understandings, both written and verbal, concerning the fate of Germany.[26] There were agreements signed that allocated the territory of Germany to the four (soon to be) victorious powers. In addition, there were agreements concerning the division of the spoils of war and the agricultural

---

nuclear weapons, and by July 1946 it had only seven. David Alan Rosenberg, "U.S. Nuclear Stockpile, 1945 to 1950," *Bulletin of the Atomic Scientist* 38, no. 5 (May 1982): 26. Barry M. Blechman and Stephen S. Kaplan found no evidence that the United States engaged in any "shows of force" to put pressure on the Soviet Union during the Iranian crisis. *Force without War: U.S. Armed Forces as a Political Instrument* (Washington, D.C.: Brookings, 1978), 547.

25. Shlaim, *The United States and the Berlin Blockade*, 182. This is an extremely comprehensive work, covering the various psychological and decision-making aspects of American policy-making in the Berlin crisis. Much of the analysis that follows is drawn from Shlaim's book. Useful histories of this period can be found in Max Charles, *Berlin Blockade* (London: Allan Wingate, 1959); Lucius D. Clay, *Decision in Germany* (Westport, Conn.: Greenwood Press, 1950); and W. Phillips Davison, *The Berlin Blockade: A Study in Cold War Politics* (Princeton: Princeton University Press, 1958). For the documentary record, see U.S. Department of State, *Documents on Germany, 1944–1985* no. 9446 (Washington D.C.: Office of the Historian, Bureau of Public Affairs, n.d.) (hereafter *Documents on Germany*), and *FRUS*, 1948, vol. 2 (Germany and Austria).

26. A very useful account of the negotiating history of the various agreements governing Allied control of Berlin is found in Daniel J. Nelson, *Wartime Origins of the Berlin Dilemma* (University, Ala.: University of Alabama Press, 1978).

and industrial outputs of each region. Even though Berlin was within the Soviet sector, there was a separate agreement drawn up that divided the city among the four powers and set up a joint commission for the administration of the city. It was thought at the time that problems concerning Germany as a whole would be worked out at the level of foreign ministers while problems concerning Berlin would be worked out in the Allied Kommandatura (the council composed of the military leaders of each of the four powers in Berlin) at the level of the local military commander.[27]

Problems arose immediately as the four powers tried to run their sectors of the city in the manner that they felt was appropriate. During the first two postwar years, most of the problems were of such a basic nature that they were worked out among the four powers. These problems included the clearing of rubble, restoration of water and power supplies, and the provision of basic food rations for the inhabitants of Berlin. However, by late 1947 and early 1948, the rebuilding of the city and its economy had progressed to such a level that disputes were beginning to arise over issues like a common currency, standard economic regulations, political parties, and education. The resolution of these problems became more difficult and bitter as time went on, particularly as the three Western powers began to coordinate some of their different programs, usually in a manner that angered the Soviet representatives. These disputes would set the stage for the later confrontation over access to Berlin.

By March 1948, currency reform was the main issue in dispute between the four powers. The question of which currency to use was crucially important as whoever controlled the supply of the currency also had a great deal of influence on the economy. Political ends could be secured by manipulating the currency supply, and for this reason there were many hours of discussion between the four powers about the nature of any currency reform.

A series of disputes over currency reform and economic regulation came to a head on 20 March when the head of the Soviet delegation to the Allied Control Council abruptly left a meeting without having set the agenda for the next meeting. This was recognized by all concerned as a serious break with past practice and was seen as a signal of potential problems. On 30 March the Soviets announced that there would be significant curbs on traffic between the Western and Soviet sectors of the city, as well as between the Western sectors and the Soviet sector of Germany. The following day, President Truman authorized the sending of armed trains through the checkpoints that the Soviets had established. In their attempt to reach the checkpoints, the trains were

---

27. The Soviet sector of Germany would not become a state until 1949 when the German Democratic Republic was formed. For the purposes of this discussion, *Eastern Germany* will be used instead of *East Germany*.

shifted by Soviet railroad workers to a siding, and no confrontation came about. The Truman administration was denied an opportunity to show that it was determined to challenge the Soviets, and the Soviets were spared the problem of deciding whether or not to resist the American moves with force. Over the next week the Soviets increased their troop strength in Eastern Germany to three hundred thousand, far beyond the number of Western troops in Western Germany, and at the same time, Soviet troops began to stop and inspect trains going from the West into Berlin, in violation of a long-standing understanding that each power could send in whatever goods it wished.

This Soviet action led to what came to be called the *baby airlift*. On 1 April, General Lucius D. Clay, the military governor of Germany, ordered that a small airlift be made into the American sector of Berlin, providing supplies for the 9,415 American personnel in the city. The British followed suit, bringing in supplies for their own personnel. A week later, a Soviet fighter plane buzzed a British airliner on its approach to Berlin, causing both planes to crash. Tensions rose sharply for a few days, but there seems to have been no serious impact on subsequent events. The baby blockade was to play an important role two months later when the complete blockade was imposed as it established that an airlift was a practical response to a blockade, and when General Clay and General Curtis LeMay (head of U.S. Air Forces in Germany) met to discuss the June blockade, their concern was how to run an airlift, not whether it was a feasible idea. The baby blockade had shown that it was.

On 9 April, the Soviets announced that all trains leaving for the West (not just those coming in from the West) would have to be cleared by Soviet personnel. Two days later they put a halt to all rail traffic between Berlin and the Western zones of Germany. The next day the main highway bridge to Berlin from the West was closed by the Soviets "for repair." The following day, in a move that helped ease some of the tensions, the baby airlift that had been started on 1 April was halted as some of the restrictions that the Soviets had imposed were lifted. The immediate crisis had ended for a time.

Over the next month, there were a series of small actions taken by all sides in their efforts to assert control over their sectors of Berlin. The final series of steps that led to the full blockade started on 16 June when the Soviet representative to the Berlin Kommandatura walked out, claiming that he had been insulted. This strain in four-power relations was compounded two days later with the announcement on 18 June of a currency reform in Western Germany (not including Berlin). In response to this, the Soviet Union stopped all passenger rail and road traffic between the Western and Soviet zones, along with decreasing freight rail traffic coming into the Western zones. The reason given for this was to "protect currency" in Berlin, implying that Berlin was part of the Soviet occupation zone. The next day all barge traffic from the West was halted as well.

On 21 June the Soviets announced that they would institute a currency reform of their own in Eastern Germany. On the following day this currency reform was extended to the Soviet sector of Berlin, while at the same time, the remaining land traffic from Western Germany into Berlin was halted. General Clay responded on the 23d by extending the currency reforms into Berlin, coming directly in conflict with the Soviet reforms. On the 24th, the Soviets took the final steps of imposing the blockade, closing the very few remaining routes into the city, halting the supply of electricity from power plants located in the Soviet sector, and prohibiting the distribution of any food supplies from the Soviet sector to the Western sectors. The blockade had begun, and the feeling of crisis reached its height in Washington.

For the purposes of this analysis, the crisis period of the Berlin blockade began on 24 June with the full implementation of the blockade by the Soviet Union and ended with a National Security Council meeting on 22 July.[28] It was at the 22 July meeting that the proposal for an armored ground convoy to break through the blockade line was firmly and finally vetoed, and the airlift was enlarged and made more of a routine operation. The 22 July meeting of the National Security Council marked the transition from a period of high tension and perceived danger to one of the routine implementation of a policy directive. This meeting marked a turning point because there was a major shift in the psychological perspective of the major decision makers as much of the tension of the preceding month had been reduced. An additional factor helping to relieve tensions was the fact that the Soviets had not taken any military actions that might have indicated that they were preparing to attempt to force the Western powers out of Berlin.

The time period from 24 June to 22 July provides a useful period for analysis. From the perspective of those in Washington, the crisis (the imposition of the final steps of the blockade) was unexpected and posed what was felt to be a serious threat to the position of the Western powers in Europe in general and Berlin in particular.[29] From the perspective of those in Berlin, the crisis was less of a surprise, as they had warned that a confrontation with the Soviet Union over Berlin was inevitable. The feeling that this threat to Berlin

---

28. It must be emphasized here that this time period and definition of crisis is from the American point of view. The Soviets had been taking actions designed to pressure the Western powers since March, and in one sense, the imposition of the full blockade on 24 June was simply the next logical, incremental step in the Soviet effort. Given all that had gone before, the actions taken on that date seem small in comparison. Nevertheless, it was this final step that created the impression of a crisis and propelled the Truman administration into action.

29. Shlaim, *The United States and the Berlin Blockade*, 195–96.

was a problem for the Western powers was even stronger among the relevant officials in Berlin, who were united in their belief that to back down in the face of Soviet threat would seriously undermine the credibility and standing of the United States in European eyes. Finally, both sets of decision makers felt that they had to respond quickly to the Soviet actions, both because of fears about having to supply a city of 2.5 million people and because of the great uncertainty about what the Soviets would do next. These fears had diminished greatly by 22 July because the first month of the airlift had shown great promise for being able to supply the city and because the Soviets had not taken any further steps by that point. It is interesting to note that fears about further Soviet action were much stronger in Washington than they were in Berlin. Both General Clay and State Department Advisor Robert Murphy felt that the Soviets would not escalate this crisis any further than they had.

Unlike the other crises considered in this analysis, there were four major powers involved in this crisis: the United States, the Soviet Union, Great Britain, and France. The analysis presented here will focus on the decision making of the United States and its interactions with the Soviet Union. This is not as much of a problem as it would seem because by the time this crisis began the Western powers had come to agree on most issues. There were some issues on which they did not agree, but these issues are not directly relevant here.

Another factor that distinguishes this crisis from the others is that, unlike most of the crises considered in this analysis, there were two clearly defined levels of decision making concerning American actions in Berlin. General Clay was the military governor of Germany, in charge of all aspects of the occupation, and he had wide-ranging powers to do as he wished.[30] This power allowed General Clay a great deal of room in making decisions concerning Germany and Berlin, and Clay was the sort of person who used that freedom. The second level of decision making concerned with the Berlin crisis was in Washington, and it consisted primarily of President Truman and Secretary of State George Marshall.[31] At times there were significant differences in the

---

30. John McCloy, Clay's civilian successor, had the following description of the power available in that position:

> Military governor was a pretty heady job. It is the nearest thing to a Roman proconsulship the modern world afforded. You could turn to your secretary and say, "Take a law." The law was there, and you could see its effects in two or three weeks. It was a challenging job to an ambitious man. Benevolent dictatorship.

Smith, *Clay Papers*, vol. 1, xxv, quoted here from Shlaim, *The United States and the Berlin Blockade*, 98.

31. Shlaim is useful in providing excellent descriptions of these decision makers, their backgrounds, political outlooks, their attitudes toward the Soviet Union and Europe, and their images of the United States and the role that it should play in Europe. Shlaim, *The United States and the Berlin Blockade*.

way that these decision makers viewed events, and it will be useful to point out those differences during the analyses in later chapters.

Berlin Wall Crisis

On the night of 13 August 1961, East German forces, with the backing of the Soviet Union, moved to split the city of Berlin into two parts, East and West. This was done by constructing a barbed-wire and concrete barrier that surrounded the Western (French, British, and American) sectors of the city.[32] This barrier was constructed entirely on the soil of East Germany and the Soviet sector of Berlin. As time went on, it became obvious that the intent was not to block access to East Berlin or East Germany, but to restrict the flow of East Germans to the Western sectors of Berlin. This view of events is shown in the first statement issued by the U.S. State Department on 13 August:

> Available information indicates that measures taken thus far are aimed at residents of East Berlin and East Germany and not at the Allied position in West Berlin or access thereto. However, limitation on travel within Berlin is a [*sic*] violation of the four-power status of Berlin and a flagrant violation of the right of free circulation throughout the city. Restrictions on travel between East Germany and Berlin are indirect [*sic*] contravention of the Four Power agreement reached at Paris on June 20, 1949. These violations of existing agreements will be the subject of vigorous protest through appropriate channels.[33]

The emphasis on the relationship of these actions to *East* Berlin had been noted in previous U.S. statements, much to the dismay of those in the government who supported a strong stance in Berlin.[34] Emphasis in Washington was on the question of Western access to Berlin, not on restricting exits from the Soviet sector of Berlin. As the statement noted above suggests, the wall itself was not the reason for concern in Washington, but what might come next and what might be done to restrict Western access to Berlin itself.

---

32. The wall was not presented to Western decision makers as a fait accompli. It went up in stages, starting with barbed wire, then concrete blocks topped with barbed wire, and finally a concrete and brick wall. The first cement blocks were installed on 18 August.

33. U.S. Department of State, *Documents on Germany*, 776.

34. Norman Gelb, *The Berlin Wall* (New York: New York Times–Quadrangle, 1986), 117–20. See also Honore M. Catudal, *Kennedy and the Berlin Wall Crisis: A Case Study in U.S. Decision Making* (Berlin: Berlin-Verlag, 1980), 127–50. Catudal's is a very useful work, drawing on archival resources and interviews with many of the important figures in the Kennedy administration at the time of the Berlin crisis.

The construction of the Berlin Wall marked the beginning, and end, of two different phases of this crisis. It was the beginning of a crisis because the Soviets had finally taken action on the East German refugee problem.[35] In addition, there was the Soviet threat to sign a separate peace treaty with East Germany, thus turning control of the access routes to Berlin over to the East Germans. The construction of the wall contributed to the end of a crisis because the Soviets had finally acted, bringing to an end the tense period of waiting that had existed in Washington since the Vienna Summit in June between Kennedy and Nikita Khrushchev. At that summit Khrushchev had issued an ultimatum demanding that a peace treaty with the East Germans be signed. This ultimatum was very explicit in the threats it made, and it caused a great deal of concern in Washington.

In the days following the construction of the wall there was tremendous concern about whether or not the wall was a discrete action or the beginning of a new push on Berlin. It became apparent that the Soviets were acting cautiously, making sure that they did nothing to block Western access to all sectors of Berlin. The dawning realization that the Soviets were not going to take actions against Western access was reinforced when no effort was made to interfere with an American troop convoy sent to reinforce the Berlin garrison at the time of Vice-President Johnson's visit on 18 August.

The Berlin Wall crisis had two aspects, one general and one acute, and it is necessary to make a distinction between the two. The general crisis had to do with concern about what the Soviets were going to do about Berlin, while the more acute crisis concerned what the United States should do in response to the construction of the wall. The main focus here will be on the American response to the construction of the wall, but to do so, an understanding of the larger crisis is necessary. We will talk first about the larger crisis and then move on to a discussion of the crisis prompted by the construction of the wall.

The discussion above about the Berlin blockade detailed how the four Allied powers in World War II had established various agreements relating to their occupation of Berlin. The city had been divided into four sectors controlled separately by each of the four occupying powers. Following the Berlin airlift of 1948–49, the breakdown in four-power cooperation had become almost total. By the time of the construction of the Berlin Wall, the only functioning four-power entity was the Berlin air-traffic control center, and there was concern that this would fall victim to the crisis.[36] The three Western sectors (British, French, and American) had been increasingly governed and

---

35. For the purposes of this case study, the Soviets are assumed to have made the final decisions concerning the wall. While it is clear that the Soviets were not happy with the wall as a solution, it does seem clear that its construction would not have occurred without their agreement and encouragement.

36. *New York Times*, 9 September 1961.

treated as a single unit while the Soviets, and the East German regime they had set up, worked to consolidate their hold on their sector.

Over time, as the divisions between East and West in Germany became more entrenched, one of the major sources of tension between East and West was the sovereignty of East Germany and the control that it wished to exercise over access to Berlin. Following the uprisings in East Germany in 1953, one of the frequent threats made by Khrushchev had been that he would sign a peace treaty with East Germany, with or without the participation of the Western powers. The Western powers had strongly objected to such plans and had made such objections clearly known to the Soviet Union.[37] This threat had been made repeatedly since the end of World War II, by both Stalin and Khrushchev, and there was concern that the Soviets might actually do it. The main reason for this concern was that the rights and status of Berlin were governed by a number of four-power agreements that had been signed since the end of World War II and the Western powers were uncertain as to what would happen if the Soviets backed out of these agreements. Because East Germany was not party to these agreements, actions that they might take in Berlin could not be contested under these agreements. The Soviets had always claimed that once a peace treaty with East Germany had been signed, all previous agreements concerning Western rights in Berlin would be invalid and would have to be renegotiated with the East Germans. Needless to say, this caused a great deal of concern in the West.

In 1958, the Soviet Union had provoked a brief crisis by demanding that a peace treaty be signed with East Germany. The United States refused, and after a few months the crisis died down.[38] The issue of a peace treaty had remained somewhat dormant until February 1961 when the Soviet Union delivered two notes to the West German government. One was a message from Khrushchev offering to discuss the repatriation of Germans held in the Soviet Union since World War II, while the other was an aide-memoire that suggested that the Soviets did not want to wait until a new West German government was elected in September 1961 to deal with the "German prob-lem."[39] While professing to be willing to "display maximum understanding of the wishes of the Federal Government [of Germany]" the note continued with the threat that:

An entirely different situation would arise if the Federal Government [West Germany] would continue to insist on its negative position with

37. See Jean Edward Smith, *The Defense of Berlin* (Baltimore: Johns Hopkins University Press, 1963), 151ff, for a discussion of the history of Soviet demands on Berlin.

38. See Smith, *The Defense of Berlin*, 151–208, for a detailed discussion of this period.

39. See U.S. Department of State, *Documents on Germany*, 723–27, 729–32, for the text of the two notes.

regard to a peace treaty with Germany. By this very fact it would deny itself the possibility of direct defense of its interests.[40]

The memoire went on to threaten that if the West German government chose not to sign a treaty, the Soviets would go ahead and conclude their own treaty with East German authorities, which would mean the end of "the occupation regime in West Berlin with all the attendant consequences."[41] These consequences would include the renegotiation of all air, sea, and land lines of communication with East Germany. The contents of the aide-memoire were made known to the Allied governments, and a new round of discussions was initiated to anticipate problems that might come up. President Kennedy ordered a comprehensive review of administration policy on Berlin, and this review group was headed by former Secretary of State Acheson.[42]

On 16 March, U.S. Ambassador to the Soviet Union Llewelyn Thompson warned in a secret cable that the refugee problem in East Germany (thousands of East Germans were fleeing to West Berlin every month) was viewed very seriously in Moscow. The cable warned that if the Soviets should decide to postpone the signing of a separate peace treaty, then "we must at least expect East Germans to seal off Sector boundary in order to stop what they must consider intolerable continuation of refugee flow through Berlin."[43] During an April meeting with British Prime Minister Harold Macmillan, Kennedy discussed how far the West should be willing to go to defend Berlin.[44] Throughout the spring, the various planning groups in the administration continued to meet to discuss U.S. policy on Berlin.

Concern about Soviet intentions increased sharply as a result of the Kennedy-Khrushchev summit meeting at Vienna in June. There has been a great deal of controversy over what actually transpired at the summit, and to this day it remains unclear who actually came out of the meetings looking worse.[45] It is safe to say that the question of Berlin came up at the summit and there was no meeting of minds on the issue. Khrushchev presented Kennedy

---

40. U.S. Department of State, *Documents on Germany*, 726.

41. U.S. Department of State, *Documents on Germany*, 726.

42. Catudal, *Kennedy and the Berlin Wall Crisis*, 41–44, and Smith, *The Defense of Berlin*, 235–49. This is also discussed in Arthur M. Schlesinger, Jr., *A Thousand Days: John F. Kennedy in the White House* (Boston: Houghton Mifflin Company, 1965), 380–94.

43. Catudal, *Kennedy and the Berlin Wall Crisis*, 239–41.

44. Catudal, *Kennedy and the Berlin Wall Crisis*, 52–54.

45. The debate centers around how tough Khrushchev was on Kennedy and how much Kennedy was or was not affected by the meeting. For a view that the meeting was very rough and Kennedy deeply depressed, see Gelb, *The Berlin Wall*, 83–87, and Schlesinger, *A Thousand Days*, 373–74. For a contrary view, see Kenneth P. O'Donnell and David F. Powers, *"Johnny, We Hardly Knew Ye": Memories of John Fitzgerald Kennedy* (Boston: Little, Brown and Company, 1970), 297–99, and Theodore Sorensen, *Kennedy* (New York: Harper and Row, 1965), 550.

with an aide-memoire on the German question that was an updated version of the demands put forth in 1958. Kennedy's "Address to the Nation" following his return from Vienna noted that "it was a very sober 2 days," and he stressed the need for strength and vigilance in the face of Soviet threats.[46]

Pressure on the United States increased a week after the summit when the Soviets published the aide-memoire and reiterated their demands that a peace treaty be signed. Kennedy again ordered that planning efforts be increased, and these efforts continued into the summer.[47] The main focus of these efforts was to consider what the United States would do in response to any Soviet attempt to cut off Western access to Berlin. As it would turn out, this would not be the only problem that would face the United States and its allies.

The immediate cause of the 1961 Berlin crisis was the massive outpouring of refugees from East Germany to West Berlin, and West Germany beyond that.[48] The number of refugees had grown rapidly after Khrushchev's speech of 8 July when he announced that demobilization of the Soviet armed forces was being discontinued and that the military budget was being increased by one-third.[49] The number of refugees who crossed over in July was over thirty thousand, the highest figure since June 1953 when there was serious unrest in East Germany.[50] Khrushchev, in his memoirs, paints a bleak picture of the problem facing the East Germans:

> The . . . drain of workers was creating a simply disastrous situation in the GDR, which was already suffering from a shortage of manual labor, not to mention specialized labor. If things had continued like this much longer, I don't know what would have happened.[51]

That the refugee problem was a serious concern for the East Germans was recognized in the West and in particular by the Kennedy administration. There

46. John F. Kennedy, "Radio and Television Report to the American People on Returning from Europe, June 6, 1961," *Public Papers of the Presidents of the United States: John F. Kennedy, 1961* (Washington, D.C.: GPO, 1961), 442.

47. Catudal, *Kennedy and the Berlin Wall Crisis*, 123. See also Robert M. Slusser, *The Berlin Crisis of 1961: Soviet-American Relations and the Struggle for Power in the Kremlin, June–November 1961* (Baltimore: Johns Hopkins University Press, 1973), 21–34. Slusser discusses the Berlin crisis against the larger context of Soviet foreign policy during this time.

48. See Gelb, *The Berlin Wall*, 63–67, for a discussion of the refugee situation from the standpoint of the strain it was putting on the East German economy and regime. See also Slusser, *The Berlin Crisis of 1961*, 66–68.

49. Catudal, *Kennedy and the Berlin Wall Crisis*, 163–64.

50. Smith, *The Defense of Berlin*, 259. The total number of refugees who left between 1950 and 1964 was 2,715,185. Eleanor Lansing Dulles, *Berlin: The Wall Is Not Forever* (Chapel Hill: University of North Carolina Press, 1967), 56.

51. Nikita Khrushchev, *Khrushchev Remembers* (Boston: Little, Brown and Company, 1970), 454.

were many, including the chairman of the Senate Foreign Relations Committee, William Fulbright, who expressed their surprise that the East Germans and Soviets had let this problem go on for so long. Fulbright even commented on 30 July, two weeks before the wall was constructed:

> The truth of the matter [is that the] Russians have the power to close it [the border] in any case . . . without violating any treaty. . . . I don't understand why the East Germans don't close their border because I think they have a right to close it.[52]

Although Fulbright would later deny the charge, many at the time felt that this idea was a "trial balloon" for the Kennedy administration. Fulbright's speech was reported widely in West and East Germany, with varying tones of indignation and praise.[53] Even the *New York Times* commented that:

> There has never been any East-West agreement that would prevent the Communists from closing the border between East Germany and East Berlin. Why they have not done so in the past is something of a mystery.[54]

Thus, the question of a Soviet move to stem the tide of refugees was one that had received coverage before the construction of the wall on 13 August.

At a general level, concern in the Kennedy administration revolved around what the Soviets would do about the peace treaty and what the East Germans, and the Soviets, would do about the refugee problem. Western intelligence sources had been predicting for many months that the Soviets and East Germans would have to do something about the refugee situation, and many felt that the time was ripe for some sort of action.[55] As noted above, the number of refugees was continuing to rise, and there were intelligence reports of increased unrest within East Germany. Concerns about the peace treaty centered around possible threats to Western access to the city, while the concerns surrounding the refugee problem were about the potential for unrest in East Germany. The fear was that the situation in East Germany would get so bad that there would be uprisings similar to those in 1953 or those in Hungary in 1956. An additional fear was that the Soviets might use unrest in East Germany as an excuse to finally move in on Berlin and bring it com-

---

52. *New York Times*, 3 August 1961, quoted in Catudal, *Kennedy and the Berlin Wall Crisis*, 201.

53. Catudal, *Kennedy and the Berlin Wall Crisis*, 202.

54. *New York Times*, 6 August 1961, quoted in Slusser, *The Berlin Crisis of 1961*, 94.

55. Schlesinger, *A Thousand Days*, 394.

pletely under their control. This last was the nightmare scenario for many in the Kennedy administration.

At this general level, then, the problems in Berlin did not come as a surprise to the Kennedy administration. Its planning efforts had been directed at finding solutions to any possible problems that might come up. The construction of the Berlin Wall as a solution to the serious refugee problem facing the East German authorities was not a surprise to Western authorities.[56] Many in the administration fully expected the Soviet and East German authorities to do something. The construction of the Berlin Wall as the particular form of that solution to the refugee problem was a surprise. One way of looking at this issue is to say that the construction of the Berlin Wall was a tactical surprise but not a strategic surprise. Western leaders knew that the Soviets would have to do something about the refugee problem; they were just surprised at what they did. Of all the crises considered here, the Berlin Wall crisis was the least surprising as far as American leaders were concerned.[57] What made this a crisis for Western (and, particularly in this case, American) leaders was the concern over what the Soviets were going to do next. The question of whether or not this was seen as a crisis will be taken up in detail in chapter 4.

Cuban Missile Crisis

The Cuban Missile Crisis is perhaps the most-studied event in the history of American foreign policy and possibly the second most-studied event of this century, behind the outbreak of World War I. Recent scholarship on the topic has spurred renewed interest in the crisis, as both the United States and the Soviet Union have been more forthcoming about what actually transpired.[58]

---

56. Slusser suggests that there were some clues in Soviet announcements and statements designed to set the stage for the construction of the wall. Slusser, *The Berlin Crisis of 1961*, 123–29. Bundy also makes the same suggestion in *Danger and Survival*, 364–65.

57. The history of East-West confrontation in, and over, Berlin is long and complex and far beyond the scope of this discussion. For a discussion of that history, as it relates to this crisis, see Clay, *Decision in Germany*, and Smith, *The Defense of Berlin*.

58. For the most current reviews of the debate surrounding events in this crisis, as well as the most useful bibliographies, see James G. Blight and David A. Welch, *On the Brink: Americans and Soviets Reexamine the Cuban Missile Crisis* (New York: Hill and Wang, 1989), and James G. Blight, *The Shattered Crystal Ball: Fear and Learning in the Cuban Missile Crisis* (Savage, Md.: Rowman and Littlefield Publishers, 1990). The best analysis that incorporates the new information is Raymond L. Garthoff, *Reflections on the Cuban Missile Crisis*, rev. ed. (Washington, D.C.: Brookings, 1989). The recent debates about Soviet perceptions and actions in the crisis are of great interest but of little importance to the story told here. The focus here is on American decision making and recent revelations have added little to our knowledge about American decisions. Between 1987 and 1989, there were a series of conferences on the Cuban Missile Crisis that involved former officials from the Kennedy administration, academics, and

What this new information has made clear is that perceptions, and change in those perceptions, played a very significant role in the crisis.

The drama of the Cuban Missile Crisis has become almost legendary, in part because this was a serious crisis. Robert Divine introduces his book on the Cuban Missile Crisis in following manner:

> The Cuban missile crisis marks the closest the world has yet come to nuclear destruction. For six harrowing days in 1962, from the time President John F. Kennedy informed the nation of the Soviet missile buildup in Cuba until Nikita Khrushchev agreed to pull back, the American people lived under the threat of disaster. The armed forces went from Defense Condition Five (peacetime alert) to Defcon 3 (war alert), and the Strategic Air Command was ordered to Defcon 2 (full war footing), only one step away from actual hostilities. Five of the eight divisions of the Army Strategic Reserve were placed on alert; the First Armored Division moved from Texas to Fort Stewart, Georgia; and in Florida, Lieutenant General Hamilton Howze set up a command post for the invasion of Cuba. Polaris-armed nuclear submarines left their base in Holy Loch, Scotland, to take up stations at sea within range of the Soviet Union; SAC scattered its B-47 bombers to civilian airfields around the United States and kept a major portion of its long-range B-52 bombers, loaded with nuclear weapons, in the air. These planes, together with 105 short-range missiles in Europe and 156 intercontinental missiles in the United States, were ready to deliver the nuclear equivalent of thirty billion tons of TNT upon the Soviet Union at the command of the President. The command never came.[59]

---

even Soviet specialists. During these conferences, which I will call the *glasnost revelations*, new information became available that shed some further light on both the American and Soviet sides of the confrontation. There remains some controversy over the new information, but for the most part the additional information complements the information that existed previously. There are four pieces of new information that might have had an impact on the events of 1962 had they been known at the time. First, the number of Soviet troops in Cuba at the time of the crisis was over forty thousand, not the sixteen thousand believed at the time. Blight and Welch, *On the Brink*, 356 n. 26. Second, the shooting down of Major Rudolf Anderson, Jr.'s U-2 in the final days of the crisis was not ordered by the Kremlin but was undertaken by a Soviet military commander in Cuba. Blight and Welch, *On the Brink*, 311. Third, the communication with John Scali from Aleksandr Fomin, suggesting a possible deal that might end the crisis, did not come from the Kremlin, as the members of the ExComm believed at the time, but was the result of an independent initiative of Soviet Ambassador to the United States, Dobrynin. Garthoff, *Reflections on the Cuban Missile Crisis*, 80 n. 136. Finally, it was revealed that President Kennedy had indeed been willing to trade missiles in Turkey for the missiles in Cuba. Blight and Welch, *On the Brink*, 83–84, 113–15. The discrepancies will be noted where appropriate in the discussion that follows.

59. Robert A. Divine, ed., *The Cuban Missile Crisis* (Chicago: Quadrangle, 1971), 4–5. For a detailed discussion of the extraordinary military steps taken during the crisis, see Dan

Given the tremendous amount of information available on this topic,[60] no attempt will be made here to unearth new information.[61] Rather, this discussion will adopt a different perspective than that taken by most scholars and ask what role perception and misperception played in the crisis. The question, and danger, of misperception was highlighted during the crisis in one of the communications from Premier Khrushchev:

> An even more dangerous case occurred on October 28, when your reconnaissance aircraft invaded the northern area of the Soviet Union, in the area of Chukotski Peninsula, and flew over our territory. One asks, Mr. President, how we should regard this. What is this—a provocation? Your aircraft violates our frontier, and this happens at a time as troubled as the one through which we are now passing, when everything has been put in battle readiness. For an intruding U.S. aircraft can easily be taken

Caldwell, ed., "Department of Defense Operations during the Cuban Crisis: A Report by Adam Yarmolinsky, 13 February 1963," *Naval War College Review* 32, no. 4 (June–July 1979): 83–99. For a further discussion see Scott D. Sagan, "Nuclear Alerts and Crisis Management," *International Security* 9, no. 4 (Spring 1985): 99–139. For a basic account of the crisis, see Elie Abel, *The Missile Crisis* (New York: Bantam, 1968); Robert F. Kennedy, *Thirteen Days: A Memoir of the Cuban Missile Crisis* (New York: W. W. Norton, 1969); or Graham T. Allison, *Essence of Decision: Explaining the Cuban Missile Crisis* (Boston: Little, Brown and Company, 1971).

60. See Lester H. Brune, *The Missile Crisis of October 1962: A Review of Issues and References* (Claremont, Calif.: Regina Books, 1985), for a detailed overview of the many sources of information available on the Cuban Missile Crisis. For recent material, Blight and Welch, *On The Brink*, and Blight, *The Shattered Crystal Ball*, provide the best bibliographies.

61. Prior to the glasnost revelations, there have been two major releases of new information about the Cuban Missile Crisis. In October 1983, the John F. Kennedy Library revealed the existence of tape recordings made during the ExComm meetings of 16 October 1962. These were the only transcripts that were released until 1987 when transcripts of the final meeting of the ExComm on 27 October were also released. The transcripts for the intervening days of meetings have not been released. Nevertheless, the ones that have been released do shed some new light on the deliberations of the group and suggest that some of the earlier interpretations of events might be incorrect. For a discussion of the new information coming from the first meeting, see Marc Trachtenberg, "The Influence of Nuclear Weapons in the Cuban Missile Crisis," *International Security* 10, no. 1 (Summer 1985): 137–63. For example, Trachtenberg suggests that three popular beliefs about the Cuban Missile Crisis are wrong: Robert Kennedy's opposition to an invasion, President Kennedy's refusal to consider a deal involving missiles in Turkey, and Secretary of Defense McNamara's acceptance of the argument that these missiles did have a strategic impact. Trachtenberg also provides excerpts from written summaries of three of the final Ex Comm meetings that occurred as Soviet ships were approaching the blockade and preparations for an invasion were being made. The second meeting is covered in David A. Welch and James G. Blight, "The Eleventh Hour of the Cuban Missile Crisis," *International Security* 12, no. 3 (Winter 1987–88): 5–29, and McGeorge Bundy and James G. Blight, "October 27, 1962: Transcripts of the Meeting of the ExComm," *International Security* 12, no. 3 (Winter 1987–88): 30–92. For detailed discussions of the final days of the crisis, and the thinking of the American and Soviet players, see Blight, *The Shattered Crystal Ball*.

for a bomber with nuclear weapons, and that can push us toward a fatal step. All the more so, because the U.S. Government and the Pentagon have long been saying that you continually maintain bombers with atomic bombs in the air. Therefore, you can imagine what kind of responsibility you assume, especially during such an anxious time as the present.[62]

The various accounts of the deliberations of American decision makers show that perceptions of Soviet motives and actions changed during the course of deliberations, particularly as more information about Soviet activities and statements became available. The discussion in the chapters to follow will relate these changes in information and opinion to the overall dynamic of the crisis.

Before proceeding, a note about sources is needed. Unlike many of the foreign policy events that have occurred within the past thirty years, there is a great deal of official and unofficial information available about the Cuban Missile Crisis. There are a few problems, however, that should be noted and addressed. Up until 1983, and later 1987, when the partial transcripts of the ExComm meetings were released, all accounts of the deliberations of the ExComm came from participants or from writers who had interviewed those participants. This poses a problem with respect to historical bias and objectivity, and even the glasnost revelations have not solved all such problems. The public portrayal of the handling of the crisis by the Kennedy administra-

---

62. "Chairman Khrushchev's Message of October 28, 1962," (official translation), reprinted in *Department of State Bulletin*, 19 November 1973, 653. President Kennedy and Premier Khrushchev exchanged a total of ten messages during the Cuban Missile Crisis. Only four were made public at the time (the last four sent), and these are the ones most commonly referred to. The remaining six were declassified and made public in 1973. All ten, with two sets of translations, were published in the 19 November 1973 issue of the *Department of State Bulletin*. Informal translations were made by the Moscow embassy at the time the Soviet messages were received, and official translations were provided later. There are many minor and a few major differences. When the differences are relevant to the discussion here, they will be pointed out. When discussing the impressions that American leaders might have had from Khrushchev's messages, the informal translations will be referred to as these were most likely the ones used at the time. When attempting to ascertain what the Soviets were thinking, the official translations will be used. "Messages Exchanged by President Kennedy and Chairman Khrushchev during the Cuban Missile Crisis of October 1962," *Department of State Bulletin*, 19 November 1973, 635–55. An additional ten letters sent by Kennedy and Khrushchev in the aftermath of the crisis between 3 November and 14 December were released following a conference in Havana, Cuba, in January 1992. The letters dealt with clarifications regarding the agreement reached between Kennedy and Khrushchev on the removal of the missiles from Cuba. The discussion here deals with events prior to the exchange of these letters and the information contained in them does not alter the analysis presented.

tion, and by President Kennedy in particular, has generally been favorable.[63] However, as Marc Trachtenberg notes:

> But the picture [of American actions during the Cuban Missile Crisis] that came through in the memoir literature was almost bound to be distorted: after President Kennedy's assassination, and the series of national traumas that followed in rapid succession, it was inevitable that recollections about the early 1960s would be filtered through many layers of emotion, and in fact the prevailing interpretation of the period came to have an almost mythic [*sic*] quality.[64]

Even those who had participated in the crisis have become critical of the overwhelming praise lavished on President Kennedy's handling of the crisis. As Acheson writes following the publication of Robert Kennedy's *Thirteen Days: A Memoir of the Cuban Missile Crisis*:

> It was not enough, Napoleon observed, that he should have good generals; he wanted them to be lucky generals, also. In foreign affairs brains, preparation, judgment, and power are of utmost importance, but luck is essential. It does not detract from President Kennedy's laurels in handling the Cuban crisis that he was helped by the luck of Khrushchev's befuddlement and loss of nerve. The fact was that he succeeded. However, as the Duke of Wellington said of Waterloo, it was "a damned near thing." And one should not play one's luck so far too often.[65]

As noted above, the transcripts of just two days' worth of meetings have cast doubt on many of the traditional interpretations of events. As a result, the usual cautions about the accuracy of memoir accounts must be made again.[66]

Another problem with currently available information about the crisis is its uneven coverage of events. To begin with, there is a great deal known about the decision-making process in the United States while very little is

---

63. See Brune, *The Missile Crisis of October 1962*, and Divine, *The Cuban Missile Crisis*, for useful reviews of the debate over the handling of the crisis as well as of the various revisionist interpretations of the crisis.

64. Trachtenberg, "The Influence of Nuclear Weapons in the Cuban Missile Crisis," 164.

65. "Dean Acheson's Version of Robert Kennedy's Version of the Cuban Missile Affair," *Esquire* 71 (February 1969), in Divine, *The Cuban Missile Crisis*, 206–7.

66. One of the most interesting, and disturbing, results of the glasnost revelations about the Cuban Missile Crisis is the extent to which former American officials have changed their interpretations of events, sometimes completely reversing previous positions. Cautions about this are raised in Ray S. Cline, "The Cuban Missile Crisis," *Foreign Affairs* 68, no. 4 (Fall 1989): 190–96, and Mark Kramer, "Remembering the Cuban Missile Crisis: Should We Swallow Oral History?" *International Security* 15, no. 1 (Summer 1990): 212–18.67. Michel Tatu, *Power in*

known about this process in the Soviet Union. This is true in general as well as for the decision-making process during the Cuban Missile Crisis. The works of Michel Tatu and Roman Kolkowicz, as well as that of Arnold L. Horelick, are those most frequently referred to in describing the workings of the Kremlin and the debates among various factions about the wisdom of placing missiles in Cuba.[67] Following the crisis, there were two authoritative statements made by Khrushchev about Soviet goals and intentions in providing missiles to Cuba, yet they do not provide anywhere near the degree of information that is available for the American side. The first statement was to the Supreme Soviet on 12 December 1962 and the second to the Socialist Unity Party of Germany on 16 January 1963.[68] A later, semiauthoritative statement on Soviet goals and American blame for creating the Cuban crisis was provided by Anatolii Gromyko in 1971.[69] These sources provide the bulk of information that most authors cite in their analyses of Soviet intentions and goals in the Cuban Missile Crisis, and they will be discussed further below. The Cuban Missile Crisis has received very little attention in the Soviet press, as well as in the Soviet scholarly literature, and the writings of Gromyko are the only ones that have been widely available.[70] The glasnost revelations have helped lift some of the secrecy that surrounds Soviet actions in the Cuban Missile Crisis, but unlike the American side, no high-level Soviet officials who were participants have come forth with further information.

The types of materials that can be expected to eventually appear in the *Foreign Relations of the United States* series are not yet available and probably will not be for another three to five years. It was only in 1992 that all of the messages sent between Kennedy and Khrushchev were finally made available! The most comprehensive government review of American operations and decision making during the crisis can be found in the hearings on the 1964

---

67. Michel Tatu, *Power in the Kremlin* (New York: Viking Press, 1969), Roman Kolkowicz, *The Soviet Military and the Communist Party* (Princeton: Princeton University Press, 1967); and Arnold L. Horelick, "The Cuban Missile Crisis: An Analysis of Soviet Calculations and Behavior," *World Politics* 16, no. 3 (April 1964): 363–89.

68. Nikita Khrushchev, "Report to the Supreme Soviet of the USSR, December 12, 1962," *Pravda*, 13 December 1962, and "Speech at the VI Congress of the Socialist Unity Party of Germany, 16 January 1963," *Pravda*, 17 January 1963. Both of these are reprinted in Alexander Dallin, ed., *Diversity in International Communism: A Documentary Record, 1961–1963* (New York: Columbia University Press, 1963).

69. Anatolii A. Gromyko, "The Caribbean Crisis 1: The U.S. Government's Preparation of the Caribbean Crisis," and "The Caribbean Crisis 2: Diplomatic Efforts of the USSR to Eliminate the Crisis," *Voprosy istorii*, nos. 7–8 (1971), reprinted in *Soviet Law and Government* 11, no. 1 (Summer 1972): 3–53.

70. Ronald R. Pope, ed., *Soviet Views on the Cuban Missile Crisis: Myth and Reality in Foreign Policy Analysis* (Washington, D.C.: University Press of America, 1982), ix, 1–3.

Department of Defense budget allocation.[71] The point being made here is that while there is a great deal of information available, sometimes in great detail, there is more that will become available as time goes on, possibly requiring further analysis and evaluation.

The events of October 1962 have been widely chronicled and discussed. Rather than recount the whole story, from the discovery on 15 October of the missile bases under construction to Khrushchev's letter of 28 October agreeing to remove the missiles, only those parts of the story relevant to the argument presented here will be told. The general outline of the story is well-known, and it will be assumed that the reader has that basic knowledge.[72] In the summer of 1962, the Soviet Union decided to install medium- and intermediate-range nuclear missiles in Cuba as a means of redressing its strategic weakness, a weakness that had recently become known to the entire world. The deployment continued clandestinely until 14 October when an American U-2 plane flying over Cuba took photographs of the missile deployments. Throughout the remainder of that summer, while the deployment of the missiles continued, the Kennedy administration engaged in a complicated rhetorical campaign that attempted to make clear that the installation of offensive weapons in Cuba would be unacceptable, while suggesting that defensive weapons would be OK. This effort became wrapped up in an intense domestic political battle over which party, Democratic or Republican, was too soft on communism in this hemisphere, and Cuba in particular. When the news about missiles in Cuba was broken to President Kennedy on 16 October, he had both an international and domestic problem on his hands.

With news of missiles in Cuba, President Kennedy convened what came to be called the *ExComm*, a group of his closest advisors that met together for the next thirteen days to monitor the crisis. The group considered six options: a full-scale invasion, a surgical air strike, a secret approach to Castro to try to split him from the Soviets, a diplomatic effort involving the UN and Organization of the American States (OAS), a quarantine, or, simply, doing nothing. Within forty-eight hours, the group decided to prepare for the possibility of an eventual air strike and invasion, while pursuing a quarantine against the introduction of further offensive weapons. For six days, U.S. preparations were conducted in secret, along with increased surveillance of the island, until 22 October when President Kennedy stunned the world (and especially the Soviets) with a speech describing the Soviet activities and announcing the quarantine. For the next seven days, the world watched as the United States

---

71. U.S. Congress, House of Representatives, Committee on Appropriations, Subcommittee on Department of Defense Appropriations for 1964, *Hearings*, 88th Cong., 1st sess., 1963.

72. The following brief overview is drawn from Blight, *The Shattered Crystal Ball*, 14–22.

made its preparations for an air strike and invasion, and the Soviet forces on Cuba rushed to make their missiles operational. What eventually resolved the crisis, on 27 October, was a Soviet pledge to remove the missiles from Cuba, in return for an American pledge not to invade Cuba. After thirteen days of confrontation, the crisis was over.

One useful way to discuss the crisis is to divide it into four broad stages. The first stage is from the summer of 1962 until 15 October when the presence of offensive missiles was confirmed. This phase can be thought of as the *precrisis stage*, both for the United States because it did not know a crisis was coming and for the Soviet Union because it did not know one was coming so soon.[73]

The second stage of the crisis can be called the *American crisis* or the *unilateral crisis*. This stage includes the six days from the discovery of the missiles to the public announcement by President Kennedy of their discovery on 22 October. This stage was marked by increased surveillance of Cuba, military preparations for an invasion, military preparations for an air strike against the missiles, detailed discussion of Soviet motives and intentions, and consideration of various diplomatic courses of action.

The third stage can be called the *confrontation stage*. This stage began when Dean Rusk informed Soviet Ambassador Anatolii Dobrynin of the American discovery one hour before Kennedy's speech and ended when it was announced over Radio Moscow that the missiles were being withdrawn. This stage was the most tense and dangerous, as both sides faced each other diplomatically and militarily, attempting to coerce the other side into acceding to their demands.

The fourth stage can be thought of as the *crisis resolution* or *coordination phase*. For most of the world, as well as for most scholars, the Cuban Missile Crisis ended with the public statements of Khrushchev, announcing the withdrawal of the missiles, and Kennedy, announcing a pledge not to invade Cuba. What many people overlook is the fact that there was still a high risk of conflict well into November and even December. There were ongoing debates between Castro, Khrushchev, and Kennedy over the nature and composition of the Soviet withdrawal. Preparations for an American invasion of the island continued long after the announced withdrawal, reaching a peak on 15 November. The alert status of these forces was not downgraded until 21 November. Surveillance and overflights of Cuba continued at a stepped up pace after the Soviet announcement that the missiles were being withdrawn.[74]

---

73. The question of whether the Soviets had any reason to think that they could get away with putting missiles in Cuba without being caught will be discussed in chap. 6.

74. Caldwell, "Department of Defense Operations during the Cuban Crisis," 93.

The members of ExComm continued to meet to monitor the progress of withdrawing the missiles and IL-28 bombers that had been sent.[75]

Phases two and three are the ones that are of most interest here because it was during these phases that the perceptions of both sides came into conflict. In phase two, many in the U.S. government had to confront the apparent contradiction between their belief that the Soviet Union would not install offensive weapons in Cuba and the Soviet installation of missiles in Cuba. In phase three, the Soviet Union had to confront the apparent contradiction between its belief that the response of the United States to the discovery of missiles in Cuba would not be very strong and the very extensive military preparations that the United States was making. In phase four, perceptions played a role, although to a much lesser extent than in the other phases. There were tensions that developed during this phase as the debate over verification of the removal of the medium-range ballistic missiles (MRBMs) and bombers was being resolved. This phase will figure less prominently in our discussion because it concerned bargaining over the contents of an agreed upon outcome (removal of offensive forces).

This brief summary does not do justice to the details of the crisis, but more will be filled in as the propositions in the following chapters are discussed.

October 1973 Middle East War

In contrast to the other crises considered here, the October 1973 Middle East War crisis was of very short duration. While the October 1973 War lasted almost three weeks, the confrontation between the United States and the Soviets lasted less than forty-eight hours. While the crisis was short, it was the most serious confrontation between the United States and the Soviet Union since the Cuban Missile Crisis in 1962. While the war itself was a crucial event in the history of Arab-Israeli relations, it is the interaction between the United States and the Soviet Union during the war, and the confrontation that grew out of that interaction, that is of interest here. As President Richard Nixon put it in his 26 October news conference, he viewed the confrontation between the United States and the Soviet Union as "a real crisis. It was the most difficult crisis we have had since the Cuban confrontation of 1962."[76] While critics at the time and later have questioned the extent of the crisis, and

---

75. It is somewhat disheartening to learn that the number of missiles counted as leaving Cuba was larger than the number discovered by American intelligence sources. Allison, *Essence of Decision*, 303–4 n. 12.

76. Richard M. Nixon, "Press Conference of 26 October 1973," *Department of State Bulletin*, 12 November 1973, 583.

the need for a nuclear alert on the part of the United States, it is interesting to ask how the United States and the Soviet Union came to be in such a confrontation. The process of détente had been given a strong boost by the 1972 Moscow Summit and the 1973 Washington/San Clemente Summit. It seemed that relations between the two countries were the best they had been in many years and the lines of communication between them were relatively open. Nevertheless, the most serious confrontation between the two in ten years would come out of the Arab-Israeli war. The general question to be asked is "To what extent did misperceptions contribute to this crisis?"

The fourth major war between the Arabs and Israelis began with a coordinated attack against Israeli positions by both the Egyptians and Syrians at 2:00 P.M. (Cairo time) on 6 October 1973.[77] On the Egyptian front, the war began with an artillery and rocket attack across the Suez Canal and a simultaneous crossing of the canal by commandos to begin the process of building the necessary bridges to carry the troops that would follow. For the Syrians, the war began with a massive artillery attack and tank assault into the Golan Heights. Both attacks were initially successful, but in time their momentum began to falter. Israel was caught in total strategic surprise, and almost total tactical surprise, and was forced to mobilize under fire. Along with the Israelis, the United States was surprised by the outbreak of the war. The State Department's Bureau of Intelligence and Research had concluded on 30 September that:

> In our view, the political climate in the Arab states argues against a major Syrian military move against Israel at this time. The possibility of a more limited Syrian strike, perhaps one designed to retaliate for the

---

77. The following discussion relies on Sunday Times Insight Team, *Insight on the Middle East War* (New York: Doubleday, 1974), as it is the most comprehensive account as well as the most commonly cited source. A very useful source for American perspectives on the crisis is Alan Dowty, *Middle East Crisis: U.S. Decision-Making in 1958, 1970, 1973* (Berkeley: University of California Press, 1984), 199–320. With respect to the details of the interaction between the United States and the Soviet Union, we are forced to rely for the most part on Henry Kissinger, *Years of Upheaval* (Boston: Little, Brown and Company, 1982), 450–613. There is always a problem with relying on a single source or a source that cannot be verified by independent means. Aside from President Nixon, no other major official of the time has written memoirs, and Nixon's account is of questionable accuracy. Marvin Kalb and Bernard Kalb, *Kissinger* (Boston: Little, Brown and Company, 1974), is based on much inside information and is consistent with what Kissinger later wrote in *Years of Upheaval*. Given the almost single-handed way in which Kissinger made and carried out the foreign policy of the United States during this crisis, one is left with having to rely heavily on his account until the relevant documents become available. Dowty's account, which relies on numerous interviews with American civilian and military officials at the time, substantially corroborates Kissinger's account, adding credibility because of its many different sources.

pounding the Syrian Air Force took from the Israelis on September 13, cannot of course be excluded.[78]

The Defense Intelligence Agency reported on 3 October (three days before the war) that the movements of Syrian and Egyptian troops "are considered to be coincidental and not designed to lead to major hostilities," while on the day before the outbreak of the war, the CIA reported that Egypt did not appear to be preparing for war with Israel.[79] The Egyptians and Syrians had been able to make their preparations for war in almost complete secrecy—even though many of their actions were known to Israeli and Western intelligence sources. As a result, the first week of the war was one of overwhelming victory for the Egyptians and Syrians. In contrast to the previous Arab-Israeli wars, the Arab forces performed extremely well, taking advantage of the planning and training of the previous eighteen months.

In addition to taking advantage of a long lead time in training and planning, as well as carrying out a successful deception, the Syrians and Egyptians started this war with limited goals. Previous wars had begun with the goal of defeating Israel and regaining Arab control over the region. As the *London Times* Insight Team puts it:

> for Egypt and Syria, who launched their attack after months of meticulous planning, the war was different than the previous three. This time their stated war plans contained no intention of destroying Israel; nor were the claims of the Palestinians among their main considerations. Israel's principal offence by now, as far as Egypt and Syria were concerned, was not its existence, but its continued occupation of the Arab land it had conquered in 1967.[80]

Syria and Egypt almost reached their goals in the first week of the war. By the end of that week, on 12 October, Egyptian and Syrian troops were continuing to cross the borders, coming close to their planned points of advance. The strategy in this war was to take as much land from the Israelis as possible, thus

---

78. Kissinger, *Years of Upheaval*, 464. The Israeli air force shot down thirteen Syrian planes in an ambush a week earlier. For a detailed discussion of the way in which the U.S. intelligence community was fooled, see 459–67. A useful discussion of the nature of surprise and its use in this war is in Alex Roberto Hybel, *The Logic of Surprise in International Conflict* (Lexington, Mass.: D. C. Heath and Company, 1986). Dowty provides a detailed account of the various intelligence assessments available to American decision makers prior to the crisis. *Middle East Crisis*, 209–12.

79. Kissinger, *Years of Upheaval*, 464–65.

80. Sunday Times Insight Team, *Insight on the Middle East War*, 14.

proving that the Arabs could put up a substantial fight, and then call for negotiations to work out a political settlement. This, however, did not work out as planned.

By not accepting a cease-fire proposal that was put forth on the 12th, Egypt gave the impression that it was heading for a new offensive that would go beyond its stated aims of a limited recovery of territory.[81] Had Egypt accepted the cease-fire, it would have halted the fighting before Israel had a chance to complete its mobilization, and such a halt would have consolidated Arab territorial gains. By the beginning of the second week it was clear that the high hopes of the week before were beginning to fade. The Soviet Union had begun a massive airlift of military supplies to Egypt and Syria on the 10th, but this was not enough to blunt the Israeli counteroffensive that began in the Golan Heights on the 11th and in the Sinai on the 13th. Israel's strategy was to conduct a holding action in the Sinai while defeating Syria in the north, and following the stabilization of the Golan front, to turn its full attention to the Sinai. The American airlift had begun on the 13th and was in full swing when the Israelis were able to cross the canal and begin undermining the Egyptian offensive. By the end of the second week (16–22 October) the tide had turned in the favor of Israel, thus setting the stage for confrontation between the United States and the Soviet Union. As the Israelis moved to the offensive and began winning the war, it became obvious that they were only interested in ending the war on their own terms (a cease-fire dictated by them) rather than ending the war to suit anyone else's needs.[82]

The Soviet Union, in an effort to halt the deterioration of Egypt's position, extended an invitation on 19 October to Secretary of State Kissinger to travel to Moscow and work out a cease-fire. Kissinger's trip to Moscow followed Soviet Premier Alexei N. Kosygin's visit to Cairo (16–19 October), where pressure was put on Anwar Sadat to accept a cease-fire.[83] Kissinger's stay in Moscow lasted until the 22d, when a cease-fire agreement was worked out. Kissinger then returned to Washington via Tel Aviv where he informed the Israeli government about the terms of the cease-fire. By this time, the Egyptian Third Army was in serious trouble in the Sinai, and President Anwar Sadat was making urgent appeals to the United States and the Soviet Union for assistance in the imposition of a cease-fire. The text of the first cease-fire (Resolution 338) agreed upon by the United States and the Soviet Union was

81. The title of the Sunday Times Insight Team's chapter on the first week of the war is "Week One: The Victory Egypt Threw Away."

82. Lawrence L. Whetten, *The Canal War: Four-Power Conflict in the Middle East* (Cambridge: MIT Press, 1974), 290.

83. Mohamed Heikal, *The Road to Ramadan* (London: Colling; New York: Quadrangle, 1975), 232, 245–46; Anwar Sadat, *In Search of Identity: An Autobiography* (New York: Harper and Row, 1978), 258–59; and Whetten, *The Canal War*, 288–89.

passed unanimously (fourteen to zero with China abstaining) by the UN Security Council on 22 October. This cease-fire held for less than twenty-four hours as both sides moved to consolidate their gains. The second cease-fire, Resolution 339, closed some of the gaps in the wording of Resolution 338 and was passed unanimously by the Security Council (fourteen to zero) on 23 October. By the time Resolution 339 was adopted, the Egyptian Third Army was in serious danger of being totally encircled in the Sinai. This would be the pivot point on which the confrontation between the United States and the Soviet Union, and between the United States and Israel, would rest in the next forty-eight hours.

The Israeli government continued to make it clear that it was intent on achieving a complete military victory in the Sinai and was not willing to let the political concerns of either the United States or the Soviet Union slow it down.[84] It was the realization of this Israeli determination to conduct the war on its own terms, as well as the steadily worsening situation of the Egyptian Third Army in the Sinai, that caused President Sadat to seek the help of first the United States and then the Soviet Union.[85] This included sending urgent appeals to both Washington and Moscow to send observers or troops to the area.[86] Sadat's intent was to have these troops see that Israel was violating the cease-fire, thus leading the United States (and possibly the Soviet Union) to pressure Israel to adhere to the cease-fire. On 24 October, President Sadat made a public appeal for troops from the United States and the Soviet Union to enforce the cease-fire in the Sinai (all previous appeals had been through a private diplomatic channel). The Soviet Union let it be known through informal conversations with the American delegation to the United Nations that it was willing to go along with the idea if another country introduced it into the Security Council. The United States was strongly opposed to the idea of Soviet troops enforcing a cease-fire, and Kissinger made this clear to

---

84. Kissinger, *Years of Upheaval*, 571–73.

85. Heikal, *The Road to Ramadan*, 250–54. Dowty provides a detailed examination of the specific events surrounding this event, as seen by the American participants. *Middle East Crisis*, 255–60.

86. Heikal provides an interesting note about the actual requests that were made to the Soviet Union and the possible confusion that might have resulted. He notes that Syrian President Hafez Asad asked Sadat whether or not the Soviets were sending "forces" (*quwat* in Arabic) and Sadat replied that they were sending seventy observers. Heikal notes that the word *quwat* can mean either "personnel" or "forces" ("troops") in Arabic, and he speculates that these messages were intercepted by the Americans and given the second ("troops") interpretation. "It is possible that they gave the impression that somebody was asking for Soviet forces to be sent to the area." Heikal notes that Kissinger later said there was "concrete evidence" that the Soviets were about to intervene and [Heikal] suggests that "there could be no other conceivable source for such a statement apart from these Asad-Sadat exchanges." *The Road to Ramadan*, 253–54. While there appear to be no other accounts that mention this possibility, it would truly be ironic if the U.S.-Soviet confrontation was the result of a misunderstood Arabic word.

Dobrynin. As Kissinger notes in his memoirs: "We were determined to resist by force if necessary the introduction of Soviet troops into the Middle East regardless of the pretext under which they arrived."[87]

On the 24th Soviet Premier Brezhnev sent a letter to President Nixon suggesting that the United States and the Soviet Union jointly send forces to the Middle East to enforce the cease-fire. The letter, at the same time, threatened that the Soviet Union would act unilaterally if the United States chose not to cooperate:

> Let us together, the USSR and the United States, urgently dispatch to Egypt the Soviet and American military contingents, to insure the implementation of the decision of the Security Council of October 22 and 23 concerning the cessation of fire and of all military activities and also of our understanding with you on the guarantee of the implementation of the decisions of the Security Council.
>
> It is necessary to adhere without delay. I will say it straight that if you find it impossible to act jointly with us in this matter, we should be faced with the necessity urgently to consider the question of taking appropriate steps unilaterally.[88]

Prior to the arrival of this letter, intelligence sources of the United States had received indications that Soviet airborne troops had been put on alert in the Ukraine, leading some to believe that they were about to be sent to the Sinai to monitor, or enforce, the cease-fire. In addition, it was learned that some of the aircraft that had been in use in the airlift to Damascus and Cairo had been diverted to bases in the Ukraine. Marvin and Bernard Kalb note that the high-level working group that had been dealing with this crisis since the beginning, the Washington Special Action Group (WSAG), learned late on the 24th that four more airborne divisions had been put on alert (bringing the total to seven divisions—about 50,000 troops), that five or six transport ships had entered the Mediterranean bringing the number of Soviet ships in the region to an unprecedented eighty-five, that intelligence sources had acquired intercepts of "special military orders" that "suggest[ed] the Russians might be preparing to intervene," and that a flight of Soviet transports, capable of carrying 1,600 troops, had taken off in the direction of Cairo.[89] With these bits of informa-

---

87. Kissinger, *Years of Upheaval*, 580.

88. Kissinger, *Years of Upheaval*, 583.

89. Kalb and Kalb, *Kissinger*, 488. See also Kissinger, *Years of Upheaval*, 584, 589; William B. Quandt, *Soviet Policy in the October 1973 War*, report prepared for the Office of the Assistant Secretary of Defense, International Security Affairs, R-1864-ISA (Santa Monica: RAND Corporation, May 1976), 33; Galia Golan, "Soviet Decision Making in the Yom Kippur War, 1973" in *Soviet Decision-Making for National Security*, ed. Jiri Valenta and William Potter (London: George Allen and Unwin, 1984), 209; and Dowty, *Middle East Crisis*, 255–60.

tion, the president (or Kissinger, depending on which account one reads) ordered an alert of U.S. military forces. All elements of the armed forces of the United States not normally at DefCon III (a situation of increased readiness without there having been a determination that war is likely) were raised to that status. What President Nixon and Secretary Kissinger hoped to do was send a strong signal to the Soviet Union that the United States was determined to resist the introduction of Soviet forces into the region.[90] The following day the Soviets had not moved any of the forces the United States had been monitoring. All indications were that they had been taken off of alert status, and the United States responded by calling off its alert. The fighting on the ground ended shortly thereafter. The end of the war, and the end of the confrontation between the United States and the Soviet Union, came as quickly as it had started.

Conclusion

These short summaries have provided the basic information needed to begin the discussion of perceptions and crises. The detail has been necessary to provide as much as possible of the situation as it was seen by the decision makers of the time. Additional information on each crisis will be presented as needed. Each of the crises helps fill in information needed to consider the theory and propositions presented here. Not everyone will support the theory, but taken together the crises provide strong support for it. It is now time to begin the discussion of the propositions.

---

90. Sadat had expelled all Soviet advisors from his country in July 1972 as a result of continuing disagreements over Soviet arms shipments to Egypt. This breach did not last long, and the Soviets were in the process of rebuilding their position in Egypt at the time of the October 1973 War.

CHAPTER 3

The View from the Top:
The Origins of Crises

This study began a number of years ago with a simple question: What happens
to the interaction between two states when they do not see eye to eye? That is,
when the view that each has of the world, and of the other, is radically
different? Having been influenced by game theoretic approaches, the initial
questions took the form of "What happens when parties to a dispute see the
choices and payoffs differently?" and "What if country A's assessment of B's
preferences were different than B's own assessment—would that increase or
decrease the likelihood of conflict?" The initial suspicion was that relations
would be more likely to be tense or conflictual. The supposition was that
actors would from time to time find themselves in situations where their views
of events were different and that this would increase the likelihood of conflict.
Part of the puzzle was whether or not countries could stumble into a crisis—
that is, find themselves in a crisis unintentionally or by accident. If indeed
they could, a logical question to ask would be whether or not misperceptions
played a role.

This chapter begins the discussion of the theoretical elements of crisis
decision making being considered here. It, and the four that follow, consider
five different propositions about the origins, continuation, and termination of
crises. In doing so, each looks at the cases selected, noting both the strengths
and weaknesses of the propositions as applied to the cases. As noted in
chapters 1 and 2, not all cases will fit the propositions, but in sum they
provide a strong case for the theory being presented here. Let us now turn to a
discussion of the propositions and an examination of the crises themselves.

> *Proposition One*: Actors will tend to assume that their opponent(s) see
> the world in the same way as they themselves see it, and see their acts,
> motives, and preferences as they intend them to be seen.

Proposition One restates what seems to be a commonplace observation:
people tend to believe that what they say and do will be clear to others (unless
they are actively attempting to be deceptive). Jervis argues quite persuasively

that this will be the case in international relations as well, and that point of view is accepted here.[1] The main argument here is that actors will not consider how different events will look to another actor. This proposition sets the groundwork for part of the explanation of why crises will occur—clashing points of view.

In the language of game theory, Proposition One can be stated as "Actors will assume that the matrix of choices and payoffs will appear to both sides in the same manner." A constant theme in many accounts of the crises studied here was the inability of decision makers on one side of a dispute to realize (1) that the world might look different to their opponent, (2) that their actions might not be as clear as they believed them to be, and (3) that their ability to influence their opponent's views of their own motives was very limited. All of these points have been made by others, Jervis in particular, but they are worth discussing in greater detail to point out those elements that are relevant to the discussion here.[2]

Many of the tools available to game theorists make explicit or implicit assumptions similar to that behind Proposition One. To take the most simple and well-known example, consider the basic 2×2 matrix used to model the Prisoner's Dilemma (fig. 1). By representing the choices and outcomes in a single matrix, this approach assumes that both players see the same relationship of choices and outcomes. While this approach has provided a number of useful insights, there are limitations as it is not always the case that each party will have the same image of choices and outcomes. Thus it can frequently be useful to attempt to model the "world" from the point of view of each actor. Analysis that allows for the possibility of different perceptions of events on the part of each actor will be more accurate than that which assumes that each actor will have a similar view of the situation at hand.[3] In *Conflict Among Nations*, Snyder and Diesing used a combined matrix that contained each player's own estimates and valuations of their opponents' outcomes. The authors note that if one was to be completely rigorous in factoring in the role of perception, it would be necessary to provide as many subjective matrices as there are players as well as provide an objective matrix that would show the reality of the situation:

---

1. Robert Jervis, "Hypotheses on Misperception," *World Politics* 20, no. 3 (April 1968): 473.

2. Jervis, "Hypotheses on Misperception," 473–77.

3. It may turn out to be the case that the sides to a dispute did have similar views of the situation and thus the interaction could be portrayed in a single matrix. What is being suggested here is that one cannot assume this to be the case. S. Plous provides an example of actually attempting to ascertain the views of relevant elites in the United States and the Soviet Union about the arms race. "Perceptual Illusions and Military Realities: The Nuclear Arms Race," *Journal of Conflict Resolution* 29, no. 3 (September 1985): 363–89.

	Cooperate	Defect
Cooperate	3,3	0,5
Defect	5,0	1,1

Fig. 1. Prisoner's Dilemma

A complete portrait of a crisis would have to show a subjective matrix for each player, consisting of his own valuations of possible outcomes and his estimate of the valuations of the other player. Each player's matrix describes his estimate of the situation and to a certain extent explains his behavior, though the estimate may change during the crisis as he acquires more information. Of course, the subjective matrices will be different if one or both players misestimate the other's payoff rankings.[4]

Using a single matrix to represent the players' views can be either a convenient shortcut or an accurate reflection of reality. The point here is that one should not assume this to be the case, and in not doing so we can develop a more complete understanding of crisis behavior.

Proposition One starts with this observation and builds from there. It suggests that actors will be unlikely to consider the possibility that an opponent could possibly not see clearly an act that they believe to be clear.[5] Acts that are taken with a cooperative or noncooperative intent will usually be assumed to have been seen by the opponent in the intended light. When an act is taken that is believed to be nonthreatening or cooperative and the opponent responds as if the opposite were true, decision makers will tend to assume that it is because of a malevolent intent on the part of the opponent and not because the act might have been ambiguous in the first place. Research on the outbreak of World War I has shown that attempts to "put oneself in the other's shoes" were few, adding to the difficulty of understanding the way that other actors were responding to one's own actions. Not only was there little effort to ask how one's actions might be seen by others, but the "1914 documents are virtually devoid of any empathy for the dilemmas of the opposing leaders."[6] A

---

4. Glenn H. Snyder and Paul Diesing, *Conflict among Nations: Bargaining, Decision Making, and System Structure in International Crises* (Princeton: Princeton University Press, 1977), 85.

5. This is leaving aside situations where the actor is intentionally trying to deceive an opponent. This proposition deals only with situations in which the first actor believes that the actions the actor takes are clear and therefore should be clear to the other side.

6. Ole R. Holsti, *Crisis, Escalation, War* (Montreal: McGill-Queen's University Press, 1972), 168.

leader who ignores potential differences from an opponent increases the likelihood of misperception or conflict.

The root of this problem, it seems, rests on a reluctance to consider the possibility that there might be other ways of interpreting events or signals. To do so would imply two contradictory thoughts: I am correct in my interpretation of events, and my opponent is correct in his or her (different) interpretation of events. This phenomenon has been documented in a number of different ways, leading to the development of avoidance mechanisms and different ways of interpreting events to avoid such a contradiction. The concept of *balance of belief* has found a great deal of support in the psychological literature, in particular in research on cognitive dissonance. One description uses friendship to illustrate the concept of balance:

> A person has a balanced set of beliefs about his acquaintances if he believes that all of his friends like each other, all of his enemies like each other, and each of his friends dislikes and is disliked by each of his enemies.[7]

The implication of this for the discussion of misperceptions is clear: actors will seek to adjust incoming information to keep the various parts of their cognitive map in balance with each other. This simply adds to the likelihood of misperception and error.

A related point follows from this discussion: people will have difficulty believing that their opponents do not understand them. Most people no doubt assume that when they think they are being clear they are. As Jervis notes, "[W]hen people spend a great deal of time drawing up a plan or making a decision, they tend to think that the message about it they wish to convey will be clear to the receiver."[8] It is hard for people to believe that others cannot understand what they are sure they are making clear. An example of this can be seen in U.S. policy statements leading up to the 15 January 1991 deadline for Iraqi forces to pull out of Kuwait. American leaders repeatedly stated their intention to use force if necessary to compel Iraqi leaders to order their troops out of Kuwait and repeatedly emphasized how clear they were being in making this known. Not surprisingly, many expressed puzzlement that Saddam Hussein had not understood what they thought was a very clear message. After Secretary of State James Baker and Iraq's Foreign Minister Tariq Aziz met inconclusively in a last-minute effort to avoid war on 9 January 1991, Aziz commented that the United States seemed to have assumed that it needed to make clear to the Iraqis its message, when, in fact, its message to Iraq (that it

---

7. Robert Axelrod, "Schema Theory: An Information Processing Model of Perception and Cognition," *American Political Science Review* 67, no. 4 (December 1973): 1248.

8. Jervis, "Hypotheses on Misperception," 474.

could avoid war by pulling out of Kuwait) had been quite clear. The Iraqis simply chose not to respond to it. Throughout the Cold War, American presidents have frequently proclaimed that the United States had no intention of attacking the Soviet Union and, as such, any buildup on the Soviet's part could only have been for offensive purposes. The common refrain had always been "Why can't they [the Soviet Union] see that we mean them no harm?" American leaders knew that peace was their top priority and for the most part tended to assume that the Soviet Union (and others) would be aware of that. This can create obvious problems:

> When state A reacts with anger and suspicion to what it incorrectly believes to have been a double cross by state B, state B will not be able to understand A's reaction. B knows that its own behavior was unexceptionable. So A's outburst must be an unpleasant bargaining tactic, a smokescreen for its own devious plans, or a refusal to observe the standard rules of diplomacy.[9]

A state that takes what it thinks to have been a cooperative action will be less willing to repeat such an act if that state's opponent, from its particular perspective, sees that act as noncooperative and responds accordingly. Hostile acts will be seen as being the deliberately hostile acts of others because it will be difficult for the observers of the hostile acts to understand that it was their interpretation of the acts that made them hostile—not necessarily the acts themselves.

Support for Proposition One will be seen in four cases: the Berlin blockade, the Berlin Wall, the Cuban Missile Crisis, and the October 1973 War. The strongest support for the proposition comes from the Cuban Missile Crisis, during which American leaders repeatedly asked why the Soviets did not see things as they did, and the October 1973 War, when American leaders (Kissinger in particular) acted as if they believed that the Soviet Union would understand the viewpoint of the United States and act accordingly. In the Berlin cases there is more limited support for the ideas embedded in Proposition One. In the Iranian case no evidence was found to support or negate Proposition One. Let us turn to a discussion of the cases, looking to those with the strongest support first.

Cuban Missile Crisis

Unlike the other crises studied here, the Cuban Missile Crisis arose when secretive behavior was discovered. While there is fairly widespread agree-

---

9. Robert Jervis, *Perception and Misperception in International Politics* (Princeton: Princeton University Press, 1976), 341.

ment that the Soviets intended to use the presence of these missiles as a
bargaining tool,[10] no one has suggested that the Soviets wished the presence
of the missiles to become known when they did.[11] The situation created a
crisis for the United States before it became a crisis for the Soviet Union. The
United States found itself in a crisis when the missiles were discovered, and
the Soviets found themselves in a crisis when President Kennedy made this
information public. In this sense, the crisis can be said to have been unintended by the Soviets with respect to the timing but not with respect to the
overall nature of the situation.

Turning directly to the crisis, the record on Proposition One is generally
favorable. The leaders of the United States certainly felt that their repeated
statements about the undesirability of the stationing of offensive missiles in
Cuba had been clear and easily understood. As Bundy writes later:

> One obvious but insufficient reason for our silence [with respect to
> Soviet weapons shipment to Cuba in early 1962] in the spring is our
> unexamined assumption that Khrushchev needed no warning. If it was
> self-evident to us that Soviet nuclear weapons in Cuba would be intoler-
> able, should not that be obvious also to the Kremlin?[12]

A common theme in the early ExComm meetings, as recorded in the transcripts as well as by commentators, was surprise at the apparent Soviet misunderstanding of American statements on this matter. The reactions of American
policymakers to the discovery of the missiles made clear the fact that they
thought they had been clear about what would be tolerated and what would
not.[13] During the second ExComm meeting in the afternoon of 16 October,

---

10. See Secretary McNamara's opening statement to the Subcommittee on Defense Appropriations, 6 February 1963, for an elaboration of this point. U.S. Congress, House of Representatives, Committee on Appropriations, Subcommittee on Department of Defense Appropriations
for 1964. *Hearings.* 88th Cong., 1st sess., 1963, 2–4. (Hereafter *Hearings.*) For a useful review
of the various explanations advanced about Soviet behavior, see Lester H. Brune, *The Missile
Crisis of October 1962: A Review of Issues and References* (Claremont, Calif.: Regina Books,
1985), 15ff. This is probably the best preglasnost bibliography and source book. For more recent
interpretations, see Raymond L. Garthoff, *Reflections on the Cuban Missile Crisis*, rev. ed.
(Washington, D.C.: Brookings, 1989).

11. John Hughes of the Defense Intelligence Agency testified that he believed that the
Soviets intended to have a "full operational capability of all systems by early December 1962 in
order to confront the United States, at that time, with a fait accompli." U.S. Congress, *Hearings*, 6.

12. McGeorge Bundy, *Danger and Survival: Choices about the Bomb in the First Fifty
Years* (New York: Random House, 1988), 415.

13. Garthoff reports that Kennedy felt that he was quite sure that his two statements in
September about the inadmissibility of offensive weapons had been very clear. Garthoff, *Reflections on the Cuban Missile Crisis*, 33. Bundy notes that the words of the two statements were
"entirely clear." Bundy, *Danger and Survival*, 393.

President Kennedy expressed his concerns about whether his previous messages had carried through clearly to the Soviet Union:

> It seems to me, uh, my press statement was so *clear* about how we *wouldn't* do anything under these conditions and under the conditions that we *would*. He [Khrushchev] must know that we're going to find out, so it seems to me he just, uh . . . [14]

Later in the same meeting, Kennedy expressed a similar concern for possible Soviet misinterpretation of his messages:

> I don't know whether his, they're *aware* of what I sai- . . . I can't understand their viewpoint, if they're aware of what we said at the press conferences. [15]

The sense of puzzlement expressed by American leaders was strong as various spokespersons for the United States had made a number of statements with regard to the placing of offensive missiles in Cuba and most thought that the messages had been very clear. [16]

Once American decision makers became aware of the missiles' presence, and made that knowledge known to the Soviet Union, there was concern that the Soviet Union would misinterpret the actions of the United States, particularly with regard to the steps being taken to implement the blockade. Robert Kennedy's *Thirteen Days: A Memoir of the Cuban Missile Crisis* has a chapter titled "The importance of placing ourselves in the other country's shoes," and in it he argues that one cannot assume that actions will always be clear to an opponent. [17] Kennedy's comments are directed more to actions than policy statements (such as the stopping of Soviet ships during the blockade and the flying of U-2s over Cuba), and it is quite clear that he believed that the messages and statements that the United States had sent to the Soviets had been clear. Kennedy makes it clear that he believed that the Soviet move had not been based on a misunderstanding but was a deliberate move. [18] James G.

---

14. John F. Kennedy, "Cuban Missile Crisis Meetings, October 16, 1962." *Presidential Recordings Transcripts* (Boston: John F. Kennedy Library), part 2, 11. (Hereafter *Transcripts of 16 October 1962*.) Emphasis in original and the statement trails off as noted.

15. John F. Kennedy, *Transcripts of 16 October 1962*, part 2, 32. Emphasis in original and the statement trails off as noted.

16. Elie Abel discusses the various messages and warnings that had been given to the Soviet Union about the unacceptable nature of offensive missiles in Cuba. *The Missile Crisis* (New York: Bantam, 1968), 6–12.

17. Robert F. Kennedy, *Thirteen Days: A Memoir of the Cuban Missile Crisis* (New York: W. W. Norton, 1969), 102–6.

18. Robert F. Kennedy, *Thirteen Days*, 2–6.

Blight and David A. Welch report that ExComm members later admitted that prior to the crisis they had not paid enough attention to how the Soviets might have viewed U.S. actions such as the continued efforts by the CIA to undermine Castro, with the Bay of Pigs incident and others, as well as the continued heated debate in the United States about what to do about Castro.[19]

Once the crisis began, the United States went to great lengths to ensure that the message being sent was loud and clear. Tatu reports one action that the United States took that is indicative of an effort to ensure that there were no misunderstandings of American resolve. In the days after President Kennedy's announcement of the quarantine, U.S. Polaris submarines exchanged uncoded messages about targeting with their home ports. On the one hand, this might have been a bluff but:

> to those [in the Soviet Union] who had to make decisions and knew the quantitative superiority of the American strategic capabilities, it was no trifling matter.[20]

On the other hand, it might have been a deliberate attempt to ensure that there was no misunderstanding of American determination and resolve. There is also evidence that the commander in chief of the Strategic Air Command (SAC) ordered a message emphasizing the strength of U.S. nuclear forces be sent in the clear to ensure that the Soviets knew of SAC's readiness.[21] What is clear is that they did get the message: according to one account, "near panic broke out" in Moscow when this message was received.[22]

One way to consider Proposition One is to look at American beliefs about the clarity of their messages to the Soviet Union in the context of their beliefs about what the Soviets would and would not do in Cuba. Because most American leaders assumed that the Soviets would not install offensive missiles in Cuba, it was easy for them to believe that their warnings had been clear. Their warnings concerned an action (installing missiles in Cuba) that they did not believe would happen in any event. During the recent meetings between U.S. and Soviet experts on this crisis, one of the main themes to emerge was the considerable doubt as to why the Soviets had acted the way

---

19. James G. Blight and David A. Welch, *On the Brink: Americans and Soviets Reexamine the Cuban Missile Crisis* (New York: Hill and Wang, 1989), 302.

20. Michel Tatu, *Power in the Kremlin* (New York: Viking Press, 1969), 264.

21. H. R. Haldeman, *The Ends of Power* (New York: Times Books, 1978), 93. This is noted in Scott D. Sagan, "Nuclear Alerts and Crisis Management," *International Security* 9, no. 4 (Spring 1985): 108 n. 22. See also Blight and Welch, *On The Brink*, 75, and Garthoff, *Reflections on the Cuban Missile Crisis*, 61–62.

22. James G. Blight, *The Shattered Crystal Ball: Fear and Learning in the Cuban Missile Crisis* (Savage, Md.: Rowman and Littlefield Publishers, 1990), 20. See also Blight and Welch, *On the Brink*, 75.

they did.[23] What remained clear was the belief that the Soviet Union had acted deliberately to create a situation where it would benefit at the expense of the United States.

Roberta Wohlstetter argues that the prevalent view on the part of American government officials prior to the crisis was that the Soviet Union would not engage in such risky behavior and that this clouded their outlook with respect to intelligence information. The *Stennis Report*, which reviewed American intelligence and policy-making prior to the Cuban Missile Crisis, notes that there was a "predisposition [toward Cuba] of the intelligence community to the philosophical conviction that it would be incompatible with Soviet policy to introduce strategic missiles into Cuba."[24] All in all, there were very strong beliefs about what the Soviets would, and would not, do in Cuba. These beliefs contributed to a strong dispositional misperception about Soviet activities in Cuba that prevented some decision makers from accurately assessing the information that was available. These beliefs about what the Soviets would and would not do served to reinforce the decision makers' beliefs about the clarity of their warnings about installing missiles in Cuba.

The overall picture that emerges from a review of American decision makers' thinking prior to the crisis is that they thought the warnings made to the Soviets about offensive weapons in Cuba had been clear. As the crisis moved into phase 2, doubts began to creep in about the clarity of those messages, yet many remained convinced that they had been clear, and this provided a strong case for taking action against the Soviet Union. What is evident in examining this crisis is that the context in which the crisis emerged (U.S. domestic political concerns about Castro and concerns about Soviet efforts to arm Cuba) also played a central role in the way American leaders viewed the crisis.

Turning briefly to the Soviet side in this issue, they certainly wanted to make it seem that they believed their messages to the United States had been clear about the defensive nature of the armaments that they were sending to Cuba. As Ronald R. Pope points out, the defensive nature of the missiles sent to Cuba is a very prominent theme in Soviet accounts of the crisis.[25] In their statements, before and after the crisis, Soviet leaders stressed the defensive nature of these weapons, going to great lengths to make a distinction between

---

23. Blight and Welch, *On the Brink*, 116–19.

24. Roberta Wohlstetter, "Cuba and Pearl Harbor: Hindsight and Foresight," *Foreign Affairs* 43, no. 4 (July 1965): 701.

25. Ronald R. Pope, ed., *Soviet Views on the Cuban Missile Crisis: Myth and Reality in Foreign Policy Analysis* (Washington, D.C.: University Press of America, 1982), 227–33. This has been a very prominent theme in the new Soviet openness about the "Caribbean Crisis." Its accuracy remains open to question.

defensive weapons (which the United States could not justifiably object to) and offensive weapons (which it might legitimately object to). These Soviet statements were discussed in the ExComm meetings in an effort to understand where the Soviets had misunderstood the United States. Even in the messages that Khrushchev sent to Kennedy, the theme of acceptable defensive weapons appeared repeatedly, along with the suggestion that the United States had, deliberately or not, misinterpreted the nature of these missiles.[26]

October 1973 Middle East War

The Cuban Missile Crisis provides the best test case for Proposition One, and the October 1973 War crisis the next best example. Unlike the Cuban Missile Crisis, this crisis came about very quickly and ended very quickly—lasting less than twenty-four hours. While there was very little time for impressions to form or change, we can still find sufficient information about this crisis to test Proposition One.

In one very important way, this crisis is similar to the Cuban Missile Crisis: it came about because the Soviet Union took actions that American leaders had confidently expected it would not do, catching American leaders off guard. U.S. leaders felt they had been clear about the importance they attached to the Soviet Union remaining on the sidelines in the October 1973 War and were quite surprised when it seemed that it was about to intervene with troops. Kissinger's view was that he had been quite clear about what the United States would and would not tolerate, and he was surprised when the Soviets appeared to have not understood.

The crisis that arose between the United States and the Soviet Union came as the result of two decisions, the first made by the Soviet Union and the second made by the United States. The first was the apparent decision made by the Soviet Union to prepare to send troops into the Middle East in response to Sadat's request to have Soviet troops help enforce the cease-fire. This created a crisis situation for the United States in which a response was felt to be necessary. It is worth noting that there is a lively debate about whether or not the Soviet Union actually intended to send its troops into the Sinai. The second decision, by the United States, was to put U.S. military forces on alert in response to the Soviet decision. This created a crisis for the Soviet Union, forcing it to decide whether or not to carry out its (apparent) plans to move troops into the area. At this stage, the existence of the dilemma created by the American alert has to be assumed. The almost complete lack of information about Soviet decision making during the October 1973 War limits the analysis to assuming certain events or situations. At this stage, then, there are two

---

26. "Messages of 23 and 26 October," *Department of State Bulletin*, 19 November 1973.

related assumptions being made: first, that the Soviets intended to move some troops into the Middle East and, second, that the American alert created a dilemma for the Soviets.

The evidence available about the American perspective on the crisis does allow for some conclusions even though there was little time for opinions to be formulated, debated, modified, or acted upon.[27] Kissinger's detailed account of the maneuverings before American forces were put on alert makes clear his efforts to communicate to the Soviet Union the American position that the introduction of Soviet troops into the Middle East could not be tolerated.[28] Clearly, Kissinger felt that the Soviets had not understood the seriousness with which the United States took the question of Soviet troops in the Middle East, as he described the alerting of American troops as a way to back up the message that was being sent, warning once again about American opposition to the introduction of Soviet troops.[29] Kissinger's actions support Proposition One.

Turning to the remaining three crises, we find limited, but suggestive, support for Proposition One. Each of these three illustrates the difficulties inherent in sorting out the views of decision makers in crisis situations. The discussion will begin with the Berlin blockade.

Berlin Blockade

The Berlin blockade crisis presents a picture different than other crises considered here. Looking at the issues that brought the crisis into focus for American leaders (the Soviet cutoff of electricity to the Western sectors of Berlin and the closing of railways and roads into Berlin), there were very few direct confrontations between U.S. and Soviet leaders. There were few statements made by American leaders that would indicate whether or not they thought they were being clear and had been misunderstood. American leaders had made it clear that they felt a commitment to Berlin, but it was never made clear how strong that commitment was. Even as the crisis unfolded, there was considerable debate in Washington, inside and outside of government, about

---

27. In outlining the perceptions and views of the major parties, Kissinger's view will be taken as being the most important for understanding the actions of the United States. With respect to the Soviet Union and its views on outcomes, this discussion relies on Kissinger's reports of his conversations with Dobrynin, the contents of messages from the Soviets to the United States as reported by Kissinger, and assessments of the Soviet views as reported by other authors. There were no public statements from the Soviet Union during the crisis, and comments made by Brezhnev after the crisis only claimed that the United States had overreacted and made no mention of the nuclear aspect of the alert.

28. Henry Kissinger, *Years of Upheaval* (Boston: Little, Brown and Company, 1982), 578–91.

29. Kissinger, *Years of Upheaval*, 587.

the desirability of attempting to maintain a presence at all in Berlin.[30] In the context of Proposition One, it is not clear what there was for American leaders to feel they had been clear about or to feel that the Soviets had misunderstood. As the crisis went on, there was discussion about acts that the United States was considering (such as sending armed trains to attempt to break through the blockade) and how these acts would appear to the Soviets, but there were very few statements made or actions taken before the crisis that American leaders felt the Soviets had misunderstood or misinterpreted. As noted above, Proposition One is primarily concerned with actions or statements that are felt to be misunderstood by an opponent and have thus led to a crisis.

One of the reasons for this difficulty is that by the time the American leadership felt this was a crisis, the Soviets had taken all the steps that they could, without resorting to military force, to put pressure on the city. With all access to the city cut off and all supplies to the city withheld, there was little else the Soviets could do without actually attempting to remove the Western powers by force. The feeling that problems were coming was felt much earlier by those in Berlin than in Washington, but there was little that those in Berlin did prior to 24 June that they felt had been misunderstood.[31]

Once the crisis had begun (from the American point of view), there was little left for the Soviets to do, short of a direct attack on Berlin or an attempt to interfere with the airlift that was under way. American leaders had made it very clear that these actions would not be tolerated. Once the crisis had begun, the actions taken by the United States were chosen carefully, with an eye toward making sure that the Soviets did understand what the Americans were doing.

In looking at the record of this crisis, it is difficult to find direct support for Proposition One. Rarely did decision makers say, "The Soviets must understand us; their apparent misunderstanding is actually a ploy." The American leaders seem to have understood that they were involved in a political confrontation with the Soviet Union and that statements made in this political confrontation to influence the public were just that—statements made to influence the public. While the American leaders continually discounted Soviet accounts of events, there seems to have been an understanding that their

---

30. Walter Millis, ed., *The Forrestal Diaries* (New York: Viking Press, 1951), 452–55, 459.

31. After the breakdown of four-power government on 22 March, General Clay and the military commandant of Berlin, Colonel Frank Howley, prepared plans for a number of eventualities, including a blockade of the city. Avi Shlaim, *The United States and the Berlin Blockade, 1948–1949: A Study in Crisis Decision-Making* (Berkeley: University of California Press, 1983), 119–21. As the crisis in June unfolded, Clay and Howley argued that the Soviets would not use force to press their demands. Those in Berlin were prepared much earlier for a blockade, but when it happened, they were not as alarmed as those in Washington.

(American) statements could be subject to the same objections in this political battle. It seems that the Americans were aware that they were involved in a propaganda battle and that, "One could not expect that others would believe you—you had to make them believe you." What was happening was a propaganda battle, and in order to win, one side had to convince the other that its point of view was the one to accept. This seems to have been understood by both sides in this dispute.

It is interesting to note that there is one instance of an American decision maker suggesting that the Soviet view of events, while different than the American, might nonetheless be legitimate. Following the American announcement of a currency reform for Western Germany (18 June), the Soviet Union imposed further restrictions on all incoming traffic. The State Department's political advisor for Germany, Robert Murphy, noted that:

> Certain of these measures are not unreasonable in view of natural defensive action to protect Soviet Zone from influx of old currency.
>
> General Robertson [UK Berlin Commander] telephoned General Clay this morning suggesting that a vigorous protest be made immediately regarding the new Soviet traffic regulations. Clay replied, it seems to me correctly, that it would be better to wait for two or three days because the regulations themselves are not immoderate, stating his opinion that were the situation reversed, we on our side would have been required to take rather similar precautions.[32]

In summary, this case provides limited material to actually test Proposition One. There were very few steps taken during the crisis that the Americans felt that the Soviets had misinterpreted. Once the crisis began, American leaders were not always willing to assume that their actions would be clear to the Soviets, particularly if these actions were ones that had not been taken before—in partial contradiction to the premise of Proposition One. One of the reasons that the Americans did not deviate from many existing practices (e.g., allowing Soviet officials to walk through trains as they entered the city, or staying within the existing air traffic routes) was their fear that the Soviets would see these steps in a way that was unintended by the United States.[33]

Turning to the Berlin Wall crisis, a similar situation of tentative support for Proposition One can be seen.

---

32. Telegram from Murphy to Marshall, 19 June 1948. U.S. Department of State, *Foreign Relations of the United States*, 1948, 2:910–11. (Hereafter *FRUS*.)

33. The issue of whether or not to discontinue this practice was the subject of two teleconferences during the March crisis that focused on established rights and practices and how they should be observed. Jean Edward Smith, ed., *The Papers of General Lucius D. Clay: Germany 1945–1949*, vol. 2 (Bloomington: Indiana University Press, 1974).

Berlin Wall Crisis

The Berlin Wall crisis is similar to the Berlin blockade crisis in its minimal support for Proposition One but for different reasons. The construction of the Berlin Wall occurred in the context of an ongoing confrontation between the Soviet Union and the Western powers over the status of Berlin. The confrontation became more intense with Khrushchev's speech on 9 July and President Kennedy's speech on 25 July 1961. Khrushchev's speech was seen as an effort to increase the pressure on Berlin, and Kennedy's speech was seen as a response to that pressure.[34] In his speech, Kennedy called for a renewed commitment to the security of Berlin and Western Europe in the face of an increased threat from the Soviet Union.

This crisis generated many of the same kinds of concerns that had confronted American leaders during the Berlin blockade: Would the Soviets attempt to enforce their demands with military action? Would they fight if challenged by the Western powers? And would the Soviets use this crisis as an excuse to challenge the Western position in Berlin? Even after the wall went up:

> the possibility remained the intention [behind the construction of the wall] might be far more sinister: that the Wall might represent the unfolding of an unalterable Soviet plan, based on a conviction of American irresolution, to drive the West out of Berlin.[35]

As discussed in chapter 2, the Kennedy administration had framed the question of any Soviet threat to Berlin in the context of Western access to Berlin. From the summit in June right up to, and after, the construction of the wall, the United States had made its position clear: it would not tolerate any action that threatened Western rights in, or access to, Berlin. The issue that is relevant here is whether or not American leaders believed that their statements about access to Berlin were understood by the Soviets. American leaders were quite confident that the Soviets would understand their position on Berlin and were quite surprised when it appeared that they did not. The most interesting element of this crisis is that the Soviets understood very clearly what the Kennedy administration was saying. What became clear was that many in the Kennedy administration did not understand the message they themselves were sending. What makes this crisis somewhat unique is that it occurred when one

34. Robert M. Slusser, *The Berlin Crisis of 1961: Soviet-American Relations and the Struggle for Power in the Kremlin, June–November 1961* (Baltimore: Johns Hopkins University Press, 1973), 61–67, 77–87, discusses Khrushchev's and Kennedy's speeches and how they responded to each other.

35. Arthur M. Schlesinger, Jr., *A Thousand Days: John F. Kennedy in the White House* (Boston: Houghton Mifflin Company, 1965), 395.

party clearly understood what the other was saying. This was not what was anticipated in the development of the theory here, but it does not negate the value of the theory either.

In most of the crises studied here, if the statements that decision makers have made are understood by the opponent, there is no crisis because the statements reflect a commitment to defend a particular interest. What makes this crisis interesting is that the Kennedy administration was perfectly clear about what it would, and would not, defend, and the Soviets appear to have understood that distinction. Nevertheless, there was still a crisis, and many felt that the Soviets had misunderstood the United States. Why? The apparent reason is that many thought that the Kennedy administration had made it clear that it would protect access by all to Berlin when in fact a careful reading of administration statements and actions would suggest that the administration was willing to protect Western access to Berlin. As mentioned above, critics of the Kennedy administration frequently point to this aspect of the handling of the Berlin crisis and suggest that this reflected the Kennedy administration's decision not to protect its rights and access in East Berlin. What makes this case interesting is that the Soviets appear to have understood that distinction very well because they were extremely careful not to hinder Western access to Berlin. Robert M. Slusser argues that Soviet acquiescence to the reinforcement of West Berlin with American troops at the time of Vice-President Johnson's visit is further evidence of Soviet caution with respect to Western rights.[36] In one respect, this seems to be similar to the problems seen in the recent Iraq-Kuwait crisis. The Iraqis seem to have understood all too well what the United States was saying about any Iraqi-Kuwaiti dispute in the spring and summer of 1990. American leaders had left the impression that they would not act to defend Kuwait, and the Iraqis appear to have acted on that basis. Once they did, however, the U.S. commitment changed quickly, leading to the confrontation and showdown between the Iraqi and Allied forces.

Iranian Crisis of 1946

The final crisis to be considered here is the Iranian crisis of 1946. This crisis was the most difficult to apply Proposition One to because there were so few statements about U.S. interests in Iran that the Soviets could have misinterpreted, in the American leaders' view. There is, as a result, little to contradict or confirm Proposition One. What information there is, however, is instructive.

Looking at the record of this crisis, we can see why it is difficult to apply

---

36. Slusser, *The Berlin Crisis of 1961*, 137.

Proposition One directly.[37] The discussion of crises in chapter 1 was built on a view that saw misunderstandings giving rise to crises because actors would assume that their opponents' views of events would be the same as their own. In the Iranian crisis of 1946 it is difficult to see this type of behavior. American leaders made a number of statements about the need for the Soviet Union to withdraw its troops from Iran, but this was only after it appeared that they might not. An additional complication was that the United States never took any serious actions (e.g., military maneuvers or diplomatic threats) to attempt to coerce the Soviets into a particular course of action.[38] The removal of Soviet troops was never the target of any threat from the United States.[39] The demand that the Soviets remove their troops from Iran in accordance with

---

37. Most of the analysis that follows will be concerned with the American side of this crisis. There is very little evidence to suggest that the situation in Iran was seen by the Soviet Union as a crisis. Some commentators suggest that the Soviets were concerned about the course of events in Iran and that they were also concerned about pushing the conflict in United Nations over Iran too far, but none suggest that they viewed it as a crisis. See Adam B. Ulam, *Expansion and Coexistence: Soviet Foreign Policy, 1917–1973*, 2d ed. (New York: Praeger, 1974), 425–29; George Lenczowski, *Russia and the West in Iran, 1918–1948: A Study In Big-Power Rivalry* (New York: Greenwood Press, 1968), 284–303; and Bruce Robellet Kuniholm, *The Origins of the Cold War in the Near East: Great Power Conflict and Diplomacy in Iran, Turkey, and Greece* (Princeton: Princeton University Press, 1980), 328–30.

38. On 24 April 1952, President Truman stated in a news conference that "in 1945 [this was later corrected to 1946] I had to send an ultimatum to the head of the Soviet Union to get out of Persia. They got out because we were in a position then to meet a situation of that kind." Later in the same press conference, Truman said, "It was a message from me to Stalin to get out of Persia. Unless he did get out, we would put some more people in there. And he got out." Harry S. Truman, *Public Papers of the Presidents of the United States: Harry S. Truman, 1952–1953* (Washington, D.C.: GPO), 291, 294. Truman also discusses this matter in his *Memoirs, Volume II: Years of Trial and Hope, 1946–1952* (Garden City, N.Y.: Doubleday, 1956), 94–95. John R. Oneal notes an article that Truman wrote that appeared in the *New York Times* on 25 August 1957, which said in part:

> For example, shortly after the end of World War II, Stalin and Molotov brazenly refused to keep their agreement to withdraw from Iran. They persisted in keeping their troops in Azerbaijan in northern Iran. Formal steps were taken through diplomatic channels and the United Nations to get the Russians to withdraw. The Soviet Union persisted in its occupation until I personally saw to it that Stalin was informed that I had given orders to our military chiefs to prepare for the movement of our ground, sea, and airforces. Stalin then did what I knew he would do. He moved his troops out.

Oneal notes that Byrnes, Allen Dulles, Averell Harriman, and other policymakers involved at the time have said they knew of no such ultimatum and that they do not believe one could have been sent without their knowledge. *Foreign Policy Making in Times of Crisis* (Columbus: Ohio State University Press, 1982), 133 n. 78. The Historical Office of the State Department conducted a review of its files and could find no record of any ultimatum. *FRUS*, 1946, 7:348–49. See Kuniholm, *The Origins of the Cold War in the Near East*, 320 n. 45, for further discussion on this issue.

39. It is being assumed that the State Department's assessment about Truman's ultimatum is correct: there was no ultimatum.

their prior obligations was not accompanied by an "or else" statement. The protest delivered to the Soviet Union on 6 March 1946 only reminded it of its pledge to withdraw its troops from Iran by 2 March and noted that the United States could not remain indifferent to the situation in Iran. The note was sent "in the spirit of the friendly association which developed between the United States and the Soviet Union in the successful effort against the common enemy and as a fellow member of the United Nations," and it reminded the Soviets of the "heavy responsibility resting upon the great powers" to observe their obligations to the smaller powers.[40]

There were no steps taken by the United States that its leaders felt had been misunderstood by Soviets. In fact there were few steps taken by the United States that the Soviets could have misunderstood. American leaders do not appear to have believed that this crisis was the result of a Soviet misunderstanding of anything they had done or said. Their view of the crisis (which will be discussed further under Proposition Two in the next chapter) generally took one of two forms: that the Soviets were working to protect their historical sphere of interest in Iran or that they were working to increase their influence in Iran, possibly working to create a situation in which they could annex (de facto or otherwise) the northern provinces of Iran. With respect to Proposition One, it seems that members of the U.S. government did not think that they had been misunderstood—merely that the United States and the Soviet Union had different goals with respect to Iran and that these goals were in conflict.

Conclusion

This assessment of Proposition One has provided a useful starting point for the discussion of crises and perceptions that began in chapter 1. Proposition One is built on the view that one potential source of crises is the assumption (sometimes unconscious) that both sides to a dispute will see choices and preferences in the same fashion. The empirical testing of the proposition revealed that most of the cases were supportive, but it also revealed some problems.

This proposition has a great deal of intuitive appeal to it, and it would seem to capture a great deal of what happens in the interaction of states. It is similar to one of Jervis's "hypotheses on misperception" that deals with the way decision makers will see others.[41] Jervis's hypothesis reads, "[W]hen actors have intentions that they do not try to conceal from others, they tend to assume that others accurately perceive these intentions." Interestingly enough, it turned out to be very difficult to find direct proof in these case

---

40. *FRUS*, 1946, 7:340–42.

41. Jervis, "Hypotheses on Misperception," 476.

studies to support Proposition One. There were very few instances of decision makers claiming that an opponent had misunderstood them or claiming that there should have been no misunderstanding because things were so clear. One reason for this is that the decision makers might just be right: states can generally communicate to others about their interests and concerns without tremendous difficulty. The assumption behind Proposition One, that there is a great deal of misunderstanding in communications between states, might not be as widely true as originally thought. This possibility will be taken up in greater detail in the final chapter.

CHAPTER 4

"He can't do that to me!"

The previous chapter discussed how decision makers will tend to believe that their perspective on the world will be shared by others. When a decision maker believes that his or her actions are clearly nonthreatening, the decision maker will be truly puzzled when others respond in a negative fashion. It is this certainty about the meanings of actions that leads to the discussion of the next proposition. There is a strong tendency to attribute things that go wrong to the actions of others or to external factors.[1] It will be argued here that this is particularly true during times of crisis. Decision makers who are confronted with a crisis that is not of their own making will tend to assume that the crisis is a deliberate act by an opponent, designed to cause problems. Jervis's observation that decision makers tend to see others, particularly adversaries, as more dangerous or hostile than they really are is an important insight.[2] Another way of putting this is that actors will assume that the reasons for another's actions (usually seen as hostile or detrimental to their interests) are the result of internal factors (hostility, aggressive intentions) rather than as a result of external factors (pressure from associates or allies, misperceptions of the original actor's intentions). These findings have been shown in research on a number of different crises. One of the strongest findings comes from Holsti, who presents impressive evidence, derived from content analysis of documents generated in the weeks leading up to World War I, that leaders tended to perceive their options as being more restricted than their opponents' and that their perceptions of these constraints (and of the freedom of their opponents from these constraints) increased with stress. In addition, Holsti found that leaders will tend to assume that the lack of positive steps from their opponents suggests hostile intent:

> Most European leaders tended to view their own freedom of choice and that of their allies as severely restricted. At the same time they

---

1. White provides a useful overview and bibliography of the literature supporting this idea, as well as the concept of *motivated misperception*. Ralph K. White, "Motivated Misperceptions" in *Psychology and the Prevention of Nuclear War: A Book of Readings*, ed. Ralph K. White (New York: New York University Press, 1986): 279–301.

2. Robert Jervis, *Perception and Misperception in International Politics* (Princeton: Princeton University Press, 1976), 321–23.

generally believed that in order to slow down or reverse the escalation it remained only for leaders in the other alliance to take some "reasonable" steps. The failure of adversaries to do so only confirmed the suspicion that their intentions were aggressive.[3]

This tendency has been demonstrated experimentally as well: subjects will frequently attribute greater freedom of action to others than they see themselves as having.[4] In general, the argument here is that leaders will assume that it's the opponents' fault. This builds on the assumption built into Proposition One in chapter 3 about assuming a shared view of events. If one assumes that an opponent sees events in the same way, then actions that one feels threaten interests must be deliberate because opponents will know that they threaten these interests. This is the connection between Proposition One and Proposition Two. This discussion sets the stage for consideration of the next proposition, which suggests how leaders view the intentions of their opponents.

Proposition Two: Decision makers will tend to see crises as the result of deliberate actions by their opponents in pursuit of outcomes beneficial to the opponent and detrimental to themselves.

This proposition rests on findings in the psychological literature that deal with the concept of the *fundamental attribution error*. The main finding in this literature that is relevant here is that there is a "pervasive tendency for actors to attribute their actions to situational requirements, whereas observers tend to attribute the same actions to stable personal dispositions."[5] To put this in the language of interstate relations, when State B does something that State A finds objectionable, State A will assume it was because of some internal motivation on the part of State B. This finding is well established within the psychological literature,[6] and there is growing acceptance of this idea within the political science literature.[7] Actors will tend to explain their actions as

---

3. Ole R. Holsti, *Crisis, Escalation, War* (Montreal: McGill-Queen's University Press, 1972), 167–68.

4. Sharon B. Gurwitz and Lawrence Panciera, "Attribution of Freedom by Actors and Observers," *Journal of Personality and Social Psychology* 32, no. 3 (September 1975): 531–39.

5. E. E. Jones and R. E. Nisbett, *The Actor and the Observer: Divergent Perceptions of the Causes of Behavior* (Morristown, N.J.: General Learning Press, 1971), quoted in Kelly G. Shaver, *Principles of Social Psychology*, 2d ed. (Cambridge, Mass.: Winthrop Publishers, 1981), 136.

6. For a review of the various studies demonstrating this type of behavior, see Richard Nisbett and Lee Ross, *Human Inference: Strategies and Shortcomings of Social Judgment* (Englewood Cliffs, N.J.: Prentice-Hall, 1980), 21–23, 122–27.

7. Robert Jervis provides a political scientist's perspective on attribution theory in "*Perception and Misperception*: An Updating of the Analysis," paper presented at the annual meeting of the International Society of Political Psychology, Washington, D.C., 24–27 June 1982, 17–30.

being the result of factors within their environment rather than as the result of internal motives or desires, while observers of the same behavior will tend to have the opposite view, attributing motives for behavior to internal characteristics of the actor. Consider the example of a person giving money to a beggar:

> For example, the actor who gives a dollar to a beggar is apt to attribute his behavior to the sad plight of the beggar, but the observer of the behavior is apt to attribute it to the actor's generosity. From the actor's perspective, it is the constantly changing features of the environment that are particularly salient or "available" as potential causes to which his behavior can be attributed. From the observer's perspective, the actor is the perceptual "figure" and the situation merely "ground," so that the actor himself provides the most available causal candidate.[8]

The implications of this phenomenon are clear: there is a strong likelihood that decision makers will have a different view of the motives, or sources of action, of an opponent than will that opponent. Jervis argues that decision makers have a strong tendency to assume that unfavorable occurrences are the result of deliberate actions:

> Accidents, chance, and lack of coordination are rarely given their due by contemporary observers. Instead, they suspect that well-laid plans give events a coherence they would otherwise lack.[9]

As was discussed in chapter 3, decision makers will have difficulty believing that there are other valid interpretations of events. As a result, decision makers will tend to assume that the opponent is fully aware of their feelings on the matter at hand and will conclude that the taking of actions detrimental to their position can only be purposeful. An example of this behavior can be seen during the Cuban Missile Crisis, when President Kennedy is reported to have exclaimed, "He [Khrushchev] can't do that to me!" assuming that Khrushchev's actions were purposeful and aimed at Kennedy.[10] Shaver calls

---

8. Nisbett and Ross, *Human Inference*, 22. It should be noted that the use here of the terms *situational* and *dispositional* is slightly different than that found in the social-psychological literature. Psychologists use the terms to describe the sources of observed behavior, not the sources of misperceptions. Situational behavior is when the actor is responding to external stimuli (such as giving money to homeless persons because of their terrible plight) while dispositional behavior is when the actor is responding to internal motivations (giving money to the homeless because one is kind and generous). In psychological terms, situational and dispositional point to different sources to explain an actor's behavior. Here the terms are used to explain different ways information is processed and perceptions changed.

9. Jervis, *Perception and Misperception*, 321.

10. Graham T. Allison, *Essence of Decision: Explaining the Cuban Missile Crisis* (Boston: Little, Brown and Company, 1971), 193.

this the "credit for success, blame for failure" syndrome.[11] When events tend to go well for an individual (e.g., passing a difficult exam), the explanation given by that individual will tend to stress internal factors (native intelligence, hard work, etc.) whereas when events go poorly (failing the exam) the results tend to be attributed to external factors (difficulty of the exam, insufficient time to study, etc.). This can be the case in foreign policy behavior as well. Secretary John Foster Dulles's elastic views of the Soviet Union would be just such an example. When things went the way the United States wanted, it was attributed to American pressure or persuasion. When things did not go in the desired direction, it was the fault of the Soviets and their aggressive tendencies.[12]

The impact of this type of behavior on crisis action is indirect but important:

> When the other behaves in accord with the actor's desires, he will overestimate the degree to which his policies are responsible for the outcome. When the situation is fluid, there is a less pronounced tendency for the actor to overestimate his potential influence. When the other's behavior is undesired, the actor is likely to see it as derived from internal sources rather than being a response to his own actions.[13]

It is the third suggestion that is of interest here. Because a crisis by definition involves actions of one party that are undesired by the other, we should expect that problems will be attributed to the other actor:

> If the other's behavior has the *effect* of injuring the actor, he is apt to believe that this was the other's *purpose*. Research on how we form impressions of others has found a "tendency [for perceivers] to assume that people always intend to do what they do and intend it to have the effect it has." In international relations this is especially pronounced when the other's behavior is undesired.[14]

There is no reason to expect that this type of behavior will not be found in the crises studied here. Crises are situations in which at least one party is unhappy about the situation, and thus it can be expected that at least one party will exhibit this type of behavior.

Having discussed the theoretical background, let us now turn to an exam-

---

11. Shaver, *Principles of Social Psychology*, 137.

12. Ole R. Holsti, "The Belief System and National Images: A Case Study," in *International Politics and Foreign Policy: A Reader in Research and Theory*, rev. ed., ed. James N. Rosenau (New York: Free Press, 1969), 543–50.

13. Jervis, *Perception and Misperception*, 343.

14. Jervis, *Perception and Misperception*, 350. Emphasis in original.

ination of the cases. As the theoretical basis of this argument is developed, the evidence in support of the theory becomes stronger. More of the cases will be shown to support Proposition Two than were found for Proposition One, and there will be even greater support for later propositions. We will once again begin with the two most recent crises, the Cuban Missile Crisis and the October 1973 Middle East War.

Cuban Missile Crisis

For the Kennedy administration, and President Kennedy in particular, Cuba was an extremely sensitive issue. The views of many American leaders of the time about the prospects for Soviet actions were twofold: most American leaders assumed that the Soviet Union would not install offensive missiles in Cuba. When they did, however, these same leaders had no difficulty believing the fact that they had and that it had been a deliberate attempt to cause problems for the United States. The reasons why American officials did not believe that the Soviets would take the unprecedented step of putting missiles in Cuba are not directly relevant to the discussion of Proposition Two. As was discussed above under Proposition One, the belief that the Soviet Union would not run such risks allowed American leaders to believe that their messages about the unacceptable nature of such activity were clear. This contributed to the strength of the American leaders' belief that this was a deliberate crisis. This belief is what is under consideration here, not the sources of it.

With respect to the discussion of Proposition Two, it is safe to say that the American leaders agreed that the Soviets had taken a serious step and that it had been deliberate. The degree of seriousness of this move,[15] and the motives behind it,[16] was not agreed upon, but for the purposes of the discussion here, this is not relevant. These issues will become important in our later

---

15. As noted in chap. 2, there were extensive discussions about the seriousness of this move. With the exception of McNamara, and possibly President Kennedy, all of those present felt that this was a very serious military crisis as well as a serious political crisis. McNamara joined the others in the belief that this was a serious political crisis.

16. There are a variety of explanations for the Soviet move. See Lester H. Brune, *The Missile Crisis of October 1962: A Review of Issues and References* (Claremont, Calif.: Regina Books, 1985), 15–32, for a discussion of these explanations. The two most prominent explanations, accepted by those in the ExComm, were that this was a move to boost the Soviet's strategic position as well as an effort to provide some bargaining leverage with respect to Berlin. McNamara's later explanation emphasized the Berlin aspect. U.S. Congress, House of Representatives, Committee on Appropriations, Subcommittee on Department of Defense Appropriations for 1964. *Hearings*, 88th Cong., 1st sess., 1963, 23. As Raymond L. Garthoff notes, *"No one* in the U.S. government believed that the deployment of Soviet missiles was intended to deter a U.S. invasion of Cuba," a view shared by the Soviet experts within the administration. *Reflections on the Cuban Missile Crisis*, rev. ed. (Washington, D.C.: Brookings, 1989), 45–46. Emphasis in original.

discussions, but for the moment, they can be ignored. There is little doubt that American leaders felt that the crisis had been part of a deliberate effort by the Soviets to gain some advantage at the expense of the United States.

The view from the other side of the crisis was quite different. The Soviets argued that this situation was a deliberate crisis caused by the United States in order to provide an excuse for attacking Cuba and Castro. Both Khrushchev and, later, Anatolii Gromyko argued that the United States had deliberately overreacted to the presence of defensive missiles in Cuba. Gromyko argues, "an intentional crisis was manufactured in the American capital," to provide a pretext for invading Cuba.[17] The main culprit, according to Gromyko, was the "American military clique" whose "final aim . . . was clear—the annihilation of the popular national government of Cuba."[18] The strongest claim that Gromyko makes about the U.S. desire to create a crisis stems from the meeting between Soviet Foreign Minister Andrei Gromyko and President Kennedy on 18 October. One of the questions that the United States had to deal with was whether or not to ask Gromyko about the missiles at this meeting (they had been discovered on the 15th), and it had been decided not to mention them unless he did. Anatolii Gromyko argues that this proves that the United States was deliberately creating a crisis, for if they were concerned about the missiles in Cuba, all they had to do was ask![19] Whether or not it actually was telling the truth, the Soviet government wanted to make it appear that it thought the crisis had been a deliberate act on the part of the United States. Bundy notes that the United States considered doing just that, going quietly to the Soviets with its knowledge about missiles in Cuba, but concluded that the risks were too great. The primary fear was that the Soviets would go public with their legal argument that they had the right to install missiles in Cuba, in the same way that the United States had installed missiles in Turkey—an argument that Bundy notes that the United States was afraid it would not be able to counter.[20]

There was no doubt on the part of the American leadership that this crisis was the result of deliberate Soviet actions designed to disadvantage the American position. The support for Proposition Two, that decision makers will

---

17. Anatolii A. Gromyko, "The Caribbean Crisis 1: The U.S. Government's Preparation of the Caribbean Crisis," *Voprosy istorii.* no. 7 (1971), reprinted in *Soviet Law and Government* 11, no. 1 (Summer 1972): 16.

18. Anatolii A. Gromyko, *Through Russian Eyes: President Kennedy's 1036 Days* (Washington, D.C.: International Library, 1973), 173. This line has been maintained, and even elaborated, in recent discussions of the crisis. See James G. Blight and David A. Welch, *On the Brink: Americans and Soviets Reexamine the Cuban Missile Crisis* (New York: Hill and Wang, 1989), chap. 5, passim.

19. Gromyko, "The Caribbean Crisis 1," 20–23.

20. Blight and Welch, *On the Brink*, 244–46.

assume that hostile actions are deliberate, is strong, and the October 1973 War case will provide further support.

October 1973 Middle East War

The history of this crisis provides a great deal of support for Proposition Two. American leaders in general were quite convinced that Soviet actions were designed to cause trouble for the United States. The strongest statement of that view comes from Kissinger, who saw Soviet actions as being deliberately intended to take advantage of whatever opportunity arose:

> And while the Soviet Union would no doubt maneuver warily [once the war broke out], it could not be expected to rescue us from our dilemmas; indeed, it would probably do all it could to intensify them.[21]

This certainty about the deliberateness of Soviet actions stayed with Kissinger throughout the course of the war. In his discussion of the series of communications that surrounded Sadat's call for troops, Kissinger writes that "While we were waiting to see whether the Cairo report would turn out to be a false alarm, the Soviets stepped up the tension."[22] Later Kissinger writes, "Then suddenly at 7:05 P.M. that Wednesday evening, October 24 (2:05 A.M. Moscow time), the Soviet leaders decided on a showdown."[23] The tone of his discussion of Soviet activities leaves little doubt about Kissinger's beliefs about the deliberateness of Soviet actions. Nixon's view was equally clear. He felt that Soviet actions were quite deliberate and were no doubt aimed at taking advantage of the domestic difficulties of the Nixon administration—in particular, Watergate.[24] Alan Dowty's review of the attitudes of American leaders in the earlier 1970 crisis over Jordan and the 1973 crisis showed that there was little change in the basic view of the Soviet Union: it was an opportunist ready to take advantage of any opportunity that came up, although not necessarily at the expense of détente.[25]

In this crisis there is little doubt that Kissinger would have seen the Soviet decision to send troops as a deliberate one. Dobrynin had even told him so. In phone conversations with Kissinger at 7:15 and 7:25 P.M. on Wednesday, 24 October, Dobrynin informed Kissinger that the "Soviet Union now

---

21. Henry Kissinger, *Years of Upheaval* (Boston: Little, Brown and Company, 1982), 467.

22. Kissinger, *Years of Upheaval*, 579.

23. Kissinger, *Years of Upheaval*, 581.

24. Richard M. Nixon, *RN: The Memoirs of Richard Nixon* (New York: Grosset and Dunlap, 1978), 921, 941.

25. Alan Dowty, *Middle East Crisis: U.S. Decision-Making in 1958, 1970, 1973* (Berkeley: University of California Press, 1984), 213–15, 245–47.

wanted the United Nations to send troops—including Soviet troops" and later "that in Moscow 'they [the Soviet leadership] have become so angry they want troops.'"[26] As noted in chapter 2, a letter from Brezhnev confirmed the Soviet desire to send troops, either in conjunction with the United States or unilaterally, and it is worth reprinting here:

> Let us together, the USSR and the United States, urgently dispatch to Egypt the Soviet and American contingents, to insure the implementation of the decision of the Security Council of October 22 and 23 concerning the cessation of fire and of all military activities and also of our understanding with you on the guarantee of the implementation of the decisions of the Security Council.
>
> It is necessary to adhere [Dobrynin later claimed that he said "act here"] without delay. I will say it straight that if you find it impossible to act jointly with us in this matter, we should be faced with the necessity urgently to consider the question of taking appropriate steps unilaterally.[27]

There was little to suggest that Kissinger was wrong in thinking that Soviet actions were not deliberate. In addition, Kissinger saw these steps as being taken to benefit the Soviet position in the Middle East and hurt the American position:

> But the impact [of Soviet troops arriving in the Middle East with apparent U.S. approval] would go far beyond Egypt. If Soviet forces appeared dramatically in Cairo with the United States as an appendage, our traditional friends among Arab moderates would be profoundly unnerved by the evident fact of US-Soviet condominium. The strategy we had laboriously pursued in four years of diplomacy and two weeks of crisis would disintegrate: Egypt would be drawn back into the Soviet orbit, the Soviet Union and its radical allies would emerge as the dominant factor in the Middle East.[28]

Kissinger saw Soviet actions as being both deliberate and calculated to achieve the largest possible gain, and he responded to the Soviets accordingly. Dobrynin's comments and actions only served to confirm the suspicion that Kissinger had had from the beginning of the crisis. Nixon's view was equally

---

26. Kissinger, *Years of Upheaval*, 582.
27. Kissinger, *Years of Upheaval*, 583.
28. Kissinger, *Years of Upheaval*, 584.

clear: the Soviet message was "a scarcely veiled threat of unilateral Soviet intervention" that would seriously affect U.S. interests in the region if not effectively countered.[29]

We know very little about the Soviet views of this crisis. There is little evidence available about what the Soviets thought about the crisis or the American response. Brezhnev claimed later that the United States had over-reacted in what TASS called an attempt to intimidate the Soviet Union.[30] Brezhnev is said to have felt that the American actions were simply an effort to overdramatize the crisis as a way of sending a message to the Soviets—a message he rejected.[31] As Galia Golan notes in her review of this crisis, it is difficult to find evidence about the views of the Soviet leaders or the positions that they took on the various questions that must have come up during this crisis:

> If it is difficult to identify policy positions of the Soviet leadership, it is no less difficult to determine who actually participated in the decision-making process regarding the Middle East, and the lines of command. Formally, of course, the Politburo was the unit of primary responsibility. Just what role was played by others is entirely speculative.[32]

Only the whereabouts of Aleksei Kosygin on the 24th (immediately before the United States went on alert) were mentioned in the Soviet press. No other information was provided about the activities or whereabouts of any other Soviet leader.[33]

The examination of the October 1973 War crisis has yielded support for the theory being developed here. Although American leaders had an initially benign view of Soviet behavior in the early days of the war, this changed quickly as new evidence arrived that suggested the Soviets were about to intervene to help the Egyptian Third Army. American leaders were convinced that the actions were part of a deliberate effort to undermine U.S. interests. Let us now turn to the Berlin blockade.

---

29. Nixon, *RN*, 938–39.

30. *Foreign Broadcast Information Service, Soviet Union*, 29 October 1973, B4.

31. Mohamed Heikal, *The Road to Ramadan* (London: Colling; New York: Quadrangle, 1975), 255.

32. Galia Golan, "Soviet Decision Making in the Yom Kippur War, 1973," in *Soviet Decision-Making for National Security*, ed. Jiri Valenta and William Potter (London: George Allen and Unwin, 1984), 191.

33. Golan, "Soviet Decision Making in the Yom Kippur War," 211. Kosygin was attending a diplomatic reception at the time.

Berlin Blockade

The Berlin blockade provides strong support for the idea embodied in Proposition Two, that decision makers will see hostile acts by others as being deliberate. It was clear in the minds of American decision makers that the Soviets were attempting to create a serious problem for the United States with the actions they were taking in, and around, Berlin. All of the major decision makers involved in setting policy for the crisis (Truman, Marshall, Clay, and others) felt that the Soviets were engaged in actions deliberately calculated to drive the United States (and the other Western powers) out of Berlin and possibly out of Germany as well. There were major differences between these leaders in their views about the overall nature of the Soviet Union and its goals in Europe, but with respect to their views of the source of this crisis, the answer was clear and unanimous: the crisis was the result of a deliberate action on the part of the Soviet Union designed to put pressure on the Western powers.[34] Because of these differences of view on Soviet motivations, some detail on each participant's view will be useful.

Turning to the question of whether or not the Soviets were to blame for the crises, Truman was the strongest in assigning blame to Moscow. As he writes in his memoirs:

> Russia was caught off guard by the Marshall Plan. Moscow quickly realized that when the Marshall Plan began to function, the opportunity to communize western Europe by exploiting her economic miseries would be lost. Failing to prevent Allied cooperation for European recovery, Russia sought to retaliate by two moves. The first move was to set up a counterpart for a Marshall Plan under Russian auspices for her satellites. . . . The second and even more provocative move was to risk a military incident in Berlin designated to test our firmness and our patience.[35]

Later, Truman writes:

> What the Russians were trying to do was get us out of Berlin. At first they took the position that we never had a legal right to be in Berlin.

---

34. There were those who thought of the Soviets as reckless and risk taking (Marshall) while there were others who thought of them as calculating, deliberate, and generally risk averse (Clay, Truman). Avi Shlaim does an excellent job of outlining the views of these actors on this and other points. *The United States and the Berlin Blockade, 1948–1949: A Study in Crisis Decision-Making* (Berkeley: University of California Press, 1983).

35. Harry S. Truman, *Memoirs, Volume II: Years of Trial and Hope, 1946–1952* (Garden City, N.Y.: Doubleday, 1956), 120.

Later they said that we had the right but that we had forfeited it. . . .What was at stake in Berlin was not a contest over legal rights, although our position was entirely sound in international law, but a struggle over Germany and, in a larger sense, over Europe. In the face of our launching of the Marshall Plan, the Kremlin tried to mislead the people of Europe into believing that our interest and support would not extend beyond economic matters and that we would back away from any military risks.[36]

Truman also believed that the Soviets knew that they were involved in a political battle with the Western powers and, as a result, they knew that the claims they were making were just propaganda, adding to the argument here that leaders will see the actions of an opponent as deliberately calculated to create problems. In commenting on the Soviet reply (14 July) to a presentation of the Western position on Berlin by the ambassadors of the three Western powers in Moscow, Truman notes that the "Soviet reply, given on July 14, dropped all pretenses of 'technical difficulties' and made it abundantly clear that the blockading of Berlin by the Russians was a major political and propaganda move."[37] Truman has many further comments, scattered throughout his discussion of the Berlin crisis, which make it clear that he felt that the Soviet moves were deliberate and designed to maximize American difficulties and Soviet benefits. In all of his references to the blockade, right up until its termination on 12 May 1949, Truman consistently took this line.

As for the other major actors on the American side, there was no doubt about Soviet deliberateness or intentions. Secretary of State Marshall appears to have believed that Soviet actions were deliberate and part of an overall plan to drive the United States in particular, and the other Western powers in general, out of Germany.[38] It seems that Marshall saw the Soviets as moving to extend their domination in Europe and this belief served to motivate Marshall's actions in the Berlin crisis. In a telegram sent in February 1948 to the U.S. ambassador to England, Lewis Douglas, Marshall transmitted his private views on Soviet moves in Western Europe:

At present Eastern Zone of Germany under Soviet occupation is being reshaped in a totalitarian pattern, both economically and politically,

---

36. Truman, *Memoirs, Volume II*, 122–23.

37. Truman, *Memoirs, Volume II*, 123.

38. The note of caution in describing Marshall's view is necessary because of the lack of information available on his views on the issues of Germany and Berlin. As Shlaim notes, "Marshall made few utterances in public on the subject of the Berlin crisis and wrote no memoirs, and this makes it difficult to reconstruct his images [of the Soviets in general, and the Berlin crisis in particular]." *The United States and the Berlin Blockade*, 182.

along lines similar to developments in Eastern European satellite countries. Economy of Eastern Germany is being reoriented to fit into Eastern European economic system developing under Soviet aegis. Accordingly, Western Powers have no alternative except to undertake to integrate both economy and political life of Western Germany with Western Europe. Unless Western Germany is effectively associated with Western European powers, through economic arrangements and, ultimately perhaps, through mutual political understanding, Western Germany too may be at some time drawn into Eastern orbit with all obvious consequences which such an eventuality would entail.[39]

As Avi Shlaim notes:

The blockade of Berlin startlingly confirmed Marshall's suspicions that Russia aimed to extend her domination over the whole of Germany. Since he regarded this eventuality as the greatest threat to the security of the United States and her European allies, Marshall was clearly predisposed to resist the Soviet move. . . .The evidence we have concerning Marshall's images, incomplete as it is, does permit the conclusion that he perceived the Soviet Union as an expansionist power, the United States as a status quo power, and the relations between them in the German arena as a zero-sum game in which any Russian gain would be at Western expense.[40]

In sum, it is probably safe to say that Marshall's view of the Soviet Union and its actions during the Berlin crisis supports Proposition Two.

The third major decision maker during the Berlin crisis was General Clay. It is perfectly clear from his writings at the time and later that Clay saw the Soviet actions in Berlin as a series of calculated moves designed to put pressure on the Western powers over the issues of Berlin and Germany. During both the small baby blockade of April 1948 and the full-scale blockade of June 1948–May 1949, Clay continued to express his view that the Soviets were engaged in a deliberate attempt to force the Western Allies out of Berlin. While Clay later describes the Soviet effort as "one of the most ruthless efforts in modern times to use mass starvation for political coercion,"[41] an assessment that is more consistent with other comments is:

---

39. Telegram from Marshall to Douglas, 20 February 1948. U.S. Department of State, *Foreign Relations of the United States* 1948, 2:71–73. (Hereafter *FRUS.*)

40. Shlaim, *The United States and the Berlin Blockade*, 96–97.

41. Lucius D. Clay, *Decision in Germany* (Westport, Conn.: Greenwood Press, 1950), 365.

The blockade of Berlin by the Soviets was caused not by their desire to take over the city . . . It came primarily from their desire to weaken our position in Europe. . . .It [the Soviet government] was fully aware of our traditional policy of remaining free of foreign entanglements and it determined to test our intent by a blockade of Berlin, which was obviously the most vulnerable and difficult spot for us to defend. I am sure the Soviet Government expected the Western Allies to withdraw from Berlin. The consequence would have been to destroy the confidence of a defenseless Western Europe in the determination of the United States to support and defend it until it could recover.[42]

During a teleconference on 10 April 1948 between Clay and General Omar Bradley (Army Chief of Staff) about the miniblockade of April 1948, Bradley speculated about the possible course of the blockade and asked Clay what his suggestions were for avoiding being forced out of Germany.[43] Bradley's speculations (which turned out to be accurate) and Clay's responses are worth quoting in full:

Bradley: At present with our passenger trains completely stopped, Russians in effect have won the first round unless some way to get this changed. Do you see any such likelihood? If not, will not Russian restrictions be added one by one which eventually would make our position untenable unless we ourselves were prepared to threaten or actually start a war to remove these restrictions? Here [in Washington] we doubt whether our people are prepared to start a war in order to maintain our position in Berlin and Vienna.

What are your comments and if you agree should we now be planning how to avoid this development. . . .

Clay: Relative to your first question, I do not believe anything will come from protest to Moscow except rejection accompanied by legal argumentation. . . . Reference to your second question. I do not believe that we should plan on leaving Berlin short of Soviet ultimatum to drive us out by force if we do not leave. . . . There can be no question but that our departure would represent a tremendous loss of prestige and I would greatly deplore incurring such a loss of prestige unless it were forced by military action. Of course, I realize that this final decision is a matter of high Government policy. Nevertheless, I cannot believe that Soviets will apply force in Berlin unless they have deter-

---

42. Lucius D. Clay, "Berlin," *Foreign Affairs* 41, no. 1 (October 1962): 51–52.

43. This was a type of conference frequently held between Washington and Berlin in which both parties communicated by means of a teletypewriter.

mined war to be inevitable within a comparatively short period of time. . . . Why are we in Europe? We have lost Czechoslovakia. We have lost Finland. Norway is threatened. We retreat from Berlin. . . . After Berlin, will come western Germany and our strength there relatively is no greater and our position no more tenable than Berlin.

If we mean that we are to hold Europe against communism, we must not budge. We can take humiliation and pressure short of war in Berlin without losing face. If we move, our position in Europe is threatened. If America does not know this, does not believe the issue is cast now, then it never will and communism will run rampant. I believe the future of democracy requires us to stay here until forced out. God knows that this is not heroic pose because there will be nothing heroic in having to take humiliation without retaliation.[44]

This quote makes clear Clay's view that Soviet policy was deliberate and that when they decided to increase the pressure on the West they would do so. It also clearly shows Clay's determination to stay in Berlin in the face of Soviet pressure, a determination that never wavered during the entire crisis.

The one area in which there were important differences relevant to our discussion of later propositions is with respect to the leaders' assessments of the willingness of the Soviet Union to use force to achieve its goals in Berlin and run the risk of war. The fear of such a course of action tended to increase the farther the decision maker was from Berlin. Both Clay and the State Department's political advisor, Murphy, repeatedly stated that they did not think that the Soviets were willing to go to war over Berlin. In the first teleconference with Washington since the beginning of the crisis, Clay expressed his view about the small likelihood of war, a view he repeatedly made known during the crisis:

Clay: If Soviets go to war, it will not be because of Berlin currency issue but only because they believe this the right time. In such case, they would use currency issue as an excuse. I regard this probability as rather remote although it must not be disregarded.[45]

In Washington, at the State Department, White House, and Department of Defense, the fears of Soviet escalation were greater. These fears of escalation would consistently cause Clay's superiors in Washington to deny his requests to use force to attempt to break the blockade.

With this discussion of the Berlin blockade, the support continues to

---

44. Jean Edward Smith, ed., *The Papers of General Lucius D. Clay: Germany 1945–1949*, vol. 2 (Bloomington: Indiana University Press, 1974), 622—23. (Herefter *Clay Papers.*)

45. Smith, *Clay Papers*, vol. 2, 702.

grow for Proposition Two's position that decision makers will view the detrimental actions of others as being hostile. What was also seen was that there were some differences of opinion about the Soviet Union's ultimate intentions. There was, however, no doubt about the Soviet desire to cause problems for the United States. This certainty, however, will not be as strong when the next case is considered.

Iranian Crisis of 1946

Our examination of the events of March 1946 suggests partial support for the theory presented here. The lack of communications from the Soviets, as well as the possibility of different interpretations of Soviet motives, made U.S. decision makers hesitate before concluding that Soviet actions were directed against U.S. interests. In order to understand the way in which American leaders viewed the March 1946 crisis, a brief review of the events of late 1945 and early 1946 will be useful. The context of this crisis is significantly different than that of the others considered here, coming as it did before U.S.-Soviet relations had begun to harden into the pattern of the Cold War. Because Proposition Two rests on the views that leaders have of their opponents, a more detailed discussion of this crisis and its background is needed.

In the fall of 1945, concerns about Soviet interests in Iran had become pronounced. In November, Soviet activities in Iran were taken up at the cabinet level when Truman asked Secretary of State Byrnes to make a presentation outlining the situation there.[46] What had brought the issue to Truman's attention were armed uprisings, with Soviet agitators involved, in the northern Iranian province of Azerbaijan. In addition to the agitators, twelve thousand new Soviet troops had been sent into that part of Iran.[47] As a result of this cabinet meeting, a strong note of protest was sent to the Soviet Union, reminding it that the Big 3 had issued a declaration at Tehran on 1 December 1943 pledging to maintain "the independence, sovereignty, and territorial integrity of Iran" and requested that the Soviets pledge to remove their troops by 1 January 1946.[48] The Soviets refused to remove their troops at that time, noting their rights to remain in Iran until 2 March 1946.[49]

---

46. Truman, *Memoirs, Volume II*, 93.

47. Useful reviews are Gary R. Hess, "The Iranian Crisis of 1945–46 and the Cold War," *Political Science Quarterly* 89, no. 1 (March 1974): 126–28; Bruce Robellet Kuniholm, *The Origins of the Cold War in the Near East: Great Power Conflict and Diplomacy in Iran, Turkey, and Greece* (Princeton: Princeton University Press, 1980), 270–82; John R. Oneal, *Foreign Policy Making in Times of Crisis* (Columbus: Ohio State University Press, 1982), 86–88; and *FRUS*, 1945, 8:430–526.

48. *FRUS*, 1945, 8:448–50.

49. *FRUS*, 1945, 8:468–69.

As December 1945 progressed, the question of Soviet interference in Iran grew. Soviet-inspired actions in Azerbaijan increased in intensity, and there were concerns in Washington about Soviet efforts to annex the region. These concerns caused American leaders to consider placing the matter before the United Nations.[50] As mentioned in the previous chapter, putting this issue before the United Nations was no simple or trivial matter. It would be a direct challenge to one of the five permanent members of the United Nations, and many in Washington were reluctant to do this.

There were other elements that played a role in contributing to the feelings of uncertainty and crisis felt by leaders in Washington. In late 1945 information became available about previous Soviet involvement with Iran that cast current Soviet activities in Azerbaijan in a more ominous light. In reviewing files captured from the German Foreign Office, two secret protocols to the Nazi-Soviet Non-Aggression Pact of 1939 had been found and one related to Soviet interests in Iran. Protocol One showed that the two parties had agreed that certain areas of northern Iran were part of the Soviet sphere of influence and "the center of the aspirations of the Soviet Union" in the Persian Gulf. Such a finding could only have increased concerns in Washington about Soviet intentions in Iran.[51]

As 1946 began, concerns about the direction of Soviet policy had begun to grow, both in Iran and in Washington. On 9 January 1946, the American vice-consul at Tabriz sent a cable that ended on an alarming note. After discussing various measures that Soviet authorities had taken to exercise greater control in Azerbaijan, the message ended with "Unless some sort of energetic action is soon taken Azerbaijan must be written off."[52] During this same time period, the Iranian government had made requests to the United States for assistance in slowing or reversing the growth of Soviet influence in Iran and in helping speed up the removal of Soviet troops from Iran. These activities kept Iran in the minds of many in Washington, and more officials were to become concerned as time went on.

In early February, concern about Soviet actions increased as newspaper accounts began to report a new direction in Soviet foreign policy. On 6 February, Soviet Foreign Minister Vyacheslav M. Molotov had delivered a strong speech, attacking the Western powers for rumors of war and antagonism toward the Soviet Union.[53] Two days later, Soviet Premier Stalin deliv-

---

50. Adam B. Ulam, *Expansion and Coexistence: Soviet Foreign Policy, 1917–1973*, 2d ed. (New York: Praeger, 1974), 425–26, and Hess, "The Iranian Crisis of 1945–46," 128–29.

51. Oneal, *Foreign Policy Making in Times of Crisis*, 91. See also Kuniholm, *The Origins of the Cold War in the Near East*, 293–94.

52. *FRUS*, 1946, 7:298–99.

53. *New York Times*, 7 February 1946.

ered a very harsh speech that ignored Western contributions to the victory in World War II and blamed current world problems on capitalism.[54] The speech had quite an impact in Washington. Acheson later commented that the speech marked the beginning of "Stalin's offensive against the United States and the West" and that this marked the "start of the 'Cold War'."[55] Justice William O. Douglas commented to Secretary of Defense James V. Forrestal that it was "The Declaration of World War III."[56] This speech had a significant impact on the thinking of many leaders in Washington, moving most to view the Soviets in a less than favorable light and contributing directly to the concerns about Iran.[57]

Nine days after Stalin's speech, officials in Washington received the news that a Soviet spy ring had been discovered in Canada and that its purpose had been to steal secrets concerning atomic weapons.[58] Amidst rising concerns about Soviet intentions, this event had a strong impact in Washington, increasing concerns about how much the Soviets could be trusted and raising doubts about the possible incompatibility of Western and Soviet aims.[59]

The arrival of George Kennan's famous "Long Telegram" on 22 February 1946 provided the intellectual framework that many were looking for to help interpret recent Soviet actions. Bruce Robellet Kuniholm, and others, have suggested that the telegram had a "profound" impact on leaders in Washington, coming as it did at a time of concern about Soviet activities and motives.[60] Kennan's analysis of Soviet behavior served to reinforce the views of those who already mistrusted the Soviets, provide a framework for those who were not sure of how to interpret Soviet motives, and cause those who supported the Soviets to begin to question that support. Two factors that contributed to the impact of Kennan's telegram were the fact that it came at a time when many were having trouble understanding Soviet behavior and the fact that it received a wide circulation among the top echelons of government.

---

54. *New York Times*, 10 February 1946.

55. Dean Acheson, *Present at the Creation: My Years in the State Department* (New York: W. W. Norton, 1969), 194.

56. Walter Millis, ed., *The Forrestal Diaries* (New York: Viking Press, 1951), 134.

57. Joseph L. Nogee and Robert H. Donaldson, *Soviet Foreign Policy since World War II* (New York: Pergamon, 1981), 56–61, and Daniel Yergin, *Shattered Peace: The Origins of the Cold War and the National Security State* (London: Andre Deutsch, 1977), 166–67.

58. Kuniholm, *The Origins of the Cold War in the Near East*, 315 and n. 32. This news became public in the first week of March. *New York Times*, 5 March 1946.

59. Robert J. Donovan, *Conflict and Crisis: The Presidency of Harry S. Truman, 1945–1948* (New York: W. W. Norton, 1977), 187.

60. Kuniholm, *The Origins of the Cold War in the Near East*, 311; John Lewis Gaddis, *The United States and the Origins of the Cold War, 1941–1947* (New York: Columbia University Press, 1972), 303–4. Kennan's telegram is found in *FRUS*, 1946, 6:696–709.

Forrestal had it circulated to members of the cabinet, and it was circulated among the upper levels of the State Department as well.[61]

In early February, the State Department received information that suggested that the Soviets might not be planning to leave Iran by the 2 March deadline. Information was received that the Soviets were making no moves to leave and were even signing six-month contracts with local merchants for supplies for their troops.[62] The *New York Times* reported on 22 February that "With four days to go to evacuate their troops from Iran under the terms of the Anglo-Soviet Treaty, there is no outward sign that the Russians are moving." George Lenczowski notes:

> The approach of March 2 was watched in Washington and London with growing uneasiness and tension. The failure of the Soviets to evacuate would place before the West a new violation of an international agreement by the Russians and thus complicate the whole matter. It would also call for more positive action on the part of the West, as non-evacuation, in contrast to internal interference, would be easy to ascertain.[63]

What seems to have finally pushed Washington into a feeling of crisis was a series of cables in early March from the consul at Tabriz about Soviet troop movements in northern Iran. On 5 March 1946, Robert Rossow, Jr. cabled his concerns to the secretary of state, noting that "Exceptionally heavy Soviet troop movements have been going on since yesterday."[64] That report was followed the next day, 6 March, by a more alarming one:

> Soviet troop reinforcements continue arriving night and day by truck and rail from Soviet frontier, and are being constantly redeployed from here. . . . General Bagramian, Soviet Army Commander with spectacular combat record, has arrived and taken command of Soviet troops in Azerbaijan, superseding Lieut. General Glinsky who is only Corp Commander and has no extensive combat experience. . . . All observations and reports indicate inescapably that Soviets are preparing for major military operation. . . .[Rossow then notes the arrival of more Soviet tanks.] General Bagramian is said to be specialist in tank warfare.[65]

---

61. Kuniholm, *The Origins of the Cold War in the Near East*, 312 and n. 23.
62. Rossow to Byrnes, 11 February 1946, *FRUS*, 1946, 7:332–34.
63. George Lenczowski, *Russia and the West in Iran, 1918–1948: A Study In Big-Power Rivalry* (New York: Greenwood Press, 1968), 296–97.
64. Rossow to Byrnes, *FRUS*, 1946, 7:340.
65. Rossow to Byrnes, *FRUS*, 1946, 7:342–43.

This was followed on 7 March by another alarming message:

> I cannot overstress the seriousness and magnitude of current Soviet troop movements here. This is no ordinary reshuffling of troops but a full scale combat deployment. . . .[Rossow goes on to detail further military deployments] I expect communications to be cut at any moment.[66]

These telegrams created quite a stir in Washington. As Walter LaFeber puts it, "The State Department panicked."[67] These concerns increased when the American ambassador in Iran reported a recent conversation with Iranian Foreign Minister Amhad Qavam. Qavam had just returned from a long visit in Moscow, and in the course of a discussion with Stalin and Molotov, Qavam reported that both "Stalin and Molotov had burst out with the statement that, 'We don't care what US and Britain think and we are not afraid of them.'"[68] The pressure continued to build as did the belief that the Soviets were determined to cause problems. With this background, it is now time to turn to a discussion of Proposition Two.

Recall that Proposition Two has two elements: a belief about the deliberateness of the act and, second, a belief about the motives behind the act. With respect to Soviet actions, there was little doubt on the part of American leaders that the Soviets knew that what they were doing would cause concern in the West, in particular in Washington and London.[69] Truman was so concerned about events in Iran that he pointed to the danger and risk of war stemming from the conflict over Iran as a means of persuading Averell Harriman to accept the post of ambassador to London.[70]

Secretary of State Byrnes also believed that Soviet actions were part of a deliberate effort to create problems in the region. In a briefing he was given on 7 March concerning the reports from Rossow, Byrnes is reported to have commented:

> that it now seemed that the USSR was adding military invasion to political subversion in Iran, and beating one fist into the other [Byrnes said] "Now we'll give it to them with both barrels."[71]

---

66. Rossow to Byrnes, *FRUS*, 1946, 7:344–45.

67. Walter LaFeber, *America, Russia, and the Cold War, 1945–1980*, 4th ed. (New York: Wiley, 1980), 35.

68. Murray to Byrnes, *FRUS*, 1946, 7:352.

69. Truman, *Memoirs, Volume II*, 93–95.

70. Kuniholm, *The Origins of the Cold War in the Near East*, 324–25. U.S.-British relations were felt to be crucial in dealing with events in Iran. Truman's argument to Harriman was that things were so dangerous that he needed someone he could trust in London.

71. *FRUS*, 1946, 7:347.

At a meeting of high-level officials on the next day, it was agreed that only one conclusion could be drawn from Soviet actions and behavior: the Soviets had clearly violated their agreement to leave Iran and "were determined to face Iran and the rest of the world with a *fait accompli*."[72]

There were, however, doubts elsewhere about Soviet motives. Many still saw the dispute as just another chapter in a long-standing dispute between the Soviet Union and Great Britain for control in the Middle East. In early February, the dispute was portrayed in the *New York Times* as an Anglo-Soviet dispute, and many in Washington saw it the same way.[73] Later scholars have also made similar claims. Daniel Yergin argues that the conflict in Iran between the United States, the Soviet Union, and Great Britain was really nothing more than a classic struggle for influence—and oil.[74]

What was unclear in the minds of American leaders was what the Soviets wanted to accomplish by creating this crisis. The long history of Soviet (and Russian) involvement in this region led some to conclude that this crisis was simply another chapter in the long battle between the Soviets (Russians) and the British for spheres of influence in the region. Others saw this as merely a local effort to gain some amount of influence in Iran—not to make trouble for the United States. The final point of view (most clearly expressed by Truman) was that this was a crisis designed to create problems for the United States. Most leaders in Washington were willing to believe that the Soviets were deliberately creating a crisis that would bring them benefits as well as cause problems for the United States. There were also those who were unsure about the deliberateness of Soviet moves, a situation we will see again when we examine the case of the Berlin Wall, necessitating a similarly detailed discussion of events.

Berlin Wall Crisis

The problem that arises in attempting to assess Proposition Two in the context of the Berlin Wall crisis concerns the degree to which the Kennedy administration felt that the construction of the Berlin Wall was a crisis. There is no doubt that most in the Kennedy administration viewed the Soviet threats to make a separate peace with East Germany, and Khrushchev's increased rhetoric and military preparedness around Berlin, as part of a crisis. As noted in the case history summaries, many in the administration were afraid that the Soviets would go through with their threats to conclude a peace treaty with the East

---

72. *FRUS*, 1946, 7:347.

73. *New York Times*, 1–9 February 1946. This theme would be picked up later in the month as well. See *New York Times*, 24 February 1946. See also Hess, "The Iranian Crisis of 1945-46," 128–30.

74. Yergin, *Shattered Peace*, 179–82.

German regime, and the prospect of having to defend American and Western interests in that eventuality was viewed with some alarm. There was also little doubt on the part of leaders in Washington that the Soviets were making these threats and demanding these changes in order to gain some advantage at the expense of the Western position in Berlin. In early 1961, former Secretary of State Acheson was asked to chair a review committee on America's policy in Berlin. He concluded that the Soviets were going to "force the issue" in 1961 and that the United States ought to embark on a rapid military buildup to be prepared when the crisis came.[75] In its public statements, the Kennedy administration began to take a similar line. In his remarks accompanying the Western powers' response (19 July 1961) to a Soviet aide-memoire of 4 June demanding that a peace treaty be signed soon, Kennedy remarked:

> The world knows that there is no reason for a crisis over Berlin today—and that if one develops, it will be caused by the Soviet Government's attempt to invade the rights of others and manufacture tensions.[76]

By the time of Kennedy's 25 July speech, in which he declared that the United States would defend its rights in West Berlin and asked for the economic and military measures to do so, Kennedy had clearly laid the blame at the Soviet Union's door:

> The world is not deceived by the Communist attempt to label Berlin as a hot-bed of war. There is peace in Berlin today. The source of world trouble and tension is Moscow, not Berlin. And if war begins, it will have begun in Moscow and not Berlin.
>
> For the choice of peace or war is largely theirs, not ours. It is the Soviets who have stirred up this crisis. It is they who are trying to force a change. It is they who have opposed free elections.[77]

With respect to the general Berlin crisis, the evidence strongly supports Proposition Two. American leaders, Kennedy in particular, felt that the Soviets were deliberately fostering a crisis to make gains at the expense of the Western, and American, position in Berlin.

Turning to the phase of the crisis that included the construction of the wall, it is much harder to decide if the evidence supports Proposition Two.

75. Arthur M. Schlesinger, Jr., *A Thousand Days: John F. Kennedy in the White House* (Boston: Houghton Mifflin Company, 1965), 380, and Theodore Sorensen, *Kennedy* (New York: Harper and Row, 1965), 583–84.

76. John F. Kennedy, *Public Papers of the Presidents of the United States: John F. Kennedy, 1961* (Washington, D.C.: GPO, 1961), 523.

77. Kennedy, *Public Papers of the Presidents of the United States*, 538.

The reason is that it is unclear how much decision makers in the Kennedy administration viewed the construction of the wall as a crisis. As noted in chapter 2, the literature on this crisis contains an interesting split between those who argue that the Kennedy administration was very concerned about the wall and the impact that it was having on free movement in Berlin and those who argue that the Kennedy administration almost welcomed the wall because it helped alleviate a much larger worry: the potential steps that the Soviets and East Germans might take if the refugee situation continued to get worse or if unrest was to develop in East Germany. The strongest statement of this view is given by Kenneth P. O'Donnell and David F. Powers:

> It was said and written at the time that the building of the wall shocked and depressed Kennedy. Actually, he saw the wall as the turning point that would lead to the end of the Berlin crisis. He said to me, "Why would Khrushchev put up a wall if he really intended to seize West Berlin? There wouldn't be any need of a wall if he occupied the whole city. This is his way out of his predicament. It's not a very nice solution, but a wall is a hell of a lot better than a war."[78]

Kennedy, in fact, had once even suggested that a wall might be the solution that the Soviets would decide to impose, noting the difficulty that the United States might have in challenging it, commenting in early August 1961:

> Khrushchev is losing East Germany. He cannot let that happen, if East Germany goes, so will Poland, and all of Eastern Europe. He will have to do something to stop the flow of refugees—*perhaps a wall*. And we won't be able to prevent it. I can hold the Alliance together to defend West Berlin but I cannot act to keep East Berlin open.[79]

Jean Edward Smith and Eleanor Lansing Dulles present the strongest case for the view that the Kennedy administration had already decided by the time the wall was constructed not to challenge any action that limited access to West Berlin as long as it did not affect Western access to East Berlin.[80] Dulles and

---

78. Kenneth P. O'Donnell and David F. Powers, *"Johnny, We Hardly Knew Ye": Memories of John Fitzgerald Kennedy* (Boston: Little, Brown and Company, 1970), 303.

79. Jonathan M. Roberts, *Decision-Making during International Crises* (New York: St. Martin's Press, 1988), 47. Emphasis added by Roberts. See also McGeorge Bundy, *Danger and Survival: Choices about the Bomb in the First Fifty Years* (New York: Random House, 1988), 368.

80. Jean Edward Smith, *The Defense of Berlin* (Baltimore: Johns Hopkins University Press, 1963), 293–98, and Eleanor Lansing Dulles, *Berlin: The Wall Is Not Forever* (Chapel Hill: University of North Carolina Press, 1967), 61–65.

Smith make the argument that these events, while worrisome to the Kennedy administration, did not actually constitute a crisis in the sense that has been discussed here. Their main argument is as follows: the Kennedy administration, in its review of the Berlin situation, had decided in early 1961 that it was not worth going to war over small issues in Berlin (such as access from the east) and as a result had chosen not to challenge the various encroachments made by the East German authorities in the preceding months. The Kennedy administration was afraid that an uprising in East Germany would lead to Soviet intervention, as it had in Hungary, and that the administration would look bad when it was clear that there was nothing it could do about it. Kennedy made no statement about the situation in Berlin until nine days after construction on the wall had begun, and some point to this as reflecting a lack of concern on the part of the president and other soft-liners in the administration.

The argument here is that the Kennedy administration did feel concern about events immediately after the construction of the wall and it can be argued that there was a sense of crisis. But the crisis was not about the wall per se but rather about what might come next. The initial comments of government spokesmen were low-key and did not threaten the Soviets in the event that they did not remove the wall. Diplomatic notes from the Western commandants in Berlin (15 August) and the United States (17 August) merely protested the Soviet actions.[81] When it became clear that the wall was not part of a larger push against Western interests, the crisis became much less pronounced. This aspect will be discussed further under Proposition Four.

One further element seemed to have helped limit the feelings of crisis. This was Soviet restraint in hindering Western access to East Berlin. While it was immediately obvious that those wishing to leave East Berlin were seriously constrained from doing so, it was very apparent that Soviet forces were under orders not to interfere with those from the West (namely uniformed military personnel and diplomats) who wished to enter East Berlin. There were steps taken by the United States to reinforce the principle of Western access that involved the use of American military forces, but for the most part the Soviets were very careful not to hinder the access to East Berlin from West Berlin or to West Berlin from West Germany that President Kennedy had so strongly said he would defend.[82] It is unclear how much the Kennedy administration would have resisted further Soviet moves. Honore M. Catudal suggests how the Kennedy administration looked at this crisis:

---

81. U.S. Department of State, *Documents on Germany, 1944-1985*, no. 9446 (Washington, D.C.: Office of the Historian, Bureau of Public Affairs, n.d.), 776–78.

82. See Smith, *The Defense of Berlin*, 309–10, 319–24, and Norman Gelb, *The Berlin Wall* (New York: New York Times-Quadrangle, 1986), 247–58, for a discussion of these events.

President Kennedy and other top American officials fully expected the East German government (with the permission and assistance of the Soviet Union) to take strong measures to stem the damaging flow of refugees into West Berlin. . . . these same officials recognized that the division of Berlin—by barbed wire and perhaps a wall—was one possibility. Moreover, it reveals that JFK and his advisers decided in advance to acquiesce in this and that they conveyed this message, intentionally or unintentionally, to the Russians.[83]

In summary, the evidence on the general Berlin crisis supports Proposition Two, while the evidence for the portion that included the construction of the wall is less supportive. Once people began to feel that the construction of the wall was not the prelude to a more serious effort to take Berlin, some of the pressure was off. Thus, the examination of this crisis provides mixed support for the proposition.

Conclusion

The evidence provided by these case studies is stronger and more direct for Proposition Two than that found for Proposition One. Proposition One's claim that actors will assume that others see the world in the same way and Proposition Two's claim that decision makers will see crises as the deliberate acts of opponents have been supported. The general assumption on the part of American leaders seems to have been that "If it is causing us problems and the other side is doing it, then they must be doing it for just that reason." In general, decision makers seemed to believe that the opponents knew that their actions were going to cause problems for the United States and that was the reason for their actions. This sentiment was particularly clear in the Berlin blockade, Cuban Missile Crisis, and the October 1973 Middle East War. American leaders were very firm in their beliefs about Soviet culpability and deliberateness in these crises. There almost seems to have been a reverse application of Proposition One: decision makers assumed that the Soviets knew what they (the Soviets) were doing and, if what they were doing was detrimental to American interests, then it must have been because that is what the Soviets wanted. This suggestion is similar to one of Jervis's hypotheses: "[A]ctors tend to see the behavior of others as more centralized, disciplined, and coordinated than it is."[84] This type of behavior occurred frequently in the cases studied here.

---

83. Honore M. Catudal, *Kennedy and the Berlin Wall Crisis: A Case Study in U.S. Decision Making* (Berlin: Berlin-Verlag, 1980), 251.

84. Robert Jervis, "Hypotheses on Misperception" *World Politics* 20, no. 3 (April 1968), 474.

There were two partial exceptions to Proposition Two in these case studies. The first was found in the Iranian crisis of 1946. One of the uncertainties that contributed to the feeling of crisis on the part of American leaders concerned Soviet motives: Why were the Soviets taking these actions and how far did they intend to go? Were Soviet actions aimed at gaining influence at the expense of Western interests or were the Soviets simply acting to protect what they felt were their own interests? The long history of Soviet involvement in the region had been noted frequently in the State Department's reviews of events, and there were many in and out of the government who argued that, for this reason, the United States should not get involved. In addition, many suggested that the problems in Iran were part of a dispute between the United Kingdom and the Soviet Union in an area of traditional rivalry and that the United States should not get involved in this great power rivalry. A final point made by some who argued that the United States need not get involved was that the Soviet Union did have legitimate concerns about the security of its southern regions along the Iranian border. These factors served to keep some from immediately concluding that Soviet moves were designed to hurt the United States.

This same confusion about what constituted legitimate concerns (or at least understandable concerns) was also found in the Berlin Wall crisis. As noted in chapter 2, there were those who recognized that the mass exodus of refugees from East Germany to West Berlin was placing a tremendous political and economic burden on the East German regime and, indirectly, on the Soviet Union. The political burden was the embarrassment faced by the regime at having so many of its citizens want to flee the country, while the economic burden was the impact on the economy of having so many skilled people out of the work force. Many in the administration fully expected the Soviet Union (through East Germany) to take some sort of action to limit the flow of the refugees. The result of this was that many were not willing to believe that the Soviet actions on the refugee issue were designed to create problems for the United States or that the crisis was a deliberate creation. On the question of the Soviet demands for a peace treaty with East Germany, there was total agreement that the Soviet Union was attempting to create problems for the United States and the other Western powers that would benefit the Soviet Union. There was strong support to resist Soviet efforts to put pressure on the United States and West Germany on the issue of a peace treaty, but this support did not always carry over to resisting the construction of the wall.

These examples fit Lebow's description of spinoff crises that was noted in chapter 1 and will be taken up in greater detail in chapter 5. These are crises that arise as the result of actions taken by an actor that brought it in conflict with a third party. They also suggest a possible limitation on the application of

Proposition Two: Proposition Two might be less useful in describing behavior during spinoff crises. It is certainly true that American officials felt the Iranian and Berlin Wall situations to be crises, but as compared with the other crises considered here, the officials were not as eager to assume that they were the result of deliberate actions on the part of the Soviet Union vis-à-vis the United States.

Proposition Two builds on the assumptions embedded in Proposition One, namely that one's acts will be clear to others, and makes a statement about the way that decision makers will view hostile acts of others. If a decision maker feels that his or her actions or statements have been non-hostile, then it is likely that that decision maker will believe that actions taken by others that seem to be hostile will be because of a hostile intent on the part of the other state. There is a strong interplay between Proposition One and Proposition Two that has come through clearly in the case studies. States that find themselves in a crisis that they have not initiated will tend to see it as the result of hostile actions of another and will assume that the other has misunderstood their position on a particular issue. Proposition Three is useful in attempting to understand where crises originate and how a state (or two states) might be in a crisis it did not intend.

CHAPTER 5

Crises and Their Origins

The question we turn to now relates to the origins of crises: Why do they start? This chapter presents the core of the theoretical discussion of perceptions and crisis decision making being developed here. In doing so, a more detailed inquiry into the case studies will be undertaken. The discussions in chapters 3 and 4 have laid the groundwork for the argument that will be made here. The main thrust of that argument rests on a view of crises that sees some of them beginning by accident or unintentionally. From this point of view, a crisis can start in one of two ways:

1. When one state takes actions that it believes to be benign, only to find that an opponent has taken offense and responds accordingly.
2. And/or when a state sees the actions of another state as benign, only to find out that they are not.

In both of these cases, the actions are based on interpretations or perceptions of events that turn out to be incorrect.

This discussion suggests an issue that must be addressed before proceeding: Can crises be accidental or unintentional? In each of the two situations described above, there was an element of accident or unintended crisis involved. To develop the conceptual underpinning to this question, we will look to the phenomenon of war to see what can be applied to the discussion of crises.

It has been argued that wars do not occur by accident but are the result of decision makers concluding that there was more to be gained (or less to be lost) from going to war than by not doing so. An example of this line of argument comes from Geoffrey Blainey:

> The high hopes on the eve of wars suggest a sad conclusion. Wars occurred only when both rivals believed that they could achieve more through war than peace.[1]

---

1. Geoffrey Blainey, *The Causes of War* (London: Macmillan, 1973), 127.

This runs counter to the popular notion that wars can be accidental. This idea of accidental war was one of the driving forces behind the negotiation of the "Agreement on Measures to Reduce the Risk of Outbreak of Nuclear War between the United States of America and the Union of Soviet Socialist Republics" signed in 1971. A more recent example is the signing of an agreement between the United States and the Soviet Union in May 1987 establishing nuclear risk reduction centers.[2] The assumption common in many of these approaches is that there is indeed a risk that "accidents" or misperceptions will lead to war. The argument against this assumption can be summed up in the following way:

> The idea of "unintentional war" and "accidental war" seems misleading. The sudden vogue of these concepts in the nuclear age reflects not only a justifiable nervousness about war but also the backward state of knowledge about the causes of war. One may suggest that what was so often unintentional about war was not the decision to fight but the outcome of the fighting. A war was often longer and more costly than each warring nation had intended. Above all, most wars were likely to end in the defeat of at least one nation which had expected victory. On the eve of each war at least one of the nations miscalculated its bargaining power. In that sense every war comes from a misunderstanding. And in that sense every war is an accident.[3]

The question of "accident or not" can be applied to the study of crises as well. Can crises be accidental? The question of accidental or unintended crises is an important one that should be considered in some depth. Proposition Three centers around the issue of unintended crises and their causes. Because of the centrality of this proposition to the overall theory being advanced here, a more detailed discussion of the crises will be provided.

Proposition Three: Crises that are unintended by either side will be found to be the result of misperceptions, which will frequently be situational.

Proposition Three is based on the observation that the assumption that decision makers have about the world that is embodied in Proposition One (that

---

2. The literature on confidence-building measures (CBMs) is a growing one. Two examples of different approaches to the topic are Alan J. Vick, "Building Confidence during Peace and War," *Defense Analysis* 5, no. 2 (1989): 97–113, and William L. Ury and Richard Smoke, *Beyond the Hotline: Controlling a Nuclear Crisis*, a report of the United States Arms Control and Disarmament Agency. (Cambridge: Harvard University Law School, Nuclear Negotiation Project, 1984).

3. Blainey, *The Causes of War*, 144–45.

actions and motives will be clear) is not always correct. There are many reasons why actions and motives will not be seen as the originator wants them to be seen, and this will contribute to crises under the proper circumstances. The mechanism that propels many crises is uncertainty—something that was found to be true in most of the crises discussed below. This proposition attempts to formalize two notions that are sometimes used to describe events. The first is that a state stumbled into a crisis with another state; that is, it found that actions that it had taken and thought to be unlikely to provoke a crisis did just that—provoke a crisis. This can frequently result from a misunderstanding of what the other state believes to be important or unimportant. The second notion that this proposition attempts to draw out is that of a state finding itself in more of a crisis than it bargained for. A state might engage in a particular action in hopes of gaining some foreign policy benefit with respect to another state, only to find that the response of the other state was more than expected. This type of situation can result from misperceptions as well. Proposition Three attempts to explain how crises can arise by looking at misperceptions as a source of those crises. The argument presented here suggests that there are indeed unintended crises and that misperception plays a crucial role in them. Let us expand the discussion of the concept of accidental or unintended crises that was begun in chapter 1.

Snyder and Diesing argue that there are no crises that are unintended. In their view of the crisis dynamic, there is a progression of events that includes an existing degree of conflict of interest, a *precipitant* (e.g., a feeling of strategic weakness in the Cuban Missile Crisis or the drain of East Germans to the West in the Berlin Wall crisis), a *challenge* by one of the two parties (emplacement of missiles in Cuba or the building of the wall), and then a *response* or resistance (the quarantine of Cuba or heightened military alert levels in response to the wall) that leads to a confrontation. Their argument is that the crisis will resolve either into war or some mixture of capitulation and compromise. There is no room for what might be called an unintended crisis because at each stage in their model an actor must choose to continue the confrontation or not. Snyder and Diesing found no examples of accidental crises, at least in the challenge phase of the crises, in their sample.[4] The authors do note that the prior precipitant might be considered to have been accidental or unintended, but almost by definition, a crisis that proceeds beyond the precipitant stage cannot be accidental. In their approach to defining a crisis, a crisis does not exist until the response stage, in which the second party decides to counter the actions of the first. In other words, "It takes two

---

4. Glenn H. Snyder and Paul Diesing, *Conflict among Nations: Bargaining, Decision Making, and System Structure in International Crises* (Princeton: Princeton University Press, 1977), 10–21.

to tango." Since the response has to be deliberate, the crisis must be said to be deliberate. This view can be included in the definition of unintended crisis that is being used here without doing damage to either perspective. Let us first discuss intended crises, taking Lebow's approach to crises as a starting point.

Lebow argues that there are three major types of crises, distinguishable on the basis of their origins and root causes. His first type is the "justification of hostility" crisis. In this type of crisis, the actor creating the crisis is looking for an excuse to initiate hostilities and provokes a crisis to provide such an excuse. The Austrian demands made of Serbia prior to the outbreak of World War I and the Johnson administration's creation of the Gulf of Tonkin crisis are just two of Lebow's examples.[5] The second type of crisis is what he calls a "spinoff" crisis. In this situation, the actions that a state takes with regard to a second party generate conflict with a third party. The crises involving Germany and Belgium and Germany and Great Britain prior to World War I are examples of this type of crisis:

> Spinoff crises differ from other kinds of crises in that neither side really desires a confrontation let alone the war which might result from it. But the initiator feels compelled, usually by perceived dictates of national security, to carry out policies it realizes will put its country on a collision course with a third party.[6]

The third type of crisis described by Lebow is the "brinkmanship" crisis. Half of the cases analyzed by Lebow are of this type, in which one state embarks on a certain course of action with respect to another that, it is hoped, will lead to certain concessions or changes:

> Brinkmanship crises can be said to develop when a state knowingly challenges an important commitment of another in the hope of compelling its adversary to back away from his commitment.[7]

Of the crises studied here, two (Berlin 1948 and Cuba 1962) fall into Lebow's category of brinkmanship crises. Indeed, many crises seem to be of the brinkmanship type, where crises are deliberately created in order to pursue a related goal.

To summarize the argument behind Proposition Three: states that find themselves in an unintended crisis are likely to find that the reason was a misperception about their own actions or the actions of another state. In these

---

5. Richard Ned Lebow, *Between Peace and War: The Nature of International Crisis* (Baltimore: Johns Hopkins University Press, 1981), 24ff.

6. Lebow, *Between Peace and War*, 41.

7. Lebow, *Between Peace and War*, 57.

cases, the misperceptions involved are likely to be situational, such as misin-
terpreting the actions of another as being hostile. The second path is that the
benign actions of the decision maker's own state will be misinterpreted by
others, provoking a crisis that no one intended. What is central about crises of
these types is that they rest on misperceptions about specific pieces of information. Recalling the discussion in chapter 1, dispositional misperceptions
can also play a role, but that is less likely. The reason for this is that dispositional misperceptions, which come from a decision maker's own bias and
attitudes, are more likely to affect the overall assessment of another state
rather than an assessment of specific actions. Both types of misperception can
play a role, but the expectation is that situational misperceptions will play the
larger role.

We now turn to a discussion of the origins of the crises considered here.
A few cautions are in order. This discussion will inevitably ignore what some
will argue are important elements that contributed to these crises. One of the
few things that we can say for sure about crises is that there will never be
complete agreement on the causes of any single crisis or conflict. Even that
most heavily studied of all wars, World War I, yields up a number of different,
plausible interpretations as to its origins.[8] The discussion of the origins of
crises here is taken in the context of the theory presented and will no doubt
leave out a number of elements that arguably should be included in a discussion of these crises.

Iranian Crisis of 1946

Unlike many of the other crises considered here, there were both situational
and dispositional aspects involved in the Iranian crisis.[9] Dispositional elements contributed to the delay in accepting that a crisis was occurring between
the United States and the Soviet Union, and situational factors (particularly in
March) contributed greatly to the feeling of crisis felt by many when the
Soviets refused to remove their troops. Let us address each of these in turn.

Identifying the precise point at which this issue became a crisis for
decision makers in Washington is difficult. The feeling that there existed a
crisis between the United States and the Soviet Union in Iran did not become
widespread until the Soviets had missed the 2 March deadline for the with-

---

8. Nazli Choucri and Robert C. North, *Nations in Conflict: National Growth and International Violence* (San Francisco: W. H. Freeman, 1975), 4.

9. Recall the discussion in chap. 1 of situational and dispositional misperceptions. A
situational misperception is one where the information available to the decision maker suggests a
particular conclusion that is incorrect, while a dispositional misperception is one in which the
decision maker's existing views or attitudes affect the interpretation of new information available
to the decision maker, leading to an incorrect interpretation.

drawal of their troops. It took the reports from Vice-Consul Rossow in Tabriz to convince many that there was something going on in Iran that they needed to act on. The reason suggested for this was the reluctance of many to believe that a crisis between the United States and the Soviet Union had indeed broken out. This reluctance stemmed from the hopes for U.S.-Soviet cooperation and the desire to avoid conflicts so soon after the end of World War II that was discussed in detail in chapter 4. In a sense, this attitude (and hope) delayed the crisis because many were unwilling to acknowledge that there was a serious problem. Although not clearly accounted for by Proposition Three, dispositional factors did play a role in this crisis, although in an indirect fashion. Dispositional factors prevented many from conceiving of this as a crisis until events had progressed into March. This is somewhat different than the role envisioned for dispositional elements described in this chapter and in chapter 1.

Looking at the immediate crisis (2 March–4 April), situational factors played a large role. One of the problems facing American leaders at the end of February and the beginning of March was that it was very difficult to get information about what was occurring in Iran. From January 1946 on, the Soviet Union had imposed serious travel restrictions on all foreigners in Iran. The U.S. Department of State protested vigorously about these restrictions, but to little effect.[10] The only source of information was from Vice-Consul Rossow in Tabriz.[11] There was little confirming evidence available from the British, the U.S. Army (all troops had been withdrawn except for liaison officers in Tehran), or the Iranians, who did not trust local officials in Azerbaijan because of their sympathies with the Soviet Union. Because of all these problems, American officials were unsure of what was actually happening in Iran, and this ambiguity contributed to their feeling of crisis.

A second element that contributed to the crisis was the uncertainty felt by American leaders about Soviet motives and what constituted legitimate Soviet

---

10. See U.S. Department of State, *Foreign Relations of the United States*, 1946, 7:301–2, 319, 326–27, 330–31 (hereafter *FRUS*), for a discussion of the many protests made to the Soviets about the restrictions on travel, both for those in the press and in the American government. The basic problem was that the Soviets claimed that reports of unrest in northern Iran were untrue and that all was fine, while at the same time arguing that it was unsafe for foreigners (excluding Soviets) to travel in northern Iran.

11. Some historians have suggested that Rossow's (Rossow was twenty-seven years old) reporting might have been overexcited and not actually indicative of events there. Thomas G. Paterson, *Soviet-American Confrontation: Postwar Reconstruction and the Origins of the Cold War* (Baltimore: Johns Hopkins University Press, 1973), 179. Bruce Robellet Kuniholm has examined these claims and suggests that while Rossow's descriptions might have been dramatic, they were basically accurate and reflected the nature of events in Iran. *The Origins of the Cold War in the Near East: Great Power Conflict and Diplomacy in Iran, Turkey, and Greece* (Princeton: Princeton University Press, 1980), 324 n. 50.

interests. Part of the argument that this was just another in a long series of disputes with Great Britain over spheres of influence was based on a recognition that the Soviets did have some legitimate interests in the region. What concerned some was how far the Soviets would go in pushing those interests. One of the biggest concerns was that the Soviet Union would not stop with Iran, but it would also move to put pressure on Turkey and Greece as well.[12] In both of these countries there had been unrest that many suspected was instigated by the Soviets, and the fear was that Soviet moves in Iran were part of the same effort. A primary cause of this crisis was the uncertainty about just what was happening in the region and why it was happening. The reports from Iran were sufficiently alarming that decision makers were willing to attach a negative interpretation to events, even when there was insufficient evidence to do so. When more information became available, these views did change, and that change will be taken up in the next chapter in the discussion of Proposition Four.

Before moving on to discuss the next crisis, the Berlin blockade, it might be interesting to speculate about how the Soviets might have viewed events in Iran and the Western response to them. This speculation is being done in the full realization that this is simply speculation. As mentioned above, it is unclear to what extent the Soviet Union sought as its primary goal the creation of a crisis for the United States and the other Western powers. One view is that this crisis was the result of other actions that the Soviet Union felt had to be taken. If one accepts the argument that the actions that the Soviet Union was taking in Iran were designed to protect what it felt were legitimate interests, this crisis would seem to fit Lebow's description of a spinoff crisis as already described, one in which neither side actually desires a confrontation but one nevertheless comes about because the actions that one side takes (with respect to other actors or issues) place them in a crisis.[13] Lebow argues that most states can foresee becoming involved in a spinoff crisis with a third party but they go ahead anyway because they feel they must act. In the framework used here, that would put this type of crisis into the intended crisis category—not because it was the intention of the state to create a crisis but rather because it was foreseen. This categorization is needed to separate this type of crisis (spinoff) from those which are unforeseen and, therefore, unintended.

An alternative way of viewing this crisis is to argue that the Soviets did intend to create a crisis for the United States and Great Britain in Iran, thus hoping to secure greater influence in Iran. This had long been an area that had been of concern to them. This argument can take two forms: the Soviet Union

---

12. See Harry S. Truman, *Memoirs, Volume II: Years of Trial and Hope, 1946–1952* (Garden City, N.Y.: Doubleday, 1956), 95–101.

13. Lebow, *Between Peace and War*, 41.

set out to create a crisis for the Western powers, hoping to take advantage of the confrontation that might result; second, the Soviets were engaged in probing behavior, testing to see what sorts of actions they could take without engendering too much opposition from the West. In either case, the crisis would not fall into the category of unintended crisis because it was the result of deliberate actions taken to provoke some type of response from the West.

A final interpretation of the crisis from the Soviet point of view is that the Soviets found themselves in an unintended crisis with the Americans.[14] Adam B. Ulam suggests that there were plausible reasons for the Soviets to think that they could act in Iran without interference: the recognized history of Soviet interest and involvement in Iran, the reduction of the American presence in Iran,[15] the lack of historical American interest in Iran, and American preoccupation with demobilization and conversion to a civilian economy.[16] Like the outbreak of the Korean War four years later, it might have been the case that the United States suddenly took a strong interest in a part of the world where it had shown declining interest and the Soviets were caught off guard. Ulam suggests that American "concerns about the territorial integrity of Iran might have appeared puzzling [to the Soviet Union] at this juncture in view of her acquiescence, say, in Soviet domination of *all* of Poland" particularly in light of the "ample historical precedent for a Russian sphere of interest there" and the lack of any economic stake in the country. Ulam goes on to suggest that an additional factor was the fact that the Soviet interest in the region had been repeatedly expressed during the wartime Big 3 meetings and the Allies had never objected.[17]

Having considered what this crisis might have looked like to the Kremlin, let us now turn to the next crisis.

Berlin Blockade

The Berlin blockade crisis is set against the longest crisis of the U.S.-Soviet relationship, and unlike some of the other crises, the necessary steps required for American leaders to conclude that they faced a crisis developed over a

---

14. Recall that it was pointed out that it is not clear how much this was a crisis to the Soviet Union.

15. All American troops had been removed as of 1 January 1946, and British troops had been removed by the 2 March deadline.

16. Adam B. Ulam, *Expansion and Coexistence: Soviet Foreign Policy, 1917–1973*, 2d ed. (New York: Praeger, 1974), 425–29. See Jack Stokes Ballard, *The Shock of Peace: Military and Economic Demobilization after World War II* (Washington, D.C.: University Press of America, 1983), for a discussion of the massive efforts needed to make the conversion back to a civilian economy.

17. Ulam, *Expansion and Coexistence*, 425, 429.

number of months. The crisis occurred within the context of general concern on the part of American leaders about the future of Europe and the role that the United States was going to play in that future. In addition, the crisis constituted the last straw for many in trying to deal with the Soviets, presenting final proof for those who remained skeptical that the United States and the Soviet Union were not going to be able to return to any semblance of the cooperation seen during World War II.

Looking at this crisis from the American perspective, it is difficult to conclude that this was an unintended crisis in the sense discussed in this chapter and in chapter 1. There were no actions taken by the United States that appeared to have led to the crisis (there is an argument that the lack of action on the part of the United States contributed to the crisis; this will be taken up further). There are grounds for discussing this crisis as an unexpected crisis from the point of view of those in Washington. As discussed in chapter 3 in the context of Proposition One, the decision makers in Berlin had been concerned about possible Soviet moves to put pressure on Berlin since the breakdown of four-power government in March, and as a result, they were not as surprised as those in Washington were when the blockade was finally imposed. With respect to those in Washington, the blockade seems to have become a crisis not because of situational or dispositional elements but simply because there was comparatively little attention paid to events in Germany that spring. The coup in Czechoslovakia in February 1948 and the efforts to promote the Economic Recovery Program (Marshall Plan) were all competing for the attention of decision makers in Washington, and this contributed to the unexpected nature of this crisis.

One argument that could be advanced in support of the notion that this crisis was unintended was that the Soviets had backed down from the baby blockade in March when the United States initiated its airlift and challenged the Soviet authority to impose such restrictions. Following the lifting of the baby blockade, Soviet actions became less confrontational, and leaders in Washington might have concluded that the Soviets had decided not to challenge the Western presence in Berlin. Unfortunately, this is a very difficult argument to sustain, and it suggests some of the difficulties in applying Proposition Three that will be considered in the conclusion.

In the same spirit of cautious speculation, looking at this crisis from the perspective of the Soviet Union sheds some additional light on this discussion of Proposition Three. An interesting question is whether the Soviets expected that they might be able to successfully complete the blockade against Berlin. There is very little evidence of what Soviet decision makers were actually thinking during this time period. Their actions suggest that they did believe that there was something to be gained from pushing the United States on the issue of Berlin. This pressure seems to have been aimed at three objectives:

Western agreement to discuss (on Soviet terms) the future of Germany, Western abandonment of Berlin or at least a reduction in the Western presence there, and finally, pressure on the Western Allies to reduce their commitment to Western Germany in general. Alvin Z. Rubinstein's account is representative of most commentators on Soviet foreign policy of this period:

> On June 8, 1948 [sic] the Soviet Union imposed a blockade on the Western sectors of Berlin, deep inside the Soviet zone of Germany. During the previous months Soviet authorities had periodically interfered with Western access to Berlin, but had hesitated before imposing a full blockade. Several considerations motivated the Soviets. First, by forcing the Western powers out of Berlin, and bringing the entire city under their control, the Soviets expected to enhance their prospects of controlling Germany, the ultimate prize of the Cold War. Second, they hoped to undermine efforts then being made to establish West Germany as a united and independent country within the Western camp. Third, an Allied surrender in Berlin would have strengthened Communist Party prestige in the weakened countries of Western Europe, further softening them for future subversion by local Communist Parties. . . . Allied willingness to pay the price of the airlift convinced Stalin of the futility of this tactic and a settlement was finally reached in May 1949 after months of trying negotiation. The Kremlin had suffered its first postwar defeat in Europe.[18]

What is open to debate is whether or not these actions were part of a larger Soviet plan. There is little agreement by historians about the coherence of the Soviet plan (if any existed) for Western Europe. Yergin quotes Charles Bohlen, State Department counselor, as recalling, "Although I attended most of the meetings of the Council of Foreign Ministers after the war, it was never clear to me what Soviet objectives were."[19] Ulam argues that while the "prevailing theme" of Soviet policies within the occupation zones was that of "exploitation," it is incorrect to assume that "the Soviets always operated from a master plan prepared well in advance and providing for every contingency."[20] Whether or not the Berlin blockade was part of a larger plan, there seems to be no doubt about the fact that it was the result of deliberate acts on the part of the Soviets. As a result, it is appropriate to consider this an

---

18. Alvin Z. Rubinstein, ed., *The Foreign Policy of the Soviet Union* (New York: Random House, 1960), 243. For reasons that are not clear, Rubinstein assigns the beginning of the blockade to 8 June. All other accounts put the starting date as 24 June.

19. Daniel Yergin, *Shattered Peace: The Origins of the Cold War and the National Security State* (London: Andre Deutsch, 1977), 367.

20. Ulam, *Expansion and Coexistence*, 440–41.

intended crisis and not the result of Soviet misperceptions that their actions would not cause trouble for the Western powers.

It is interesting to ask if the Soviets might have suffered from misperceptions in gauging the likely American response. From the Soviet perspective there were signs that suggested that the United States might not be willing to engage in a confrontation over Berlin. The Soviets acted as if they believed that the United States would be unwilling to shoulder a full blockade of Berlin and give in to Soviet demands about a conference to discuss the future of Germany. In a passage describing what the world situation might have looked like from the perspective of those in the Soviet Union, Ulam suggests that the Soviets were correct in thinking that the United States might not respond. After noting that the Soviets, in the spring of 1948, felt that American tradition went against direct involvement or preventive war against the Soviet Union, and that 1948 was also an election year, Ulam makes the following points:

> The Soviets were correct to deduce that under such circumstances the American government was not likely to answer a Berlin blockade with an ultimatum or military demonstration. It was probably known through intelligence channels that many American and, especially, British military figures considered the Allies' position in Berlin untenable if subjected to Russian pressure.[21]

Although the Soviet move might have been considered a dangerous game of brinkmanship, where a firm stance on the part of the Americans would face them with having to back down in humiliation, the potential gains were, according to Ulam, "enticing."[22]

Another element that might have figured into Soviet calculations was the weak military position of the United States and its allies in Europe.[23] The Soviets might have thought that the risks of military confrontation in creating the blockade were not that high given the poor state of Western military forces in Europe, particularly in Berlin.

Finally, the Soviets might have been encouraged by the lack of a strong Western response to the various steps they had taken in early 1948 to put

---

21. Ulam, *Expansion and Coexistence*, 451–52.

22. Ulam, *Expansion and Coexistence*, 451–52.

23. American and British military strength in Europe had been seriously weakened with the rapid and large demobilization that had followed the end of the war in Europe. See Ballard, *The Shock of Peace*. The total number of Allied occupation forces in Berlin numbered 20,000, of which 6,500 were military troops. They were faced by 18,000 "crack" Russian troops. Avi Shlaim, *The United States and the Berlin Blockade, 1948–1949: A Study in Crisis Decision-Making* (Berkeley: University of California Press, 1983), 187, 214.

pressure on Berlin. The United States had imposed a selective trade embargo on goods between Eastern and Western Germany at the end of March, and other smaller restrictions were placed on certain Soviet publications and activities in Berlin, but these did not appear to have affected or concerned Soviet authorities. The picture that emerges is that the lack of any serious Western or American response to the Soviet "salami tactics" probably encouraged the Soviets to keep increasing the pressure. Each step was a relatively small one in the context of those that had gone before, and few were of the type that they could not easily be reversed if the Soviets ran into strong opposition. As Ulam puts it:

> The blockade of Berlin . . . can be studied as a classic exercise of strategic-political pressure. The choice of the location was masterful: without massive supplies from the Western zones, Berlin could not be fed or provisioned with fuel. The Allies would have to leave or bow to the Soviet demands. The timing was equally dexterous. The election campaign was heating up in the United States; Britain was on the threshold of a serious economic crisis. The original Soviet explanations of the blockade were diffuse enough to allow retreat if the United States took drastic counter steps.[24]

The impression left after examining this crisis is a murky one. The type of dynamic envisioned in the discussion of Proposition Three does not emerge clearly from this examination of the history of this case. We will see the same pattern when the Berlin Wall crisis is examined.

Berlin Wall Crisis

From the Western powers' perspective, it is difficult to argue that the general Berlin crisis or the Berlin Wall crisis was unexpected. They were both clearly unintended but not unexpected. Looking at the wall crisis, there was little doubt on the part of American leaders that something was going to happen to deal with the refugee problem. The problem was that no one was sure what it was going to be. There was an unexpected element about this crisis that can be considered in the context of Proposition Three: the construction of a wall to solve the refugee problem. Unlike their reaction to the Berlin blockade, American leaders did not have many strong views about what the Soviets would and would not do.[25] There was a great deal of confusion over what the

---

24. Ulam, *Expansion and Coexistence*, 453.

25. Recall from the discussion in the previous chapter that a few Western leaders did not believe that the Soviets were attempting to push the Western powers out of Berlin by force, and many believed that they would not respond by force if challenged by Western military forces.

Soviets would do next and what their response to a Western challenge would be. As Arthur M. Schlesinger Jr., notes, there was much conflicting information in the early days of the crisis, and one possible interpretation of the information was that this was simply the beginning of an effort to "drive the West out of Berlin."[26] Seen in this way, the crisis rests on situational misperceptions that arose because the information available allowed a negative interpretation of Soviet intentions.

The problem facing Western powers was not so much that they were victims of misperceptions (because they did not have any clear views as to what the situation was) but that there was simply ambiguous information that they did not know how to deal with. They did not know what the Soviets were going to do next, and they did not how the Soviets and East Germans would react if challenged. They were unsure how to interpret Soviet military moves in East Germany and what relation, if any, they had to the construction of the wall. Thus in the narrow construction of Proposition Three, the Berlin Wall crisis does not provide much of an opportunity for a test. What can be said is that the ambiguity regarding the nature of the Soviet Union's next move contributed to the sense of crisis because it was possible that the next Soviet move would be to take all of Berlin. The available information did not rule out such a possibility, and American fears about Soviet intentions in light of the long-standing threats to deal with the German problem contributed to a crisis atmosphere.[27] When confirming information about these fears did not materialize, the feelings of crisis diminished rapidly. That will be the subject of Proposition Four. The crisis dynamic here is different than that envisioned under Proposition Three. Instead of taking actions that landed them in a crisis, American leaders found themselves in a crisis because of their inaction and subsequent Soviet actions. In some ways this is the reverse of the process described at the beginning of this chapter. What is interesting is that it is possible that the Soviet leadership found itself in just the sort of situation that American leaders were expected to be in. Let us briefly speculate what this crisis might have looked like to the Soviets.

Under one interpretation, it is difficult to see how this crisis would fall into the unintended category when seen from the Soviet side: all available evidence suggests that the Soviets were well aware that this action (building the wall) would be likely to lead to a serious Western, and in particular, American, response. One indication of how concerned the Soviets were about

---

26. Arthur M. Schlesinger, Jr., *A Thousand Days: John F. Kennedy in the White House* (Boston: Houghton Mifflin Company, 1965), 395.

27. On 18 July 1961, the West German Defense Ministry announced that the military buildup of forces within thirty miles of Berlin was "the biggest concentration of troops in the world." There were over sixty-seven thousand troops and police, along with fifteen hundred tanks and armored vehicles in that region. Three-fourths of these forces were Soviet. *Deadline Data*, 18 July 1961 (New York: Deadline Data, 1961), 48.

the possible response is that East German military forces had no ammunition in their weapons during the first day after the wall went up and they were under orders to back off if Allied troops intervened.[28] All accounts of this crisis note how careful the East German authorities were to not provoke a Western reaction or take any threatening moves with respect to Western authorities. In addition, Soviet military commanders remained discretely hidden away from the growing wall even though the West Berlin authorities were aware of their presence.

A different interpretation would be that the Soviets were indeed the victims of a situational misperception—that they would be able to get away with the construction of the wall without a confrontation with the West.[29] Bundy, pointing out that many have criticized President Kennedy for encouraging the Soviets with his emphasis on the protection of West Berlin, reluctantly concludes that Kennedy probably did encourage Khrushchev:

> That his [Kennedy's] own words may have given advance encouragement to Khrushchev, however, seems likely. . . .It must be accepted, I think, that by this process of definition and clarification [of Western interests in West Berlin] he did make it somewhat easier for Khrushchev to choose the wall.[30]

Bundy also notes that Kennedy had concluded that the whole of Berlin was not something that he could ask Americans to fight for, that it was simply not a "vital interest." It is not surprising that the Soviets might have considered that they could construct a wall to imprison the people of East Germany without serious consequence. The information available to them suggested such a conclusion, and they were for the most part correct. There was some conflict with the United States over the wall, but in the end they got away with it.

It is worth noting that a pattern is beginning to emerge here, suggesting that Proposition Three may not be as robust as originally imagined. As one of the goals of this study was to test this proposition against these case studies, failure to find support for some of the propositions in the case studies, while disappointing, still helps shed light on the nature of crises, the ultimate aim of this book. Let us now turn to a discussion of the Cuban Missile Crisis.

---

28. Jean Edward Smith, *The Defense of Berlin* (Baltimore: Johns Hopkins University Press, 1963), 276.

29. In a very unfortunate sense, they were right. They were able to get away with building the wall at no direct cost to themselves—although at great cost to the people of East Berlin and East Germany. That the wall has now finally been removed merely serves to reinforce the evidence of the moral bankruptcy of the two regimes that created it.

30. McGeorge Bundy, *Danger and Survival: Choices about the Bomb in the First Fifty Years* (New York: Random House, 1988), 368.

Cuban Missile Crisis

For American leaders, the Cuban Missile Crisis was not the type of unexpected crisis discussed above under Proposition Three. The United States took
no steps that caused affront to the Soviet Union and, as a result, caused the
Soviets to take actions that provoked a crisis.[31] One might stretch the argument a bit and suggest that American efforts to add to their strategic
capabilities in response to the "bomber gap" and the "missile gap" and the
public recounting of Soviet weakness in the speech of Deputy Secretary of
Defense Roswell Gilpatric on 21 October 1961 imply that the United States
had unintentionally set itself on a conflict course with the Soviet Union as the
Soviets sought to counter these efforts. The intention behind Gilpatric's
speech was to take some of the bluster and tension out of the relationship by
showing that many of Khrushchev's statements about the strength of their
strategic posture were untrue.[32] It seems to have worked. Following the
speech, Soviet rhetoric did moderate, along with their bombast about Cuba
and the threat that the United States posed to Cuba. American leaders might
have concluded that their efforts had succeeded and that the Soviets were
"behaving."

Most American decision makers were caught completely off guard by the
discovery of Soviet missiles in Cuba, and one of the reasons for that was that
the information coming to them about Soviet actions suggested that they had
indeed moderated their behavior. Their claims about their missile superiority
and military strength had been toned down, and they had gone to great lengths
to make clear that their efforts in Cuba were defensive. These efforts to be
reassuring about their actions in Cuba were made in response to U.S. in-
quiries, as well as independent announcements. A specific theme that was
repeated was the sufficiency of Soviet nuclear forces in the Soviet Union to
provide protection for the Soviets and their allies. Most important, there was
little information that could be interpreted to challenge this view of Soviet
quiescence.[33] In addition, American leaders simply chose to believe that the
Soviets would not install offensive weapons in Cuba, believing, it seems,

---

31. At least the United States took no direct steps that caused affront to the Soviet Union,
leading to this crisis. One might argue that the embargo against Cuba, the Bay of Pigs operation,
and the revelation of Soviet strategic weakness in the Gilpatric speech of 1961 were indirect steps
that caused the Soviets to respond in a way that provoked a crisis.

32. Elie Abel, *The Missile Crisis* (New York: Bantam, 1968), 26–27.

33. Roger Hilsman, *To Move a Nation: The Politics of Foreign Policy in the Administration
of John F. Kennedy* (Garden City, N.Y.: Doubleday, 1967), chaps. 13 and 14, provides a detailed
discussion of the information that was available and not available to decision makers at the time.
Of course, Roberta Wohlstetter, "Cuba and Pearl Harbor: Hindsight and Foresight," *Foreign
Affairs* 43, no. 4 (July 1965): 691–707, is the classic argument that there was enough information
available to decision makers.

Khrushchev's assurances that such weapons would not be installed. Bundy's retrospective view of the crisis is that American leaders might have been more attentive to just the distinction Khrushchev was making in his speech and believed that he was setting the stage for the deployment of weapons whose role would be defensive, and thus acceptable under the terms outlined by the United States.[34]

Clearly this crisis was unintended from the point of view of the United States—but in a different way than that described above. The initial discussion of crises involved situations where actions unintentionally lead to a crisis. In this case inaction led to a crisis. Even though the United States was keeping a close watch on Soviet activities in Cuba, its inaction in challenging or pursuing further questions about Soviet assurances led to the surprise of discovery.

In evaluating Proposition Three as it applies to the Cuban Missile Crisis, the conclusion must be that it does not directly support the proposition. However, it does not take much effort to adjust the theory to see that the basic idea embodied in the proposition is supported by the evidence. U.S. efforts to dampen the strategic tensions between the two countries had the reverse effect: the Soviets took steps to improve their strategic position, confronting the United States not with a chastened braggart but a devious opponent making use of lies and deception to alter the balance. An additional point to support the idea that the crisis for the U.S. side was unintended was the U.S. belief that the Soviet Union simply would not install missiles in Cuba:

> Let us return to our underlying error. We did not expect Khrushchev to put missiles in Cuba, which accounts for the relatively untroubled way in which we wrote our warnings in September.[35]

This is a clear example of a different type of misperception—a dispositional one. Theodore Sorensen reports that Kennedy drew the line:

> at what he thought the Soviets would not do. Everyone except [CIA Director] McCone had agreed that the Soviets would not put offensive missiles in Cuba.[36]

Clearly, by drawing the line at what they believed Khrushchev would not do, American leaders set themselves up for quite a surprise!

---

34. Bundy, *Danger and Survival*, 414–15.

35. Bundy, *Danger and Survival*, 415.

36. Quoted in Raymond L. Garthoff, *Reflections on the Cuban Missile Crisis*, rev. ed. (Washington, D.C.: Brookings, 1989), 33. Recall Garthoff's comments in chap. 4, n. 16, about the widespread nature of this belief.

Speculating on this crisis from the perspective of the Soviet Union, it is hard to argue that this was an unintended crisis in the way unintended crises were discussed earlier.[37] The Soviet Union intended to create a situation in which the existence of missiles in Cuba would assist it in its foreign policy goals. Doing this almost certainly would bring a response in some form from the United States. It is difficult to imagine that the Soviets believed that the American government would have no response to the introduction of Soviet missiles into Cuba. Thus, it is hard to argue that the American response was unexpected (and therefore unintended in the sense that we have been discussing it). There were, however, two elements of this crisis that were unintended from the standpoint of the Soviet Union.[38] The first concerns the timing and manner in which the missiles' presence became known. The second concerns the strength of the American response to the placement of those missiles in Cuba.

What was unintended about this crisis was the time and manner in which it became known, first to the United States and then to the rest of the world, that the Soviet Union had installed missiles in Cuba. The Soviets would have been in a better position if their missiles had been discovered after they had become operational, rather than before. Being discovered after they had become operational would have left them with a real threat to use those missiles rather than a potential threat. Let us now ask if this unintended aspect of the crisis rested on misperceptions and whether those misperceptions were situational or dispositional.

The answer to this question is that there were misperceptions involved and for the most part they were situational. Many authors have discussed whether or not the Soviets had any reason to believe that they could install missiles in Cuba and not have the United States find out until the installation

---

37. Bundy, *Danger and Survival*, 415–20, provides the most useful discussion of Khrushchev's motives, as well as the reasons why American leaders misread them.

38. This argument must proceed on the basis of speculation rather than hard evidence. There are no major analysts who accept the argument put forth by the Soviet Union that these actions were being taken simply to provide deterrence against an attack on Cuba. As this was the only explanation provided by the Soviet Union, assessments as to what it actually intended will have to depend on third-party accounts and analysis. The greater Soviet openness (the glasnost revelations mentioned in chap. 2) on this crisis evident at a series of meetings in 1989 with Western academics and officials has given rise to a debate about whether or not the purpose of the missiles was indeed the defense of Castro. The new Soviet line on this is that they were there to protect Castro from the aggressiveness of the Kennedy administration. This is simply difficult to believe. For details on the controversy see Ray S. Cline, "The Cuban Missile Crisis," *Foreign Affairs* 68, no. 4 (Fall 1989): 190–96, and Mark Kramer, "Remembering the Cuban Missile Crisis: Should We Swallow Oral History?" *International Security* 15, no. 1 (Summer 1990): 212–18. For the clearest discussion of the new Soviet line, see James G. Blight and David A. Welch, *On the Brink: Americans and Soviets Reexamine the Cuban Missile Crisis* (New York: Hill and Wang, 1989), 238ff.

was complete. Hilsman, in a discussion of the alleged intelligence failure leading up to this crisis, argues that American intelligence services could not reasonably have been expected to discover concrete evidence of Soviet missiles in Cuba before 21 September 1962.[39] In spite of his conclusion that there was no intelligence failure, one can reasonably conclude that there was a favorable chance for the Soviets to achieve operational readiness of some of those missiles without being detected. Hilsman's long discussion of the obstacles that American intelligence agencies overcame also suggests that there was always the risk that these missiles would not be detected. Alexander George and Richard Smoke discuss some of the reasons that the Soviets might have had for thinking they could install those missiles without being caught:

> There are good reasons for believing, however, that the Kremlin assessed its risks in this venture as reasonable and controllable ones. In the first place, the built-in capability of the MRBMs, especially, for very rapid deployment probably encouraged the Soviet leaders to think that these missiles could be made operational in Cuba before they were discovered by the Americans. Moreover, Moscow is presumed to have known that U.S. intelligence was not aware of this rapid-deployment feature of the MRBMs, and therefore to have hoped for a successful surprise deployment.[40]

Hilsman's discussion of the difficulties in getting information and intelligence out of Cuba suggests, in a backhanded fashion, just how complicated detecting those missiles was:

> Given the inherent difficulties of espionage and the special circumstances, the laboriousness and risk in recruiting agents, the time lag in communicating secretly with an agent once recruited, the risk of a U-2 being shot down and the possible restrictions this might impose on our best source of information, the frustrations of cloud cover, the elaborate security precautions taken by the Soviets, their efforts at deception— given all these difficulties, it is probably something to be proud of that the missiles were discovered as early as they were.[41]

---

39. The decision to send U-2s again was made on 4 October, thus allowing Hilsman to argue that at most the time lag involved would have been three weeks. *To Move a Nation*, 190. The ten-day lag between the order for the flight and its occurrence on 14 October was the result of many factors, none of which is especially relevant here.

40. Alexander L. George and Richard Smoke, *Deterrence in American Foreign Policy: Theory and Practice* (New York: Columbia University Press, 1974), 463. See also Blight and Welch, *On the Brink*, 298.

41. Hilsman, *To Move a Nation*, 190.

All in all, it would seem that there were plausible reasons for the Soviets to believe that they would be able to put missiles in Cuba. Hilsman's claim about the "elaborate security precautions" taken by the Soviets is perhaps a little self-serving, coming as it does in a defense of the American intelligence community of which he was a part. As Allison notes, the Soviets made little effort to conceal their deployment of missiles in Cuba, and one wonders what might have happened if they had made a serious effort at concealment.[42] All of the information necessary to conclude that the Soviets were installing missiles in Cuba was available to American decision makers. All that was needed was the suggestion that this was happening, a theme to tie all of the information together, for these decision makers to arrive at the correct conclusion. Wohlstetter argues that there are two ways that people come to realize that something is happening that they should be aware of. The first is that the weight of the evidence simply becomes overwhelming, forcing the recipients to alter their perspectives, changing from an existing view to a new view more in line with the new information. The second is that the recipients of ambiguous information consider a hypothesis that enables them to tie all that ambiguous information together.[43] In this case, the second did not occur because American decision makers did not want to consider such a possibility.

Returning to the argument begun earlier, it seems plausible that the Soviets might have reasonably concluded that they could put missiles in Cuba without their being detected. In the context of Proposition Three, the argument then becomes that the Soviets were the victims of a situational misperception in believing they could install those missiles. Thus, the unintended crisis (with respect to the timing of the discovery of the missiles) for the Soviets did rest on a situational misperception. The conclusion here is that there were plausible reasons for the Soviets to believe, from an operational point of view, that they could install missiles in Cuba with a minimal risk of detection.

Turning to the second unintended element of this crisis, the strong American response, one can see dispositional elements at work. Beyond the question of whether or not the missiles would be discovered, the Soviets seem to have believed (incorrectly as it turned out) that when the missiles became known to the Americans (either as the result of a Soviet announcement or American discovery) the response would not be so strong that the Soviets could not deal with it. This belief seems to be based on factors that fit the definition of dispositional misperceptions rather than situational.[44] Almost

---

42. Graham T. Allison, *Essence of Decision: Explaining the Cuban Missile Crisis* (Boston: Little, Brown and Company, 1971), 102–17.

43. Wohlstetter, "Cuba and Pearl Harbor," 695–98.

44. This discussion points to an important issue that will be discussed more fully in chap. 8: the difficulty in determining what is a situational and what is a dispositional misperception.

every commentator on the Soviet actions leading up to the Cuban Missile Crisis has suggested that the Soviet Union miscalculated the determination of President Kennedy to resist its actions. George and Smoke note that:

> The error [in thinking that they could manage the crisis as it would unfold] came partly from the Soviets' underestimation of the President. It is often remarked that Khrushchev viewed Kennedy as weak, inexperienced, and irresolute—a judgment seemingly derived from, or fortified by, the President's comparative youth, his handling of the Bay of Pigs fiasco, and his performance in Vienna in June 1961. Nearly every one who has examined the Cuban missile crisis agrees that the Soviets were operating on an incorrect image of their opponent and were genuinely surprised when Kennedy reacted as firmly as he did. Clearly, this misestimate of their opponent could only strengthen their belief that the missile deployment would not entail excessive risk.[45]

George and Smoke note that the Soviets might have believed that they were running some risk in terms of an American attack on their installations but that the risk of uncontrolled escalation would be low:

> In all probability, the Kremlin estimated that the very worst outcome it could possibly conceive would be a U.S. air strike on the missile sites while still under construction. The *loss* to the USSR in this contingency would be serious but the *risk* of uncontrollable escalation spiralling out of this event would be low, due to Cuba's isolated location, far from any other communist territory or interest. Note, furthermore, that events justified the Soviet estimate that this was an *improbable* U.S. action even if the missiles were discovered prematurely.[46]

The argument that the Soviets might have reasonably expected a sluggish response from the United States seems a plausible one:

> the Soviet leaders probably expected that the American political system would respond sluggishly to discovery of the missiles, and the Kennedy Administration would be incapable of formulating a decisive course of action in the face of Soviet threats and political pressures. Such an expectation was certainly reasonable, and it would further encourage the

---

45. George and Smoke, *Deterrence in American Foreign Policy*, 465.

46. George and Smoke, *Deterrence in American Foreign Policy*, 465 n. 20. Emphasis in original.

Soviet belief that the critical MRBM portion of the missile deployment might be completed even if discovered by the United States in process.[47]

Arnold Horelick and Myron Rush argue that the Soviets probably believed that they would be able to install their missiles quickly enough so that a sufficient number would be in operational readiness to deter any serious action on the part of the United States. In addition, the Soviets probably felt that the United States would be unable to formulate a quick response (because of the need to consult with its NATO and OAS allies), and even if it did, it would be along diplomatic lines.[48] The glasnost revelations about Soviet views on the Cuban Missile Crisis suggest that there were those in the Kremlin who saw Kennedy as being weak and irresolute, implying that they might expect a minimal response to the installation of the missiles.[49] After all, there had been no response to the Berlin Wall, an area of professed concern on the part of the Kennedy administration. All of these elements seem to have contributed to a dispositional misperception on the part of the Soviet Union with respect to any possible American response to Soviet missiles in Cuba. Some suggest that the Soviets have frequently underestimated the American political system and this seems to have been another case of them doing just that. The glasnost revelations reveal that some Soviets feel that Khrushchev "did not think through the American reaction."[50] This might account for Khrushchev's extreme shock on hearing President Kennedy's speech.[51]

On a related issue, some commentators have suggested that the Soviets might have correctly interpreted Kennedy's precrisis warnings about Soviet aid to Cuba as being intended for domestic U.S. consumption rather than as a serious threat to the Soviets. This aspect can be seen as contributing to a situational misperception about the possibility of a strong American response. Hilsman provides one of the clearest explanations of this reasoning:

> the administration fell into the semantic trap of trying to distinguish between "offensive" and "defensive" weapons. In addition, Keating,

---

47. George and Smoke, *Deterrence in American Foreign Policy*, 464.

48. Arnold L. Horelick and Myron Rush, *Strategic Power and Soviet Foreign Policy* (Chicago: University of Chicago Press, 1966), 146–49. See also Blight and Welch, *On the Brink*, 239–41.

49. Blight and Welch, *On the Brink*, 236–37.

50. Ronald R. Pope, ed., *Soviet Views on the Cuban Missile Crisis: Myth and Reality in Foreign Policy Analysis* (Washington, D.C.: University Press of America, 1982), 232–33, and Blight and Welch, *On the Brink*, 239, 298–301.

51. James G. Blight, *The Shattered Crystal Ball: Fear and Learning in the Cuban Missile Crisis* (Savage, Md.: Rowman and Littlefield Publishers, 1990), 17.

Goldwater, and the others had beaten the drums so loudly that Kennedy had been forced to not only deny that "offensive" weapons were in Cuba but to put himself on the public record that this Administration would not tolerate their being there. . . .Thus at the time they were made, the statements seemed both a necessary political response to opposition charges and a useful warning to the Soviets to reinforce their natural caution. On the other hand, if the missiles were not important enough strategically to justify a confrontation with the Soviet Union, as McNamara initially thought, yet were "offensive," then the United States might not be in mortal danger but the administration most certainly was.[52]

That this was a political crisis was the view of some in the administration as well. McNamara was very clear about how he thought this was a political crisis rather than a military one. During the first day of ExComm meetings McNamara repeatedly argued, as noted in chapter 1, that the missiles had little military significance but great political significance:

Bundy: But, the, uh, question that I would like to ask is, quite aside from what we've said—and we're very hard-locked onto it, I know—What is the strategic impact on the position of the United States of MRBMs in *Cuba*? How gravely does this change the strategic balance?
McNamara: Mac, I asked the [Joint] Chiefs that this afternoon, in effect. And they said, substantially. My own personal view is, not at all.[53]

Later:

McNamara: I, I, I'll be quite frank. I don't much think there *is* a military problem here. This is my answer to Mac's question. . . .this, this is a domestic, political problem. The announcement—we didn't say we'd go in and not, and kill them, we said we'd *act*. Well, how will we act?
....
McNamara: Because, as I suggested, I don't believe it's primarily a military problem. It's primarily a, a domestic, political problem.[54]

In addition, recall that Kennedy seconded that view as well.[55] George and Smoke conclude that:

52. Hilsman, *To Move a Nation*, 196–97.

53. John F. Kennedy, "Cuban Missile Crisis Meetings, October 16, 1962," *Presidential Recordings Transcripts* (Boston: John F. Kennedy Library), part 2, 12. (Hereafter *Transcripts of 16 October 1962*.)

54. Kennedy, *Transcripts of 16 October 1962*, 46–48. Emphasis in original.

55. Kennedy, *Transcripts of 16 October 1962*, 13. Emphasis in original.

Kennedy's statements [on 4 and 13 September regarding weapons in Cuba] were issued more out of a desire to calm the American public than to warn the leaders of the Soviet Union. . . . It seems likely that the Soviet leaders heavily discounted the President's declarations, perhaps virtually to the point of ignoring them, precisely because they were so obviously motivated by internal political needs.[56]

To finish this line of argument, it appears that the Soviets had plausible reasons for believing that they might be able to install missiles in Cuba undetected and, even if detected, for believing the American response might not be very strong. As it turned out, they were wrong.

October 1973 Middle East War

The October 1973 Middle East War presents an interesting set of problems in trying to assess Proposition Three, so more detail on the crisis will be presented to make these problems clear. Proposition Three suggests that unintended crises will rest on misperceptions, and, unlike the Cuban Missile Crisis, American leaders (specifically Kissinger) anticipated the crisis that would eventually occur—although not in the specific form that it took. While the crisis itself presented decision makers with a serious problem that they needed to deal with, it was not a surprise. American officials worked hard to avoid the crisis by trying to ease Soviet concerns about Israeli violations of the cease-fire, but these efforts were to no avail. It certainly was an unintended crisis in the sense that American leaders did not seek this confrontation, but it was not the unexpected result of American actions. Let us examine this in more detail.[57]

Two weeks after the outbreak of the war, Secretary of State Kissinger and his staff flew to Moscow to work out the details of a cease-fire between the Israelis and the Egyptians. At that point, the battle was going in favor of the Israelis, and Kissinger found the Soviets eager to reach an agreement on a cease-fire. The main goal of the Soviets was to prevent the destruction of Egypt's Third Army, which was about to be encircled by the Israelis. The cease-fire was agreed to after a brief negotiation, and Kissinger flew to Israel

---

56. George and Smoke, *Deterrence in American Foreign Policy*, 467.

57. The following discussion draws heavily on Henry Kissinger, *Years of Upheaval* (Boston: Little, Brown and Company, 1982), 568–96. As noted elsewhere, the lack of alternative information forces the analyst to rely heavily on Kissinger's memoir. With time, more information will hopefully become available that will either support or refute the interpretation presented here. The best secondary source, which draws heavily on interviews of participants, is Alan Dowty, *Middle East Crisis: U.S. Decision-Making in 1958, 1970, 1973* (Berkeley: University of California Press, 1984).

to brief the Israeli government on the agreement. After securing Israeli agreement to the cease-fire, Kissinger flew home to Washington. It was at this point that the crisis began to emerge. Israeli forces continued their attacks on Egyptian forces, in violation of the cease-fire agreements that had been worked out. These attacks, after much diplomatic maneuvering of charges and countercharges, eventually led President Sadat of Egypt to issue a series of calls for assistance from the United States and the Soviet Union to enforce the cease-fire. These calls, and the apparent Soviet response to them, led to the confrontation between the United States and the Soviet Union.

The beginning of the crisis came with communications from the Soviet Union and Egypt complaining about Israeli violations of the cease-fire. American leaders worked to bring an end to Israeli violations of the cease-fire, realizing that failure to do so increased the risk of confrontation with the Soviet Union. When Kissinger learned that the Israeli forces had finally encircled the Egyptian Third Army in the Sinai, he concluded that "A crisis was upon us."[58] The crisis was not only the breakdown of the cease-fire but also the undermining of American credibility. Even if the Israelis were to stop at encircling the Egyptian army and cutting it off from its supplies, Kissinger's view was that it would "almost certain[ly] bring about a confrontation with the Soviets. They could not possibly hold still while a cease-fire they had co-sponsored was turned into a trap for a client state." As Israeli action against the Third Army continued, Kissinger informed Israeli officials that "It was clear that if we let this go on, a confrontation with the Soviets was inevitable."[59] In this case, Kissinger knew very well that he was clearly involved in a situation that ran the risk of a crisis with the Soviets, and he worked hard to avoid that crisis.

Within this overall crisis (the risk of a confrontation with the Soviets because of Israeli violations of the cease-fire), we can see elements that support the thinking behind Proposition Three. While Kissinger fully expected that Israeli actions might lead to a conflict with the Soviet Union, it was uncertainty about the nature of the Soviet response that drove the crisis. After Brezhnev's letter threatening military action, there were additional elements that contributed to the crisis. Earlier in the war, the Soviet Union had alerted seven airborne divisions in the Ukraine, and following the arrival of Brezhnev's letter, there was information that they were being prepared for movement. This was the action that created the crisis that prompted the worldwide American alert. Kissinger's account suggests the picture of Soviet actions that was available to American leaders:

58. Kissinger, *Years of Upheaval*, 571.
59. Kissinger, *Years of Upheaval*, 575–76.

For we had tangible reasons to take the threat [of Soviet miltary intervention] seriously. The CIA reported that the Soviet airlift to the Middle East had stopped early on the twenty-fourth, even though ours was continuing; the ominous implication was that the aircraft were being assembled to carry some of the airborne divisions whose increased alert status had been noted. East German forces were also at increased readiness. The number of Soviet ships in the Mediterranean had grown to an all-time high. . . . We discovered the next day that a Soviet flotilla of twelve ships, including two amphibious vessels, was heading for Alexandria. There were other ominous reports in especially sensitive areas.[60]

This crisis was built on the misperception that the Soviets were planning to move their troops into the Middle East to support the Egyptian troops.[61] This misperception was a situational misperception: the information suggested a conclusion that later turned out to be untrue. By the next day, following the public disclosure of the alert, there had been no further movement of Soviet troops, and the Soviets had assured the United States that they had no intention of intervening. Because of this, American leaders were able to conclude, on the basis of this new information, that the grounds for the crisis had disappeared. This illustrates the dynamic of crises included in Proposition Three, adding to the evidence in support of that proposition.

Viewing this crisis speculatively from the Soviet perspective provides some additional support for Proposition Three. There are two interpretations of the indicators of Soviet intervention that were available to American decision makers. The first is that the Soviets never intended to send their troops and the actions they took were part of a bluff intended to provoke a response from the Americans. The second interpretation is that the Soviets actually intended to send troops and only the American response prevented them from doing so. Assuming that they were actually planning to send their troops, the question becomes "Was the response of the United States anticipated or was it a surprise to the Soviets?" One view leads to the conclusion that the crisis that grew out of the Soviet preparations for intervention was an intended one; the other is that it was unintended. Each will be addressed in turn.

An Intended Crisis

One way for a crisis to arise is for a state to set out to create one. In order to do so, it must have an understanding of its opponent's view of the world so that it

---

60. Kissinger, *Years of Upheaval*, 584.

61. This analysis holds true whether or not the Soviets were actually planning on intervening. The final result, no Soviet intervention, meant that the initial perception that the Soviets were about to intervene was untrue.

will know what it takes to provoke the opponent. To argue that the Soviets intended to create a crisis (why they might want to do this will be discussed later), one must argue that the Soviets knew that the United States would be unlikely to passively accept their intervention in the area.

Garthoff notes that the Soviets were in a very difficult position after the first cease-fire went into effect, and was immediately broken by the Israelis and Egyptians, and the situation got worse when the second one failed, as a result of Israeli violations, as well:

> The Soviets were in a desperate plight. Their credibility was on the line: with the Egyptians—with whom it was already low, but for whom they had just mounted a major arms resupply; with the Syrians, who had not yet accepted the cease-fire; and, indeed, with all the Arabs. The Soviets were not pursuing a forward diplomatic strategy, they were simply trying desperately to hold on. And they were urging the United States to rein Israel in, calling only for a renewed Security Council cease-fire resolution.[62]

When the second cease-fire failed after only one day, it began to look as if the Soviet Union might have been deceived by Kissinger. As a result of the two cease-fires, the Israelis had made tremendous territorial gains, and the Egyptian Third Army was about to be encircled in the Sinai. Kissinger was aware of how this would look to the Soviets and put pressure on the Israelis to halt their actions as they could lead to even greater troubles for Israel and the United States:

> I told [Israeli Ambassador] Dinitz that the art of foreign policy was to know when to clinch one's victories. There were limits beyond which we could not go, with all of our friendship for Israel, and one of them was to make the leader of another superpower look like an idiot. I said to Dinitz that if Sadat asked the Soviets, as he had us, to enforce the cease-fire with their own troops, Israel would have outsmarted itself.[63]

The Soviets needed to do something to enhance their credibility with the Arabs. One way to do this would be to show that they were willing to take bold steps to defend their clients. At the time Sadat made this request, the Israelis were enjoying a strong military advantage, and it looked as if Egypt was on its way to a severe loss. As the main supplier and backer of Egypt and

---

62. Raymond L. Garthoff, *Detente and Confrontation: American-Soviet Relations from Nixon to Reagan* (Washington: Brookings, 1985), 374. Dowty points out that many American leaders were aware of the Soviet dilemma. *Middle East Crisis*, 212.

63. Kissinger, *Years of Upheaval*, 576.

Syria, the Soviet Union had an interest in not letting Israel prevail over the Arab states. From the Soviet perspective the quickest way to bring this about was to get an immediate cease-fire. The Soviet airlift had not succeeded in turning the tide against the Israelis, and the American airlift showed no sign of stopping or slowing down. Something had to be done.

One option for the Soviets at this stage would have been to respond to Sadat's call for troops to enforce the cease-fire against the Israelis. The Soviets had put their entire airborne fleet on alert (seven divisions—about fifty thousand troops) earlier in the war, and they were presumably ready to move on short notice.[64] Such a move could have solved many of the problems facing the Soviets and their Arab clients. Sending a limited contingent of Soviet forces would have helped the Soviet position by increasing the risk to the Israelis of confronting Soviet troops. If the troop levels were kept small, they would have posed no threat to the Israelis, keeping the chance of an American intervention low, while gaining significant propaganda points for the Soviets.[65] The major problem with this option was that it ran the risk of severely antagonizing the Americans and even creating a military confrontation with them. The worst fear of the Soviets is said to have been having both Soviet and U.S. troops on the ground in the Middle East.[66] The problem facing the Soviets was how to make it appear that they were supporting their Arab clients and not antagonize the Americans. The Soviet dilemma of supporting the Arab states, without completely upsetting its relationship with the United States, became evident in this situation and forced it to decide which relationship was most important.[67] As it turned out, it seems that the Soviets decided that their relationship with the United States was more important than

---

64. Marvin Kalb and Bernard Kalb, *Kissinger* (Boston: Little, Brown and Company, 1974), 488. See also Kissinger, *Years of Upheaval*, 584; William B. Quandt, *Soviet Policy in the October 1973 War*, report prepared for the Office of the Assistant Secretary of Defense, International Security Affairs, R-1864-ISA (Santa Monica: RAND Corporation, May 1976), 33; and Galia Golan, "Soviet Decision Making in the Yom Kippur War, 1973," in *Soviet Decision-Making for National Security*, ed. Jiri Valenta and William Potter (London: George Allen and Unwin, 1984), 209, for a further discussion of the American alert.

65. This interpretation is suggested by Quandt, *Soviet Policy in the October 1973 War*, 33–34. Quandt makes this point in support of the conclusion that the Soviets probably did intend to send some forces to the region. The rest of his argument will be taken up later.

66. Golan, "Soviet Decision Making in the Yom Kippur War," 210–11, and Lawrence L. Whetten, *The Canal War: Four-Power Conflict in the Middle East* (Cambridge: MIT Press, 1974), 294.

67. Paul Jabber and Roman Kolkowicz, "The Arab-Israeli Wars of 1967 and 1973," in *Diplomacy of Power: Soviet Armed Forces as a Political Instrument*, ed. Stephen S. Kaplan (Washington, D.C.: Brookings, 1981), 438. These authors do not support the suggestion here that the Soviets created an intentional crisis. Theirs is the more common view that the Soviets were surprised by the American response. They are quoted here to illustrate the dilemmas facing the Soviet Union.

their relationship with the Arab states.[68] An apparent effort to assist the Arabs that was thwarted by the Americans (by their overreaction) would give the Soviets the credibility they needed with the Arabs without actually having to risk sending their troops to the Middle East and possibly confronting the Americans. Coral Bell suggests that the American response to the Soviet threat had to be very "loud" because the message had to be heard by many different parties, including the Egyptians: "It had to reach the Egyptians to convey the excuses of the Russians for not acting."[69] It is, of course, unlikely that this is what the Americans intended their signal to mean, but it is possible that the Soviets expected this signal to get across to the Egyptians.

There is every reason to think that the Soviets knew that the Americans would not respond favorably to such a (threatened) Soviet move. Kissinger makes clear the warnings that he repeatedly gave to Dobrynin about such a move, and U.S. Ambassador to the U.N. John Scali had also made clear the U.S. opposition to such a move. Despite this, they might have had good reasons for thinking that such an American response could work to their advantage. Paul Jabber and Roman Kolkowicz conclude their review with this assessment:

> Thus the possibility that the Soviet Union was contemplating the unilateral injection of ground forces into Egypt if it became absolutely necessary to salvage Cairo's position cannot be ruled out. But the more reasonable inference from the scanty available evidence is that Soviet diplomatic and military signals were orchestrated on October 23–25 mainly to increase pressure on Washington to restrain the Israelis.[70]

In short, what is being suggested here is that it is possible that the Soviet Union deliberately provoked the United States with the hopes that there would be a strong response, thus allowing the Soviets to plead "American overreaction" as a reason for their inaction in sending Soviet troops to help the beleaguered Egyptian Third Army. In a speech before the World Peace Congress a day after the alert (26 October) Brezhnev accused the United States of increasing tensions by distributing "fantastic rumors about the intentions of the Soviet Union in the Middle East" and suggested that the United States was to blame for the confrontation between the two countries.[71] TASS reported on

---

68. Jabber and Kolkowicz, "The Arab-Israeli Wars," 443.

69. Coral Bell, "The October Middle East War: A Case Study in Crisis Management during Detente," *International Affairs* (London) 50, no. 4 (October 1974): 538. Emphasis in original.

70. Jabber and Kolkowicz, "The Arab-Israeli Wars," 463.

71. *New York Times*, 27 October 1973, 10. *Pravda*, 27 October 1973, notes "actions such as the artificial inflaming of passions by the dissemination of various kinds of fantastic conjectures about the Soviet Union's intentions in the Near East." *The Current Digest of the Soviet Press* 25, no. 43 (21 November 1973), 3–4.

the 27th that it had been "authorized to state that such explanations [about the need for the U.S. alert] are absurd."[72] The Soviets never conceded publicly that they were about to send troops, but it is unlikely that they would have anyway because it would only serve to justify the American "overreaction."

Although the argument that Soviet actions were calculated to provoke an American response is not a common one, it is discussed in some detail here because it represents a semiplausible alternative explanation that illustrates some of the concepts behind the arguments being made here.

An Unintended Crisis

The more common interpretation of the confrontation between the United States and the Soviet Union is that the Soviets did not anticipate the nature of the American response and, because of the strength of that response, they did not go through with their plans.[73] As suggested already, some have argued that the Soviets probably saw the sending of a small contingent of troops as a move that would bring them benefits, no matter how things turned out.[74] Unfortunately for the Soviets, it was not this simple. They overestimated the willingness of the United States to tolerate Soviet troops (no matter how many) in the region and were apparently surprised by the American response:

> The Russians were predictably astonished by the American alert. Brezhnev told [Algerian President] Boumedienne and [Syrian President] Asad that he thought it was all a false alarm resulting from an American desire to over-dramatize the crisis. If, he said, it was meant as a warning to the Soviet Union, the message had the wrong address on it.[75]

This, then, can be seen as a case of misperception. The suggestion here (discussed further later) is that the misperceptions were the result of situational factors. The Soviet view of what the United States was willing to

---

72. *FBIS, Soviet Union*, 29 October 1973, B3.

73. There is controversy about whether or not the Soviets intended to send large numbers of troops or just a small token force to save face with the Arabs and create some hesitation in Israeli minds. Quandt, perhaps the most authoritative inside source on this topic, concludes that "From the evidence available, it seems unlikely that the Soviets ever contemplated a massive military intervention." *Soviet Policy in the October 1973 War*, 33. On the other hand, the chief of Naval Operations at that time, Admiral Elmo R. Zumwalt, Jr., has written that the United States was in a very vulnerable position and that Soviet actions could have supported the introduction of troops. He also notes that with respect to the naval situation in the Mediterranean the United States had never been "so ill prepared." *On Watch: A Memoir* (New York: Quadrangle–New York Times Book Company, 1976), 445.

74. Jabber and Kolkowicz, "The Arab-Israeli Wars," 457.

75. Mohamed Heikal, *The Road to Ramadan* (London: Colling; New York: Quadrangle, 1975), 255.

tolerate turned out to have been different than what the United States was willing to go along with. As more information became available to the Soviets about what the United States was, and was not, willing to accept, their perceptions of the situation changed accordingly.

It is possible that the Soviet Union was not too far off in thinking that the United States would tolerate (although not encourage) the dispatch of Soviet troops. In Kissinger's news conference of 12 October, he mentioned, then downplayed, the Soviet airlift to the Egyptians and Syrians that had been going on for two days, and he downplayed Soviet involvement in the war in general:

> We did not consider the Soviet statement to the President of Algeria helpful. We did not consider the airlift of military equipment helpful. We also do not consider that Soviet actions as of now constitute the irresponsibility that on Monday evening I pointed out would threaten detente. When that point is reached, we will in this crisis, as we have in other crises, not hesitate to take a firm stand. But at this moment we are still attempting to moderate the conflict. As of this moment we have to weigh against the actions of which we disapprove—and quite strongly—the relative restraint that has been shown in the public media in the Soviet Union and in the conduct of their representative at the Security Council.[76]

This must have appeared to be a mild comment from Kissinger, considering that Soviet clients had attacked an American ally and that the Soviets were engaging in what Kissinger later in the same press conference called "a fairly substantial airlift."[77] Robert O. Freedman comments that:

> In their analysis of this Kissinger statement [quoted earlier, note 76], the Soviet leaders may have felt that the American administration was now so wedded to detente that the USSR was free to take even further action to influence the outcome of the war. If the Soviet airlift, sealift, and vocal exhortations to the Arabs were not deemed "irresponsible," then perhaps other acts would not be either.[78]

---

76. *Department of State Bulletin*, 29 October 1973, 535–36.

77. *Department of State Bulletin*, 29 October 1973, 537.

78. Robert O. Freedman does not make the argument that there is a direct connection between this mild condemnation by Kissinger and the later Soviet move to intervene, but his comments are suggestive of the atmosphere between the two countries. *Soviet Policy toward the Middle East since 1970*, 3d ed. (New York: Praeger, 1982), 146. Dowty considers a number of factors that might have allowed the Soviets to conclude that they could have gotten away with the intervention. *Middle East Crisis*, 246.

John L. Scherer is more direct in his argument that the Soviet Union could safely conclude that the United States would not act to counter Soviet action, in particular that it would not act by putting American troops into the region:

> Prior to October 25 the United States had repeated that it would not send troops to the Middle East—Kissinger and Schlesinger had said so October 20, Kissinger, Press Secretary Gerald Warren and UN Ambassador John Scali had reaffirmed that position October 24. Moscow could assume Washington would not participate in any joint action. . . .Having promised for days to keep American troops from the Middle East, virtually inviting Moscow to act alone, the secretary prepared to go to the brink if the Kremlin moved unilaterally. . . .Kissinger may not have thought about this precedent [Acheson placing South Korea outside the American defense perimeter, only to act when it was invaded], or may have thought American restraint would reassure the Soviets. In a way, it did. It reassured them that they could act alone, and appear to save Egypt from an Israeli advance at practically no risk.[79]

Situational misperceptions on the part of the Soviet Union can explain why it took actions that led to a serious confrontation with the United States at a time when such a confrontation was no doubt not desired.

The American Response

It is interesting to speculate about Soviet perceptions of the American response because doing so provides an indirect test of Proposition Three and its corollary about intended crises. Proposition Three's concern with unintended crises and their relation to misperceptions is directly related to the question of the American response to Soviet actions. When it suspected that the Soviets were about to send troops, the United States set out to create a crisis for the Soviets, a crisis of confrontation.[80] As suggested in the discussion of Proposition Three at the beginning of this chapter, and in chapter 1, an intended crisis occurs because one side feels that there is a gap in preferences that can be exploited. In this case, the United States felt that the Soviets had underestimated the American opposition to the introduction of Soviet troops and something was needed to make clear that opposition. The nuclear alert provided that clarity. As will be discussed further under Proposition Five, the American

---

79. John L. Scherer, "Soviet and American Behavior during the Yom Kippur War," *World Affairs* 141, no. 1 (Summer 1978): 15–16.

80. This analysis assumes that the interpretation that suggests that the Soviets did not intend to create a crisis is correct.

response upped the stakes of a Soviet intervention to such a level that the Soviets were unwilling to carry through with their threat. In short, there was a gap in perceptions that the actions of the United States corrected. When the Soviet Union's perceptions were made more complete by the actions of the United States, the crisis was resolved, as the Soviets took no further actions on their airlift.

Conclusion

The examination of the crises in light of Proposition Three has produced mixed results—certainly nothing near overwhelming support. What seems clear is that the notion of a state "walking into" a crisis without knowing it needs reexamination. In the crises considered here, it was not the case that the United States took actions believed to be benign, only to find that they were viewed in a different light. The United States did find itself unexpectedly in a crisis, but it was rarely the results of American actions that the Soviets took exception to. More frequently, it seems, it was American inaction that created incentives for Soviet actions that in turn were seen by the United States as creating a crisis situation. The consequence of these findings for the theory will be taken up further in chapter 8.

It is worth repeating the definition of situational and dispositional misperceptions presented in chapter 1. Situational misperceptions involve situations where an actor's perception of the situation is plausible based on the information available, yet that perception turns out to be incorrect. The implicit assumption here is that other actors in the same situation, faced with the same information, would be very likely to come to the same (incorrect) conclusion. It is the information available that drives the actor toward a particular conclusion, and changes in the information will lead to changes in the conclusions. Only when more information about the nature of what is being observed is provided can the individual conclude with confidence that what is being seen is not what is real.

Dispositional misperceptions come from an actor's internal predisposition to see the world in a certain way or process certain types of information in a particular way. The assumption is that other actors, viewing the same information, would be less likely to arrive at the same conclusions (unless, of course, they shared the same predispositions). In cases involving this type of misperception, more information is unlikely to affect the actor's view of what is happening. Having refreshed our memories of these definitions, we now turn to a review of the performance of Proposition Three.

A complicating factor in attempting to assess Proposition Three was that most of the crises, expected or unexpected, that the United States found itself in were the result, on the American side, of dispositional elements. On the

Soviet side it appears that these crises were frequently the result of situational elements. The discussion of situational and dispositional misperceptions in chapter 1 and the discussion at the beginning of this chapter of Proposition Three envisioned situations in which states would find themselves in crises that neither side intended because of the misperceptions or misunderstandings. Ambiguous or conflicting information about the actions of an opponent would contribute to a sense of crisis that would end when information became available that suggested that there was no need for concern. The expectation was that the misperceptions involved would be situational because of the impact of ambiguous or misleading information. The evidence presented shows that crises are more complicated than that.

From the American side, all of these crises were unintended, and with the partial exception of the Berlin Wall crisis and the October 1973 War crisis, they were also unexpected.[81] The problem here is that these crises were not unintended in the way this term was discussed at the outset of this chapter: none of these crises involved actions taken by the United States that it felt would be uncontroversial, only to find that the Soviets did find them to be controversial. Rather, all of these crises involved actions taken by the Soviet Union that caused American leaders to feel that they were in a crisis situation. American leaders did not expect the Soviets to act in certain ways in certain situations. In this sense, these crises were unexpected. In each of these crises, on the American side, dispositional factors seem to have played a large role. In the case of Iran, many in the United States did not want to believe that the cooperation and harmony that existed during World War II was over nor did they want to believe that the Soviet Union was actually acting in a manner detrimental to the interests of the United States. In the Berlin blockade crisis, many of those in Washington did not feel that the Soviets were going to take action against Berlin. As noted, the Berlin Wall crisis was not a surprise but the wall was. During the Cuban Missile Crisis, the evidence strongly suggests that many simply chose not to believe that the Soviets would put missiles into Cuba—a further example of dispositional factors playing a significant role. Finally, during the October 1973 War, American leaders felt that they had been very clear with respect to the undesirability of sending Soviet troops to the Middle East and were surprised that the Soviets appeared to be doing just that.

There was also evidence that situational factors played a role in these case studies. Situational factors clearly played a role during the Iranian crisis

---

81. Recall that American leaders expected the Soviets to do something about the refugee crisis; they just were not sure what. Kissinger had the same expectation about potential Soviet action if the Israelis had persisted in their violations of the cease-fire. What he was unsure of was what the actual Soviet response would be.

and the October 1973 Middle East War. In both of these cases, military moves on the part of the Soviet Union were ambiguous enough to cause concern in the United States. The evidence for both suggested the Soviets were about to take strong military actions that the United States would be opposed to. Until information became available that suggested that this was not the case, and that there was no threat, the crises went on. The type of ambiguity or misperceptions about Soviet actions was of a tactical nature, concerning what the next Soviet move would be, given the moves that they had already taken, rather than of a strategic nature, relating to the overall goals or nature of Soviet foreign policy in a particular region.

Looking at these crises from the perspective of the Soviet Union, the picture is more complicated and harder to assess. Strong arguments can be made in favor of situational and dispositional elements in explaining Soviet behavior. The Iranian crisis, the Berlin Wall, and the October 1973 Middle East War were all spinoff crises as far as the United States was concerned (that is, the crises resulted from Soviet actions that were not aimed directly at American interests). From the Soviet perspective it seems that for many of these crises the Soviets underestimated the strength with which the Americans would respond. Strong arguments can be made that the Soviets interpreted American statements prior to the Berlin blockade and the Berlin Wall as meaning that there were certain types of actions that the United States would not oppose. In the Berlin blockade, the lack of any strong American response to the many restrictions imposed by the Soviets in the months leading up to the complete blockade might have suggested that the Americans would not respond to further steps. The emphasis prior to the Berlin Wall on the protection of Western rights in West Berlin and the emphasis on Western access to Berlin might have suggested to the Soviets that they could avoid a crisis if they acted carefully and did not infringe on any of these rights. The problem with this line of argument, as will be discussed in the concluding chapter, is that it is hard to know exactly what the Soviets were thinking.

The assessment of Proposition Three is generally favorable, but there are some issues that would need to be addressed before taking it any further. These issues concern the nature of an unexpected crisis as compared with an unintended crisis, as well as the operational differences between situational and dispositional misperceptions. These will be taken up in the concluding chapter.

CHAPTER 6

Crises and Their Termination

The theory of a crisis dynamic fueled by the perceptions and misperceptions being presented here has progressed from consideration of a decision maker's view of events and the origin of crises to consideration of the origin of crises themselves, and now it turns to a consideration of the ending or termination of crises. The theory developed here rests on a simple observation: disputants must ultimately agree (either by communication or by their actions) on an outcome to a crisis. This outcome can fall into one of three broad categories, ranging from "I win" to "Neither of us wins" to "You win."[1] Proposition Four considers how decision makers arrive at one of these conclusions. To do so, the discussion once again begins with a discussion of wars and how they end.

The parallels between the origins of crises and wars that were discussed previously can also be found in the termination of crises and wars. Wars rarely end with total victory, and crises rarely end with total capitulation. Blainey argues that wars are actually disputes that arise because states disagree (explicitly or implicitly) on the distribution of power between them. Wars end when conflict has shown the true distribution of power:

> One may suggest that the measurement of international power is a crucial clue to the causes of war. War itself is a dispute about measurement; peace on the other hand marks a rough agreement about measurement. . . .Wars usually end when the fighting nations *agree* on their relative strength, and wars usually begin when fighting nations *disagree* on their relative strength.[2]

Another way of understanding the end of wars is to say that wars end when one party sees the cost of continuing to be greater than the cost of stopping. As Schelling suggests, war termination is actually an exercise in bargaining

---

1. It is hard to imagine a crisis where win-win would be an outcome. A crisis that rests on mutual misperception that is subsequently clarified and successfully resolved is unlikely to be thought of as win-win. Thus this outcome need not be considered.

2. Geoffrey Blainey, *The Causes of War* (London: Macmillan, 1973), 122. Emphasis in the original.

over the acceptable outcome of a conflict.[3] What is being bargained about are the costs to be imposed by the victor.

In crises, a type of bargaining similar to that which occurs in war is also happening. Both sides are trying to convince the other that the cost of continuing the crisis is worse than the cost of halting the crisis on their terms. In a crisis that neither side intended, each is trying to convince the party that feels threatened that there is no cause for alarm. As in wars, crises end when the views of each party about the nature of its interactions are the same. Proposition Four deals with this issue.

Proposition Four: A crisis will continue until perceptions on both sides of the dispute match.

It was suggested in the discussion of Proposition Three that crises come about because one side deliberately provokes them or because one side has a view of the perceptions of the other that is incorrect: crises that are unintended are the result of misperceptions. In either case, the crisis will continue until one of four things happens: the actor that is being challenged gives in to the demands of the instigator of the crisis, the instigator finds the costs of continuing the crisis to be greater than expected and backs down, the perceptions of the relative merits of the various outcomes will shift so that a change in position of each actor toward a compromise agreement will be seen as acceptable, or, finally, the side that feels that the other is acting in a threatening manner comes to believe that there actually is no threat. Much of crisis behavior is an attempt to convince the opponent that the current course of action will lead to a worse outcome than that which is being demanded by the initiator. During the October 1973 Middle East War crisis, the actions the United States took (alerting its nuclear forces) were intended to suggest to the Soviet Union that the current course of action (moving Soviet troops into the Sinai) would lead to an outcome (likely confrontation with American troops) that was worse than the outcome being pushed by the United States (no troops from either side in the Middle East). Once this became clear to the Soviet Union, all indications of its preparation for the introduction of troops ceased.[4]

Lebow argues that for many of the cases he studied, the incorrect views that one side had of its opponent were quickly adjusted during the course of the crisis as more information about the strength and resolve of the opponent became available.[5] Snyder and Diesing describe this process of information change as follows:

---

3. Thomas C. Schelling, *Arms and Influence* (New Haven: Yale University Press, 1966), 30–34.

4. This case will be discussed later.

5. Richard Ned Lebow, *Between Peace and War: The Nature of International Crisis* (Baltimore: Johns Hopkins University Press, 1981), 270–71. As one anonymous reader of an early

In summary, strategy revision is initiated when a massive input of new information breaks through the barrier of the image and makes a decision maker realize that his diagnosis and expectations were somehow radically wrong and must be corrected. This leads him to be receptive to new information and to search for information to fill in the gaps, if time is available.[6]

Before proceeding further with this discussion, it will be useful to make clear the core element of the approach being taken here—the view of decision making and information flow that is being used in this analysis.

Information Processing and Decision Making

It is now appropriate to lay out in some greater detail the model of decision making that is being used here. The model is not very complex; rather it is a basic interpretation of what emerges from an examination of elements of the psychological literature on decision making. The approach taken here assumes a basically rational decision-making process without making the same assumption about the inputs into that process or the ways in which those inputs are generated. Decisions in crises are assumed to approximate the rational model in the sense that perceived alternatives are weighed and the best one (in the view of the relevant decision maker) chosen. All of the cautions and criticisms that are made about rational decision-making models and assumptions of rationality are acknowledged; this model does not assume that the decision maker surveys all alternatives, does not pick the first acceptable choice, or does not face time constraints.[7] The decision maker is assumed to make some effort to connect means and ends, but nothing is being said here about the ways in which that effort is made. There is no assumption here that the decision maker actually uses a rational process to decide which course of action to pursue—only that, by whatever mechanism, an attempt is made to

---

draft of this manuscript noted, one must be careful in examining Lebow's assessment of misperceptions on the part of leaders, as he seems to find irrational choices made by most leaders in the crises he considers. James G. Blight comments that Lebow's review of decision making during the Cuban missile crisis "see[s] irrational psychopathology at almost every turn." *The Shattered Crystal Ball: Fear and Learning in the Cuban Missile Crisis* (Savage, Md.: Rowman and Littlefield Publishers, 1990), 31. This will be considered at greater length in the conclusion.

6. Glenn H. Snyder and Paul Diesing, *Conflict among Nations: Bargaining, Decision Making, and System Structure in International Crises* (Princeton: Princeton University Press, 1977), 397.

7. Donald R. Kinder and Janet A. Weiss, "In Lieu of Rationality: Psychological Perspectives on Foreign Policy Decision Making," *Journal of Conflict Resolution* 22, no. 4 (December 1978): 707–35, provides a useful discussion of some of the convergence in the research on decision making and psychology, as well as some critiques of rationality in decision-making models.

relate goals and means. There is no corresponding assumption of rationality about the ways in which information is input into the decision-making process. The information that goes into the consideration of means and ends may come from many sources and may indeed not be rational in any sense. That would be consistent with the approach being used here.

The second element that needs to be discussed in this model of decision making is the role of information processing and the impact of new information on the decision making of leaders. Before decisions are made (rationally or not), assessments need to be made about events and actors. How much those assessments will be affected by new information will depend on the nature of those original assessments. Let us now turn to a discussion of these different elements of the decision-making process.

The model used here views the decision-making process as having a central core activity in which new information on a particular issue is received and a check is made to see if there are any existing views on the issue. If no view already exists, the decision maker will generate an initial interpretation of the information. If an interpretation of events already exists, however, the process will modify the existing interpretation to take into account the new information, or the existing view will be sustained if the new information is not deemed sufficiently contradictory to alter it.[8] The link between this view of information processing and decision making and of crisis behavior is that the information processed becomes the basis for the decisions that are subsequently made. How the decision maker processes the information available will have an influence on the outcome of the crisis.[9]

The model suggested here is similar to one put forth by Robert Axelrod in his discussion of schema theory.[10] Axelrod's intent is to describe different types of schemas, or belief-ordering principles, that people use to organize information. His main focus is on the internal adjustment process that people use to keep their schemas in balance. The main intent here is to understand the way that information interacts with perception and beliefs.

To say that an individual has a perception of an event means that that person has an interpretation of what the actual event was (e.g., sending

8. Robert Jervis, "Hypotheses on Misperception," *World Politics* 20, no. 3 (April 1968): 454–79, is the best discussion of the various ways in which this can happen.

9. Jonathan M. Roberts provides a useful review of theories and processes used in this area of research. *Decision-Making during International Crises* (New York: St. Martin's Press, 1988), 125–39. A useful review and bibliography of decision making during crises is found in Ralph K. White, ed., *Psychology and the Prevention of Nuclear War: A Book of Readings* (New York: New York University Press, 1986), 379–413.

10. Robert Axelrod, "Schema Theory: An Information Processing Model of Perception and Cognition," *American Political Science Review* 67, no. 4 (December 1973): 1248-66. While figure 2 is original, the thinking behind it was subsequently refined upon discovering Axelrod's "Schema Theory."

warships to a foreign port) and what the motivation was behind that action (attempting to influence a foreign government). What is of interest here is the step from identifying an event to arriving at an interpretation of it. An important element affecting the interpretation assigned to this new information is whether or not there is an existing interpretation that can account for the new information. An additional element that will affect how the new information is handled is the degree to which the existing interpretation is strongly held. The lack of an existing interpretation will mean that the information will "drive the conclusion"; that is, it will be assessed on its own terms. Thus, the new information will play a major role in creating a new interpretation. Similarly, having an existing interpretation that is open to reinterpretation will allow the new information to play an important role. An existing interpretation could be open to reinterpretation because of a lack of confidence in the original interpretation (i.e., it was never strongly held) or because the existing interpretation is no longer believed to be accurate. When the existing interpretation is strongly held, however, the new information will be interpreted in such a way as to maintain the existing view—a phenomenon known as *cognitive dissonance*. Figure 2 shows the structure of this process.

This description of information and interpretation change depicts a process similar to that used in attempting to forecast events. This approach is consistent with (although not identical to) Bayesian analysis, an approach that makes use of observed data about a certain phenomenon to modify existing estimates. The existing estimates may have been derived theoretically or from previous observations. In manufacturing, engineers might estimate that the mean time between failures (MTBF) of a certain electrical component might be 1,000 hours. Subsequent observations of actual occurrences (say at 950, 1,210, and 1,123 hours) would be used to modify the existing estimate to arrive at a new number.[11] The information-processing mechanism described earlier is obviously not as precise as that, yet the concept is the same: incoming information is used to create, update, or reaffirm previous interpretations of events or motives.

The link between this model of information processing and different types of misperception can now be discussed. Recall that it was argued that misperception can be the result of information made available to decision makers or it can be the result of the decision makers' own idiosyncratic ways of interpreting incoming information. It was suggested that situational misperceptions, being the result of the nature of the information available, will be more likely to change as new information becomes available. Dispositional

---

11. See Richard K. Ashley, "Bayesian Decision Analysis in International Relations Forecasting: The Analysis of Subjective Processes," in *Forecasting in International Relations: Theory, Methods, Problems, Prospects*, ed. Nazli Choucri and Thomas W. Robinson (San Francisco: W. H. Freeman, 1978), 151–53.

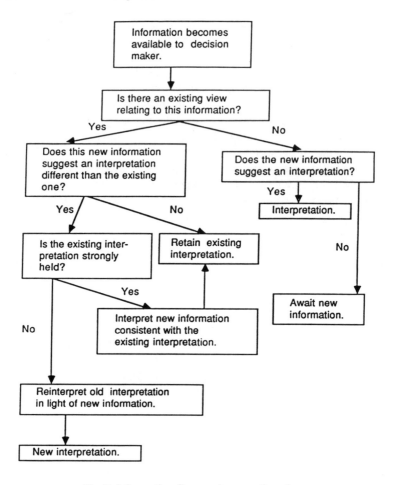

Fig. 2. Information flow and perception change

misperceptions, being the result of an actor's own internal processes, are less likely to be changed or corrected as new information becomes available. These two types of misperceptions can now be discussed in terms of the model of decision making just described.

Dispositional misperceptions can be thought of as examples of "theory over data"—situations in which the existing view will tend to play a stronger role in arriving at an interpretation of events than will incoming information. Richard Nisbett and Lee Ross describe a similar process, using *theory* in place of the term *perception* used here:

Everyday experience demonstrates that people often do not believe evidence that opposes some theory they hold. If the evidence cannot be discredited outright, it may nevertheless be given little weight and treated as if it were of little consequence. Thus, the theory often survives intact new data which ought, superficially, to force revision of confidence in the theory or perhaps even to reverse the theory.[12]

When decision makers have a certain view of events that is resistant to contradictory information, more information challenging this view will be needed before the view is changed. Decision makers having dispositional misperceptions will require more information suggesting an alternative interpretation before their views are changed than in conditions where decision makers have situational misperceptions. This follows directly from the notions advanced by Jervis in his "Hypotheses on Misperception." His Hypothesis Three states that decision makers will assimilate discrepant pieces of information into their existing view of the world (what we are calling *perception* here) more easily if the information comes in smaller pieces rather than larger ones. To put this in terms relevant to the Bayesian process described earlier, the differences between the new observations and the existing assessment will need to be larger in cases of dispositional misperception than in cases of situational misperception for the original assessment to be modified. Situational misperceptions can be altered with less discrepant information than dispositional ones. This is so because the decision maker is less wedded to the interpretation and thus better able to adjust or alter it in the face of new information.

It is important to make clear when dispositional and situational misperceptions will apply. The misperceptions that are being considered here relate to the ways in which decision makers process information that is available to them and arrive at interpretations of events. They do not apply to judgments or predictions about future events but to information that is made available to a decision maker about current or past events. As noted previously, during the Cuban Missile Crisis, most leaders held the view that the Soviet Union would not put missiles in Cuba. This turns out to have been a misperception. Let us be clear as to what type of misperception this was.

The test of whether or not this was a situational or dispositional misperception can be seen in the way that decision makers responded to the many small bits of information that suggested that the Soviets were installing missiles in Cuba. Many continued to dismiss or ignore such information, arguing

---

12. Richard Nisbett and Lee Ross, *Human Inference: Strategies and Shortcomings of Social Judgment* (Englewood Cliffs, N.J.: Prentice-Hall, 1980), 169.

that installing missiles in Cuba was something that the Soviets just would not do. This continued insistence, despite evidence to the contrary, allows one to conclude that this was a dispositional misperception. In figure 2, the progression would be to the yes arrow in response to "Is there an existing view relating to this information?" and then to the yes arrow in response to "Is the existing interpretation strongly held?" with the decision maker ignoring or interpreting the information in such a way so that the existing belief ("The Soviets would never put missiles in Cuba") remains intact. If this had been a situational misperception, the decision makers would have altered their views with the new information as it became available to them. As it was, it was not until clear, unmistakable information about the Soviet actions (photographs of the missiles and launching pads) became available that most decision makers altered their views. This same situation can be seen in the case of Pearl Harbor.[13] American military leaders in Hawaii consistently interpreted the information available to them in a way that was in line with their belief that the Japanese would not directly attack U.S. forces in Hawaii but would instead resort to sabotage.

Let us return to our discussion of Proposition Four. Proposition Four suggests that a crisis will come to an end when perceptions on both sides of the dispute match. For example, when the United States accepted the Soviet Union's argument in 1979 that its troops in Cuba were only on a training mission and, therefore, were no direct threat, the crisis came to an end. The crisis between the United States and the Soviet Union during the October 1973 Middle East War came to an end when the United States made clear its opposition to the introduction of Soviet troops and the Soviets believed that opposition and the American willingness to enforce it. Another way of putting this is that a crisis ends when both sides come to an agreement (either explicit or implicit) about the nature of the confrontation—when the views converge. The Cuban Missile Crisis ended when there was convergence between the American threat (invasion of Cuba) and Soviet belief (that the United States would actually carry out its threat).[14]

It is important to note here that there need not be any objective reality or truth to the two sides' common perception or image of events that brings about the end of the crisis. Whether or not the United States was willing to risk nuclear war with the Soviet Union in October 1973 did not matter. That was the image that the United States wanted to get across and was the image the Soviets appear to have believed. Given the apparent Soviet unwillingness to

---

13. Roberta Wohlstetter, "Cuba and Pearl Harbor: Hindsight and Foresight," *Foreign Affairs* 43, no. 4 (July 1965): 691–707.

14. It is probably more precise to say that the crisis ended when the Soviets felt that the probability of an American attack was sufficiently high to warrant backing down, rather than saying they believed the Americans would attack.

engage in nuclear war, that image of the United States and its threatened actions brought the crisis to an end. All that was required was that both sides come to agree on the outcome point—that the United States would run the risk of nuclear confrontation and that the Soviet Union was unwilling to take that risk. This is similar to Blainey's argument about the ending of wars. Wars end when both sides agree on the distribution of power between them. Crises will end when both sides agree on an image that provides for a resolution.

There are other crisis outcomes that should be addressed. A different crisis outcome could be that of a stalemate. In a stalemate, both sides find themselves in situations from which unilateral movement is considered undesirable. Neither side has an incentive to unilaterally move from its position. In game theory, this type of situation is called a *Nash equilibrium*—an equilibrium in which neither player has an interest in unilaterally changing his or her move even if the other player makes no change. In the Berlin blockade crisis the initial crisis grew out of the final imposition by the Soviets of a complete blockade of Berlin. As time went on, the confrontation settled into a situation where neither side was willing to give in to the other's demands (U.S. demand: lift the blockade; Soviet demand: discuss the future of Germany) or raise the stakes of the confrontation by an escalation of the actions taken against the other (U.S. option: force a confrontation by attempting to break the blockade with armed convoys and trains; Soviet option: interfere with the airlift). The United States found the airlift to be a satisfactory response given the options available while the Soviet Union apparently found the continued ambiguity of Berlin's and Germany's status to be tolerable. In this case, the stalemate arose because both sides seemed to understand what the other would and would not do. Both sides had a correct understanding of the views of the other; it just happened that both sides could not agree on a mutually acceptable change in position. Steven J. Brams's concept of a "nonmyopic equilibrium" is very similar to the argument being used here.[15] In Brams's usage, a Nash equilibrium can be seen as a myopic, or short-term rational equilibrium, because neither side has an immediate interest in moving from its position. In a nonmyopic equilibrium, players' consideration of the desirability of their positions takes into account the longer-term consequences of various steps by looking at the impact of subsequent moves on their positions. In this approach, a situation may be stable in the short-term but unstable in the long-term.

The argument is as follows: once a crisis has begun, it will continue as long as each side's view of what is an acceptable outcome remains different.

---

15. Steven J. Brams, *Superpower Games: Applying Game Theory to Superpower Conflict* (New Haven: Yale University Press, 1985), 66–67. Thanks go to an anonymous reader for this suggestion.

Neither side is willing to concede to the other because of the belief that the cost of doing so is greater than the cost of continuing the confrontation. With both sides having this view, the crisis will continue. The middle stage of the Cuban Missile Crisis, with Kennedy demanding that the missiles be removed, while Khrushchev was working to complete their installation, is a good example of this.

A different way for a crisis to end is for perceptions to become congruent again. One way for this to occur is the capitulation of one party to the demands of the other. The capitulation can come from either side. The target can capitulate by giving in to the demands of the initiator, or the initiator can agree to cease whatever behavior provoked the crisis because the cost of the target's response is too high.

One of the consequences of a continued crisis or stalemate is that the parties can be expected to make an effort to change the perceptions of the other side about the benefits of movement out of the situation in which they find themselves. In a situation of continued crisis, it will be in each party's interest to convince the other that the cost of continued resistance is much greater than the cost of capitulation. In a sense, this is what the Soviet Union was trying to do in the months leading up to the final imposition of the Berlin blockade. By turning up the heat through increased restrictions on the movement of Allied traffic, the Soviets were hoping to convince the Allies that the cost of these actions was much greater than going along with the Soviet proposals about the status of Berlin. The dynamics of shifting perceptions of the cost of continuing the confrontation will be discussed further under Proposition Five.

One way for parties to move out of a stalemate is for one side to believe that it will be better off moving from its current position. In the first few days following Kennedy's announcement of a quarantine, President Kennedy and Premier Khrushchev felt they were in a situation where any unilateral attempt to move away from their standoff would be too costly. The United States felt that it had to take a strong stand against missiles in Cuba while Khrushchev probably felt that he had to make an effort to redress the strategic imbalance.[16] It was not until President Kennedy began to increase the potential costs to Khrushchev of not acceding to Kennedy's demands (by increasing U.S. military might in the region) that Khrushchev began to move away from a confrontation. Only when it seemed that the cost of remaining in the stalemate (or

---

16. See Graham T. Allison, *Essence of Decision: Explaining the Cuban Missile Crisis* (Boston: Little, Brown and Company, 1971), 40–56, 102–17, 230–44, for a discussion of Soviet motives and intentions. Nikita Khrushchev reports similar considerations in *Khrushchev Remembers* (Boston: Little, Brown and Company, 1970), 488–95.

of attempting to move out of the stalemate toward his own favored position) became too high did Khrushchev move.[17]

Iranian Crisis of 1946

Proposition Four suggests that crises will end when there is a congruence of views about the nature of the interaction between parties in a dispute, in this case the United States and the Soviet Union. Unlike some of the other crises considered here, there is a fairly clear ending point for the Iranian crisis of 1946, as seen by American leaders. The Soviet announcement on 26 March that Soviet troops were being withdrawn, followed by the joint Iranian-Soviet announcement on 4 April laying out the details of the withdrawal, went a long way to relieving American concerns about the crisis. When evidence of the departure of Soviet troops reached Washington, the feeling of crisis ended.

As already pointed out, a crisis ends when both sides' images of events converge. They need not converge to an accurate representation of reality, only to one that will lead one side to back down. The reason for the decision to back down will fit one of two categories: first, one of the sides may come to feel that the cost of continuing the crisis is too high and back down; or second, the state that feels that the other has placed it in a crisis situation will change its mind. What was formerly seen as threatening behavior will come to be seen as nonthreatening, and the (perceived) crisis will end. The problem that arises in attempting to apply Proposition Four to the Iranian crisis of 1946 is that the United States made no actual threats to the Soviets that the Soviets ended up coming to believe, thus ending the crisis.[18] Unlike each of the other crises considered here, there was no agreement by both sides on the threat(s) made by the other. The Soviets appear to have backed down because they did not want to arouse American and Western opposition and jeopardize their gains in Eastern Europe.[19]

With respect to the American side of this crisis, Proposition Four is supported. The concern on the American side was that the Soviet actions were

---

17. James G. Blight and David A. Welch, *On the Brink: Americans and Soviets Reexamine the Cuban Missile Crisis* (New York: Hill and Wang, 1989), 307–8.

18. The question of Truman's ultimatum, discussed in chap. 3, is being ignored temporarily.

19. Adam B. Ulam argues that the Soviets retreated after Churchill's "Iron Curtain" speech for fear that the American public would become concerned about their actions in Eastern Europe and demand that action be taken to prevent their further consolidation of power. *Expansion and Coexistence: Soviet Foreign Policy, 1917–1973*, 2d ed. (New York: Praeger, 1974), 425. Stephen S. Kaplan makes a similar argument. *Diplomacy of Power: Soviet Armed Forces as a Political Instrument* (Washington, D.C.: Brookings, 1981), 71.

part of a larger effort to gain control of parts of Iran and use this control to expand their influence in the region. This uncertainty contributed to the crisis, and as more information became available that suggested that this was not happening, the crisis ended. When there were no further reports of troop movements, tensions decreased, and the Soviet announcements on 24 March and 2 April ended the feeling of crisis. When American beliefs about Soviet behavior changed to believing that there was no immediate threat to American interests, the crisis ended. To emphasize the point, the main component of U.S. fears, and what drove the crisis, was uncertainty about Soviet motives and intentions. Unlike other crises that American leaders would find themselves in throughout the Cold War, leaders at the time of this crisis did not have a fully formed view of Soviet intentions and motivations. That the Soviets might be intent on causing trouble for the United States was not yet a foregone conclusion, and as a result leaders were uncertain about Soviet moves.

It is interesting to speculate on why the Soviet Union was willing to back down in a situation in which it seemed that it had the local advantage. The common answer to this question centers around the Soviets' fears that their activities in Iran would stir up a strong enough reaction in the West that their efforts to consolidate their position in Eastern Europe would be hindered. Lenczowski explains events in this manner:

> During the Iranian New Years holiday of March 21–27 an armed coup by the Tudeh [Iranian Communist Party] and the Soviet agents was generally expected in the capital. Yet it never materialized. Diplomatic observers ascribed Soviet hesitation at this juncture to the stiffening of the American attitude as evidenced by the immediate publicity given the Russian troop movements by the State Department and, on the other hand, by the determined measures taken by the gendarmerie adviser, Colonel Schwarzkopf, to protect the capital.[20]

Soviet concerns about the consequences of their actions in Iran for their plans in Europe might have compelled them to reconsider the wisdom of pushing their efforts in what might have been an area of secondary importance. When the discussion turns to an area of greater American interest, Berlin, the perspective changes.

Berlin Blockade

The main cause of concern among American leaders during the initial stages of the Berlin blockade was uncertainty about how far the Soviets were willing

---

20. George Lenczowski, *Russia and the West in Iran, 1918–1948: A Study In Big-Power Rivalry* (New York: Greenwood Press, 1968), 298.

to go in pressuring the United States (and the other Western powers) to change its stance in Berlin. The main worry expressed by those in Washington during the crisis period was that the Soviets would continue escalating the pressure on Berlin with military force, including the use of force to halt the airlift. An additional worry was whether or not this was the beginning of a war with the Soviet Union over the future of Germany. Both of these worries would propel the crisis, but they would operate in sequence. The initial concerns were about larger overall Soviet plans, but as decision makers began to conclude that this was not part of a larger Soviet plan, their attention turned to Soviet intentions with respect to the airlift.

Overall, these fears were greater in Washington than in Berlin. Many of those in Washington feared that this was the beginning of a long-feared Soviet move on Western Europe and that any attempt to break the blockade would only lead to war. These fears were based on a belief that the Soviet military position in Europe was so strong that any challenge to it would be doomed to failure.[21] General Clay and Advisor Murphy had two contradictory views about the threat from the Soviet Union, views that allowed them to be less concerned about Soviet military action. The first was that if the Soviets had decided that they were going to attack the Western position in Berlin there was little that the West could do about it in the short run. The second view was that the Soviets were not likely to attack. (This second view was the underpinning of Clay's arguments in favor of attempting to break the blockade.)

As it turned out, the Soviets were not willing to interfere with the airlift or escalate the conflict by military means. Most of the steps that they had taken were passive—closing the highways because of "technical difficulties," shutting off electric power and water, etc.—which forced the Western powers to have to take the next move if they wanted to break the blockade. These passive measures also meant that if the Soviets wanted to do more to put pressure on the Western powers, they would have to start taking active measures—like shooting down planes in the airlift. It appears that the Soviets were unwilling to increase the pressure by taking any more active steps. They were willing to push hard in what has been called the *political battle* for Berlin but were unwilling to push hard in the other spheres.[22] It was the realization of this fact that brought the crisis period to a close for the American leaders.

---

21. Intelligence estimates at the time painted a pessimistic view of the relative position of Western forces vis-à-vis Soviet forces. Matthew A. Evangallista argues that Western estimates of the size of the Soviet army in Europe were much too high. "Stalin's PostWar Army Reappraised," *International Security* 7, no. 3 (Winter 1982–83): 110–38.

22. Lucius D. Clay, *Decision in Germany* (Westport, Conn.: Greenwood Press, 1950), and W. Phillips Davison, *The Berlin Blockade: A Study in Cold War Politics* (Princeton: Princeton University Press, 1958), are good sources on the political and economic steps that were taken by the Soviets to gain control of Berlin.

As the crisis went on, and no evidence emerged about a broader Soviet move against the Allied position, and there were no Soviet attempts to interfere with the airlift, American leaders adjusted their views about what the Soviets would and would not do. This adjustment in the views held by American leaders contributed to the end of the crisis phase. When American perceptions about how far the Soviets were willing to go and the Soviet unwillingness to go further came into alignment, the immediate crisis ended for the American leaders. The American decisions in Washington, of 22 July, that ruled out any attempt to break the blockade and formally instituted the airlift as a permanent program (which by then had shown that it could supply the basic needs of the city) settled the two sides into an implied status quo: the Soviets would not interfere with the airlift nor use military force to increase pressure on the city, while the Americans would not attempt to break the land blockade nor expand the airlift out of the existing air-traffic channels. This became the agreed image or perception that both sides had of the crisis, bringing the crisis to an end and providing support for Proposition Four. What had happened was that the crisis had been transformed from a situation of perceived direct confrontation (on the part of the Americans) to one of a stalemate where neither side was willing to push hard to move the other from its position. This transition in perceptions about the stakes of the crisis will be the subject of chapter 7.

Berlin Wall

The Berlin Wall crisis provides an interesting setting to test Proposition Four because of the questions that have been raised about how much of a crisis this actually was for American policymakers. The discussion of the Kennedy administration's views of the wall in previous chapters makes clear that in many ways decision makers viewed the construction of the wall with something approaching relief—relief that this might be as far as Khrushchev was willing to go in pushing the Berlin issue. It is clear that the Kennedy administration viewed the general Berlin situation in the summer of 1961 as a crisis and it viewed the uncertainty about Soviet moves surrounding the construction of the wall as a crisis as well. Sorensen and Bundy recount in some detail the mood of pessimism that hung over Washington prior to the building of the wall—a mood that deepened in the first days of the crisis.[23] The general Berlin crisis ended with the construction of the Berlin Wall because it helped ease concerns about what the Soviets were going to do about the refugee

---

23. Theodore C. Sorensen, *Kennedy* (New York: Harper and Row, 1965), 581–93, and McGeorge Bundy, *Danger and Survival: Choices about the Bomb in the First Fifty Years* (New York: Random House, 1988), 363–71.

problem and because it reduced the risk of uprisings in East Germany. The Berlin wall crisis ended for American leaders when they came to believe that (1) the Soviets were not going to push any further at this time, (2) the Soviets were not making any serious attempt to impede access to the Soviet sector of Berlin—only from the Soviet to the western sectors, and (3) there was little militarily, politically, or legally that they could do to bring down the wall. As Kenneth P. O'Donnell and David F. Powers point out, Kennedy was actually relieved when the wall went up as it suggested to him that this was as far as the Soviets were going to go, reducing some of the ambiguity and concerns that had existed in the months leading up to the crisis.[24] The explanations of both Bundy and Sorensen lead one to conclude that the wall was a turning point in the general Berlin crisis, a turning point that contributed to a decrease in concerns about the next Soviet moves. In many ways, the crisis dynamic here parallels that of the Berlin blockade, where there was similar uncertainty about Soviet moves that might follow the initial blockade. When it became clear that the blockade was as far as the Soviets were going to go, the sense of crisis diminished.

In the context of the discussion of crises that has been presented in this chapter, the central element of the Berlin Wall crisis was the fear that the Soviets would use the construction of the wall as a pretext for a further move against Berlin. The way in which the wall was constructed (entirely by East German forces on territory legally occupied by the Soviets) as well as the lack of any offensive moves against the West no doubt served to convince many in the West that this fear (of further Soviet moves) was not justified.[25] The Soviet argument was that the construction of the wall was in no way an infringement of Western rights and as a result the West had nothing to fear from it. When American leaders believed this, the crisis came to an end. Again, the course of events is seen that was suggested in the discussion of Proposition Four that opened this chapter. When both parties to the confrontation saw the same image of the crisis, that of a Soviet move to construct the wall, but no further action, the crisis ceased.

On the American side, the turning point in the crisis seems to have come when the convoy of troops sent through East Germany to reinforce the West Berlin garrison was allowed to pass without incident. Once this had occurred,

24. Kenneth P. O'Donnell and David F. Powers, *"Johnny, We Hardly Knew Ye": Memories of John Fitzgerald Kennedy* (Boston: Little, Brown and Company, 1970), 303.

25. It is interesting to note that Khrushchev and Anastas Mikoyan were out of Moscow at the time of the construction of the wall. Robert M. Slusser suggests that this indicates that the Soviets did not expect much trouble and did not intend to take any further actions that might have provoked the West. *The Berlin Crisis of 1961: Soviet-American Relations and the Struggle for Power in the Kremlin, June–November 1961* (Baltimore: Johns Hopkins University Press, 1973), 132.

American leaders began to shift their concerns away from the question of continued access to Berlin to the question of what steps should be taken to ensure that Berlin remained strong:

> Soviet acquiescence in the movement of the U.S. battle group through East German territory served as valuable confirmation of the conclusion derived from a reading of the GDR statement of August 13, that the border control measures being taken were not aimed at cutting or interfering with allied communications between West Germany and West Berlin. From this point on, Western policy in Berlin was thus directed not toward preventing the Soviets and the East Germans from splitting Berlin and sealing off its Western sectors, but toward defending Western rights in West Berlin and maintaining the city's morale and economic viability.[26]

The construction of the wall gave Khrushchev the breathing space that he needed in order to back away from the demand that a peace treaty be signed before the end of the year.[27] Plans for negotiations with the Soviets on a variety of issues were discussed at the end of August and the beginning of September, and these activities, along with the lack of any offensive moves on the part of the Soviets against West Berlin, contributed to an easing of the crisis.

Cuban Missile Crisis

Pared down to its essentials, the main component of the Cuban Missile Crisis, from the American point of view, was concern about the presence of the Soviet missiles on Cuba. Despite almost thirty years of discussion by policymakers and academics, there is still debate about just what it was about the presence of those missiles that caused concern: their military impact or their political impact. The fact remains that it was the presence of those missiles that drove the crisis. When the question of the removal of those missiles was resolved, the crisis came to an end. As noted in chapter 2, the crisis can be divided into four phases: installation, American discovery, public confrontation, and withdrawal. For the discussion here, it is the last two phases that are of interest, as Proposition Four deals with the ending of crises as perceptions change.

---

26. Slusser, *The Berlin Crisis of 1961*, 137.

27. Arthur M. Schlesinger, Jr., *A Thousand Days: John F. Kennedy in the White House* (Boston: Houghton Mifflin Company, 1965), 397–400.

The discovery of the missiles on 14 October placed American leaders in a difficult position, with two difficult and important questions to answer: When would the missiles become operational? And, second, what could the United States do to convince the Soviets of its determination to use force if necessary to compel their removal?[28] Bundy points out the speed with which American leaders arrived at the basic decision that would guide their efforts:

> Within forty-eight hours, a single objective for our policy had been identified: the removal of the missiles. Moreover, we had reduced our options to two: a conventional air strike on the missile sites, and a naval quarantine on the delivery of the offensive weapons.[29]

Bundy notes that there was debate over the consequences for the United States if those missiles were to remain depending on whether they were seen as more of a political or strategic threat, but Bundy points out that there was an overriding concern about when the missiles would become operational: "What we had been concerned with all along was the rapid and accelerating Soviet effort to make the missiles *operational*."[30] This fear was compounded by the fear that once the missiles did indeed become operational, they would be seen as the new status quo, rather than as an unacceptable challenge to the status quo, making it harder to sustain support for their removal.

These, then, were the fears that drove the crisis for American decision makers. These concerns meant that the resolution of the crisis would come when the United States was able to convince the Soviets that it would act to remove those missiles. When the Soviets came to believe that and took actions to remove the missiles (thus reassuring the Americans) and the United

---

28. Blight and Welch, *On the Brink*, and Raymond L. Garthoff, *Reflections on the Cuban Missile Crisis*, rev. ed. (Washington, D.C.: Brookings, 1989), are the best current sources on the crisis. Blight, *The Shattered Crystal Ball*, is also a useful source. *On the Brink* reports on conferences held from 1987–89 in which former American decision makers, American academics, and Soviet academics came together to discuss this crisis, while *The Shattered Crystal Ball* draws on these conferences and interviews of the participants. In these conferences new information was brought forward, as well as old information confirmed or discredited. Some care is required, however, in accepting the information presented in *On The Brink* and *The Shattered Crystal Ball*. These texts at times uncritically accept information put forth by both American and Soviet participants that runs counter to accepted wisdom and much research, only to reveal deficiencies or counterarguments buried in the footnotes. Garthoff brings out significant new information about American and Soviet thinking during the crises, particularly that of American leaders about the consequences of those missiles for the U.S. strategic position. Taken together, these three works provide a substantial base from which to discuss this crisis as seen by American and Soviet leaders.

29. Bundy, *Danger and Survival*, 397.

30. Bundy, *Danger and Survival*, 424. Emphasis in original.

States pledged not to invade Cuba (reassuring the Soviets), the crisis came to an end.[31]

A different way of interpreting the crisis, which nonetheless leads to the same conclusion about the crisis dynamic, is that what drove the crisis was nothing as concrete as fears about the operational status of the missiles, but fears about the consequences of a continued crisis. Bundy suggests by the time of the final ExComm meeting before the crisis was resolved (on 27 October) the possibility of things "spinning out of control" had become the biggest fear.[32] In this interpretation, the crisis was resolved or eased when the situation was seen to come back into control as each side took actions to steer away from confrontation.

This idea, that it was fear about the consequences of the crisis that brought leaders to a position where they could make the necessary decisions to avoid war, is argued forcefully by Blight in *The Shattered Crystal Ball: Fear and Learning in the Cuban Missile Crisis*. Blight's innovative argument suggests that the real fear that pushed decision makers on both sides of the dispute to find a way out was the fear of nuclear inadvertence, the fear that nuclear war could break out in spite of the efforts of leaders to avoid war. Blight argues that it was not the fear that the other side might use nuclear weapons should war break out that brought the crisis to an end but that the leaders "realized that the real adversary was the uncontrollable situation they had created."[33] While the evidentiary basis of Blight's argument is thin, it nevertheless lends support to the argument being made here. The crisis continued until both sides realized that the crisis had to be brought under control before it spun into nuclear war. Once both sides believed that the crisis had to be brought under control, and took steps to do so, they could rest easier.[34]

There were two elements of misperception on the part of the Soviet Union that led to this crisis. The first was the belief that it could install missiles rapidly enough to provide a sufficient degree of deterrence against an American attack.[35] The second was the apparent belief that the American response would not be a major one.[36] The crisis (for the Soviet Union) in

---

31. It has now become clear that President Kennedy also directed Robert Kennedy to communicate to the Soviets the president's intention that the U.S. missiles in Turkey be removed after the missile crisis had been resolved, but only if the Soviets made no mention of this linkage. Blight and Welch, *On the Brink*, 83–84.

32. Bundy, *Danger and Survival*, 426.

33. Blight, *The Shattered Crystal Ball*, 7–8.

34. Bundy, *Danger and Survival*, 441–45, provides a useful discussion of why Khrushchev backed down.

35. For an intriguing discussion of why Khrushchev might have felt that he could get away with it (and why he was almost right!), see Blight and Welch, *On The Brink*, 297–302.

36. Perhaps the best discussion of Soviet motivations is Garthoff, *Reflections on the Cuban Missile Crisis*, 6–42.

phase three developed when it appeared that the American response was going to be a strong military one that posed a serious threat to Cuba and possibly the Soviet Union. The source of the tension was the inherent conflict between the American determination to force the Soviets to remove the missiles and the Soviet attempt to make those missiles operational before an American attack occurred. What was at issue here was the explicit American threat to move against those missiles, along with a possible invasion of Cuba, working against the Soviet belief that the United States would not take such action.

In terms of the dynamics of this crisis, a unilateral crisis (faced by the Americans after the discovery of the missiles) became a bilateral crisis when the United States chose to publicly confront the Soviet Union over those missiles. As already pointed out, a crisis is a situation in which the views of two parties come into some degree of conflict. In this case, the first conflict arose with the discovery of the missiles in Cuba. For the American leaders, in phase two, their belief that the Soviets would not install missiles in Cuba conflicted with the apparent Soviet belief that they could do so and not be caught.[37] The second conflict, which is of greater interest here, was between the American threat to use force to compel the removal of those missiles and the apparent Soviet belief that the United States would not go this far. It is this conflict in beliefs that drove the crisis in phase three, and it is worth discussing in more detail.

The crisis for the Soviet Union began when Soviet Ambassador Dobrynin was informed by Secretary of State Rusk about President Kennedy's speech announcing the quarantine of Cuba. Dobrynin is reported to have left his meeting with Secretary Rusk "looking grim-faced and shaken," leading some to conclude that he was unaware that missiles were being placed in Cuba.[38] By the time the Soviets had been informed of Kennedy's upcoming speech, American military preparations were well under way and, as a result, the Soviets were faced with a well-developed threat by the time this became a bilateral crisis. Now the question was what it would take to end the crisis.

The crisis ended when the United States was able to convince the Soviet Union that it would indeed carry out its threat to invade Cuba if the missiles were not removed. The military preparations taken by the United States did not go unnoticed by the Soviet Union, and they apparently conveyed the correct message. Tatu notes that the Soviets started to back down on 25 October under the influence of three elements.[39] The first was the realization that Kennedy was not bluffing about the blockade and the demand that the

---

37. The reasoning behind this belief was discussed in chap. 5 under Proposition Three.

38. Elie Abel, *The Missile Crisis* (New York: Bantam, 1968), 103. This was later confirmed. See Blight and Welch, *On The Brink*, 256, and Garthoff, *Reflections on the Cuban Missile Crisis*, 29.

39. Michel Tatu, *Power in the Kremlin* (New York: Viking Press, 1969), 264–65.

missiles be dismantled and removed. The second was unprecedented American military buildup around the world (including the previously mentioned transmission of targeting codes),[40] and the third was "a much more definite danger . . . the Americans might strike at the Cuban bases, invade the island, take Castro prisoner and destroy his regime, and most probably all of these things at once."[41]

Phase three of this crisis, to which Proposition Four most aptly applies, was a race to see which side could put in place its military forces to back up its threats. These forces were needed to back up each side's demands on the other, to enforce its version of events on the other. The American efforts included diplomatic steps to get the support of OAS and NATO, as well as military preparations to back up the demand that the missiles be removed from Cuba.[42] The Soviet response to Kennedy's speech was surprisingly limited in scope. Aside from denouncing the American moves in the Soviet press, as well as the UN, and increasing the speed with which the missile bases were being constructed, little else was done.[43] The main focus of the Soviet response appears to have been a rush to create a fait accompli with respect to the installation of the missiles in Cuba.

In terms of the dynamics of the crisis, the initial Soviet assessment of the American willingness to resist the introduction of missiles changed with the arrival of new information about American actions. As the indications of the American military preparations became known, and messages from President Kennedy continued to be unyielding with respect to the demand for

---

40. See Dan Caldwell, "Department of Defense Operations during the Cuban Crisis: A Report by Adam Yarmolinsky, 13 February 1963," *Naval War College Review* 32, no. 4 (June–July 1979): 83–99, for a discussion of the various elements of this buildup. Many of the elements of the buildup could hardly have gone unnoticed by the Soviets:

> We now know that, in response [to the broadcast in the clear from SAC], near-panic broke out in Khrushchev's dacha, 30 kilometers outside of Moscow, as he and several aides rushed an immediate and conciliatory reply by car into the city for immediate transmission over Radio Moscow. Having received what he believed to be Kennedy's final offer, and with the knowledge that he no longer controlled events in Cuba and that Castro was apparently trying to provoke a war, Khrushchev could only hope that his message would reach Kennedy in time.

Blight, *The Shattered Crystal Ball*, 20. See also Scott D. Sagan "Nuclear Alerts and Crisis Management," *International Security* 9, no. 4 (Spring 1985): 108.

41. Tatu, *Power in the Kremlin*, 264.

42. See Abram Chayes, *The Cuban Missile Crisis: International Crises and the Role of Law* (Oxford: Oxford University Press, 1974), for a discussion of the extensive legal and diplomatic maneuvering used to enlist the support of allies.

43. It is interesting to note that there is no evidence that Soviet nuclear forces were alerted during this time nor, for that matter, can evidence be found of Soviet nuclear alerts at any other time in history. Bruce G. Blair, "Alerting in Crisis and Conventional War," in *Managing Nuclear Operations*, ed. Ashton B. Carter, John D. Steinbruner, and Charles A. Zraket (Washington, D.C.: Brookings, 1987), 76-77.

dismantling the missiles and removing them from Cuba, the Soviets were forced to reconsider the wisdom of continuing the crisis. The crisis came to an end when the Soviets began to believe that their assessment was wrong and that the United States actually would use force to enforce its demands. The Americans wanted the Soviets to believe this, and when they did, the crisis ended. As Bundy writes, "I think Khrushchev recognized that he was in a situation in which he had no better choice [than to back down]."[44]

One reason for the ending of the crisis was the change in Soviet perceptions of the stakes involved.[45] When it became clear to them that continued confrontation would bring about a worse outcome (war over Cuba, possibly including nuclear weapons) than going along with Kennedy's demands, the Soviets moved quickly to seek an acceptable outcome to the crisis. In spite of Soviet claims to the contrary, that their actions were simply to defend Cuba (and a newfound willingness of former policymakers and historians to believe such claims), it seems clear that the Soviets concluded that the cost of persevering in the conflict outweighed whatever gains they could have envisioned. The view that both sides to the dispute came to agree upon was that the United States would indeed use force to enforce its demands on the Soviets. Once that was understood, the way was open for the resolution of the crisis.

October 1973 Middle East War

The October 1973 War provides an interesting test of Proposition Four's assertion that crises will end when both parties share similar perceptions about the situation they are in. The crisis between the United States and the Soviet Union that grew out of the letter from Brezhnev threatening (implicitly) to intervene with troops if there was no cease-fire lasted less than twenty-four hours. This letter arrived at 9:35 P.M. on 24 October; the order to go to DefCon III was issued at 11:41 P.M. that same evening. The crisis appeared to end at 2:40 P.M. the following day when a letter from Brezhnev arrived informing the United States that the Soviet Union was sending seventy observers (nonmilitary personnel) to observe the implementation of the cease-fire. Following that letter, the alert was reduced in stages. This confrontation between the United States and the Soviet Union occurred over a very short time period, with little time for any jockeying for position or adjustment of attitudes or goals (unlike, for example, the Berlin blockade and airlift that

---

44. Bundy, *Danger and Survival*, 440. Bundy's analysis (440–46), along with that of Tatu, *Power in the Kremlin*, remain the best discussion of this decision.

45. This change may be what Blight describes as the shift to fear of nuclear inadvertence from fear of deliberate nuclear use. The role of this shift in the crisis dynamic will be considered in chap. 7.

occurred over the space of a year). Events moved quickly, and it is somewhat difficult to ascertain any solid positions taken by the parties. Nevertheless, it is possible to see some of the types of behavior suggested in Proposition Four, and it is to that behavior we now turn.

The aspect of the confrontation that will be discussed here is the unintentional crisis that developed when the Soviet Union prepared to send troops to the Middle East and the United States took strong exception to that plan. An interpretation that suggests that the crisis was intended by the Soviet Union (as a means of putting pressure on Israel and providing an excuse for the Soviets to explain their further inaction to their Arab allies) cannot be discussed under Proposition Four. Under the definition of a crisis presented in chapter 1, the Soviet action of provoking an American response, rather than demanding some sort of concession or change, would not be part of a crisis. The reason is that, unlike most crises studied, the Soviet Union was not demanding any sort of concession or return in response to its threat to intervene. All the Soviets wanted (under this interpretation of their actions) was an American response that would allow them to say that they had tried their best for the Arabs. Thus, only the interpretation that suggests that this was an unintended crisis will be tested with Proposition Four.[46]

This crisis began with a mismatch between what the Soviet Union thought the United States would tolerate and what the United States was actually willing to go along with. The Soviet perception of the American preferences was incomplete and inaccurate, and it took the response of the United States to make it more complete. The Soviet move to intervene with troops created a gap between what the Soviets were doing and what the United States wanted, and this goaded the United States into action. The actions that the United States took (the nuclear alert and the increased naval presence in the Mediterranean) forced the Soviets to reconsider their assessment of what the United States was willing to go along with. At this point, the perceptions came in line, and the Soviets had to decide what to do.

Proposition Four suggests that when perceptions match, there are two possible outcomes. The first is that each side continues to refuse to alter its course of action, choosing instead to continue to press its demands. The second outcome is that one side (or possibly both) concludes that the cost of continued confrontation is greater than conceding to the demands of the other

---

46. This does not mean that an intended crisis cannot be considered under this proposition. The Berlin blockade and airlift was an intended crisis, and it was found to conform with the suggestions of Proposition Four. The difference with the Berlin blockade was that the Soviets wanted particular concessions on the status of Berlin that the United States was aware of and was not willing to give. In the October 1973 War, the United States was not aware of what the Soviets wanted (a response to pressure Israel and provide an excuse for Soviet inaction) and therefore had nothing to refuse or concede.

side. This crisis followed the second course of action, that of a change in
behavior on the part of the Soviet Union in response to the American action
(the nuclear alert). When the vigorous American response increased the risk
of confrontation between the two countries, the Soviets appear to have concluded that the risk of confrontation was too great, and they halted preparations for intervention. The crisis then ended.

There was no room for the two countries to continue their individual
courses without heading toward a serious confrontation. Given the course of
action that each had taken, confrontation was likely. If one accepts the analysis of how the Soviet Union viewed the world (which argued that the worst
outcome for the Soviets was a military confrontation with the United States),
then for the Soviets, the nature of the crisis changed abruptly when the United
States went on alert. To continue with their planned course of action (military
intervention) would have created the worst outcome possible, and as a result
they backed down. In a sense, the Soviets saw the situation as one of Chicken,
in which mutual conflict could bring their worst outcome (this aspect is dealt
with under Proposition Five). For the United States, if Kissinger is to be
believed, a confrontation between the two powers was an outcome preferred
to having Soviet troops in the Middle East. Thus, the United States was
willing to run the risk of confrontation in order to avoid its worst outcome,
unilateral Soviet intervention.[47] From the point of view of the United States,
the situation probably looked like a Prisoner's Dilemma, where the cost of
exploitation (unilateral Soviet intervention) was worse than mutual conflict or
the creation of a crisis between the two states. With this set of preferences, it
made sense to run these risks. This will be taken up in the next chapter.

A possibility that has not been considered is that the Soviets were engaging in exploratory behavior, that is, testing the waters of the American response. This view combines aspects of both the unintended and intended
interpretations by suggesting that the Soviets were unsure about what the
American response would be and took a series of cautious, obvious steps
(gradual increase in the airlift, gradual increase in naval forces in the Mediterranean, gradual alert of airborne troops, etc.) to find out what they could, and
could not, get away with. Analyses of Soviet military behavior in situations
involving the interests of the United States have argued that the Soviets tend to
act cautiously and only move decisively when it is clear that the United States
is not going to be involved.[48]

---

47. Whether or not Kissinger was actually willing to go to the brink and seriously risk
nuclear confrontation with the Soviets cannot be proven. What matters for this discussion is that
Kissinger appeared willing to do so and the Soviets apparently were not willing to run that risk.

48. Kaplan suggests that the Soviet record in the use of military force has been one of
"great deliberation" and prudence, particularly when perceived American interests are at stake.
Diplomacy of Power, 667–69, 675–81. For the purposes of the discussion of misperception and

Conclusion

Compare with p. 146

Proposition Four, while the most simply stated of the five propositions, is the most complex. Simply put, the concept behind Proposition Four is this: disputes generally end when both sides agree on a given outcome. The agreement need not be the result of discussions or negotiations; it may simply be that both sides act in a manner that would be expected if there was such an agreement. This argument is similar to that of Blainey, noted at the beginning of this chapter, who argues that wars end when there is agreement about the distribution of power between the two disputants. In other words, both parties agree on who is the stronger party and who is the weaker party, and the war is over. This does not mean that there is any objective truth to the matter—only that the beliefs allow for an end to the war. The same model can be used to understand the end of crises. A crisis will end when both parties agree on who will back down or when one party is able to convince the other that there is no reason to believe there is a crisis. The example that opened our discussion in chapter 1, the Cuban brigade crisis, came to an end when American leaders who had believed there was a crisis concluded, on the basis of further information, that there was indeed no need to feel there was one. The agreement in this instance was between the Soviet assertion that those troops did not pose a threat and the eventual American belief of that claim. A few illustrations from the case studies will help to clarify this point.

During the October 1973 Middle East War, the crisis was caused (from the American point of view) by intelligence information that suggested the Soviet Union was about to send troops to the Middle East. When more information became available to suggest that the Soviets were not sending troops, the crisis came to an end. The agreement here was that the Soviets understood that the United States was indeed serious in its opposition to Soviet troops and that there was every reason to believe American statements that the United States would use force to keep those troops out of the Middle East. As a result of this understanding, the Soviets did not send troops, and when the Americans realized this, the crisis came to an end.

A second way for a crisis to end is for one side to convince the other that the costs of continuing the crisis are too high. It may be the initiator of the crisis who is able to convince the target that giving in to the initiator's demands will be less costly than resisting them, or it may be the target who is able to convince the initiator that the cost of getting concessions out of the

---

crises, this type of exploratory behavior does not change the predictions embodied in the propositions. Exploratory behavior of this nature merely allows the actor to confirm or modify views about the opponent's preferences.

target is too high. There were no direct examples of the first type of ending (the initiator having its demands met) found in these case studies. The closest example was in the Berlin Wall crisis, where the Soviets were able to carry out their moves (blocking exits from East Berlin and East Germany) in such a way that challenging them would have been very costly for the United States. In essence, the cost of resistance for the United States was very high.

The Berlin blockade, the Cuban Missile Crisis, and the October 1973 War all fit into the second type of situation, where the target is able to put up a stiff enough resistance to convince the initiator (the Soviet Union) to back off. In each case, the American response (or threatened response) appears to have raised the cost of continuing the crisis high enough for the Soviets to stop pushing their demands. In the Berlin blockade, the American ability to supply Berlin without directly challenging the blockade forced the Soviets to choose between further escalation of the crisis or backing down. In the Cuban Missile Crisis and the October 1973 War, the threatened American military actions raised the cost to the Soviets of continuing their military actions.

Overall, each case had elements that supported the view of crisis termination suggested by Proposition Four. A crisis will end when there is some degree of convergence on the part of the perceptions of the parties. That convergence will be to a point where the resolution to the crisis can occur, whether it be the realization that there is no crisis at all or the realization that the crisis is becoming very dangerous very quickly.

While the origins of crises can be found in many different mechanisms, the argument put forth in Proposition Four suggests that they will end for the same reasons. In the discussion of Proposition Four, the mechanism of perception change was outlined. As information is made available to decision makers, that information is checked against any existing views. If the information is suggestive enough, the existing views of events are modified to take it into account. If that information is not suggestive enough, or an existing view is very strongly held, the existing view is maintained in spite of the new information. This model of perception change was related to the termination of crises in the following way: a state believes it is in a crisis when it feels that there is a threat to important values that it holds. When the threat diminishes or the state believes itself to be strong enough to protect those values, the crisis is over. These feelings about the threat to values could be accurate or inaccurate, but the crisis will end in the same way—when the actions or inaction of the opposing state are no longer seen as threats. Proposition Four suggests that perceptions of threats (or nonthreats) will have to match on both sides before the crisis ends. The reasoning behind this is that there can be two outcomes to a crisis: the state that believes there is a crisis comes to believe that this is no longer the case (thus validating the probable claims of the other side that it meant no harm), or in a crisis that was deliberate on the part of at least one of the states, one side manages to prevail (either the challenger or defender). One way of prevailing is convincing the other side that resistance is not worth the cost. In making the other side agree with that assessment, perceptions on both sides match. How quickly this matching of perceptions occurs is the subject of Proposition Five.

CHAPTER 7

The Search for Acceptable Outcomes

The way that actors perceive the costs and benefits of a crisis will have an impact on their behavior during the crisis. The structure of the situation will affect the incentives to persist in, or seek a way out of, the confrontation. If the situation is perceived as being extremely dangerous, the actors involved are likely to exercise more caution than they might if the crisis is seen as relatively cost-free. It is also possible that a perception of danger will increase the search for mutual accommodation. To further elaborate on this theme, the concepts of *Prisoner's Dilemma* and *Chicken* will be utilized. The literature dealing with each of these terms is immense; however the interest here is only in one important difference between the two. The main elements of each that are relevant are the different outcomes that occur when both parties to a dispute choose to continue the confrontation and the impact that this has on crisis behavior. In the past four chapters, the discussion has considered the beginning and continuation of crises. It is now time to consider how they might end.

> *Proposition Five*: Crises perceived as Prisoner's Dilemmas will tend to be of longer duration than those perceived as Chicken.

Proposition Five refers to the length of the crisis and to the types of behavior that would be expected to be seen during the crisis. This proposition rests on a simple assumption about behavior: the more costly a certain course of action is likely to be, the greater the effort will be to avoid that course of action or reduce the cost.

The two types of interaction suggested in Proposition Five, Chicken and the Prisoner's Dilemma, are indicative of two perceptions that will be found on the part of the major actors in the cases covered here (fig. 3). The main difference between the two is that in a Prisoner's Dilemma mutual non-cooperation brings about the second worst outcome as seen by decision makers, while in Chicken mutual noncooperation brings about the worst outcome.[1] In their review of international conflicts, Snyder and Diesing note

---

1. Steven J. Brams provides a useful discussion of the differences and dynamics of Chicken and the Prisoner's Dilemma. *Superpower Games: Applying Game Theory to Superpower Conflict*

	Cooperate	Defect
Cooperate	3,3	0,5
Defect	5,0	1,1

a

	Swerve	Straight
Swerve	3,3	1,5
Straight	5,1	0,0

b

Fig. 3. Prisoner's Dilemma (a) and Chicken (b)

that conflicts, when portrayed as games, can be characterized as being either symmetric or nonsymmetric. Their main emphasis is on the Prisoner's Dilemma, Chicken, and asymmetric games and the types of bargaining strategies used within each.[2] The finding that is of interest here is that there was a sharp difference in behavior between parties in Prisoner's Dilemmas and parties in Chicken (and asymmetric games). Parties in Chicken and asymmetric games do not prefer the outcomes that come with mutual firmness, and thus the party that can show that it will continue to stand firm will usually prevail. In Prisoner's Dilemma situations, each party prefers war (or the noncooperative outcome) to accepting the other's demand. This outcome is intuitively believable, for as Snyder and Diesing suggest:

> When this is realized [that both parties prefer war to concession in Prisoner's Dilemma], the parties each know they must reduce their goals to something the other can accept, or the outcome is likely to be war. There occurs an internal reassessment of goals, plus probing the oppo-

---

(New Haven: Yale University Press, 1985), 7–13. Perhaps the best discussions in terms relevant to this work are Glenn H. Snyder and Paul Diesing, *Conflict among Nations: Bargaining, Decision Making, and System Structure in International Crises* (Princeton: Princeton University Press, 1977), and Glenn H. Snyder, "'Prisoner's Dilemma' and 'Chicken' Models in International Politics," *International Studies Quarterly* 15, no. 1 (March 1971): 66–103. See also Henry Hamburger, *Games as Models of Social Phenomena* (San Francisco: W. H. Freeman, 1979), 83–87, 108–110.

2. Snyder and Diesing, *Conflict among Nations*, 41–48, 488–89.

nent, to determine what is essential and what can be sacrificed, and what the opponent is willing to give up. The communication of reduced goals to the opponent is the turning point, after which the parties make reciprocal concessions leading to a compromise. In the Chicken cases . . . , one or both parties prefer to yield than risk war. Therefore when one party establishes superiority of resolve it can force the other to give way completely, and usually does so.[3]

While Snyder and Diesing are discussing situations that include crisis and war, the argument here is that this same type of behavior will be found in the crises studied here. Situations that are seen by the actors as Prisoner's Dilemmas are more likely to endure because there is less risk that they will bring about the worst outcome. A situation seen as Chicken will bring about great pressure to either (1) convince the other party that the noncooperative mode will continue or (2) work to bring about the cooperative outcome. As an example, the Cuban Missile Crisis can be seen as a game of Chicken with Kennedy's noncooperative move being continued preparations for an invasion while Khrushchev's noncooperative move was continued installation and preparation of the missiles. If both persisted in their actions, war was likely, and as a result there were efforts to find a way out of the confrontation. In the Berlin airlift and blockade, the situation was a Prisoner's Dilemma where both sides saw giving in to the other's demands as being worse than continuing the confrontation. The shift in thinking about the consequences of continued confrontation during the Cuban Missile Crisis, described by Blight and Bundy, is indicative of the type of distinction being discussed here.[4] As the crisis reached its final stages on 27 October, the concern of leaders had shifted from the deliberate use of nuclear weapons to a concern about uncontrolled nuclear weapons use. This shift in fear added impetus to the search for a solution to the crisis, with Khrushchev deciding to withdraw the missiles from Cuba and Kennedy deciding that, if necessary, a deal with the Soviet Union about the missiles in Turkey would be acceptable.

Another way of looking at the difference between the Prisoner's Dilemma and Chicken is to consider it from the point of view of the bargaining dynamics. One of the things that an actor facing a single play game of Chicken would like to do is convince the opponent that he or she is determined to carry through the noncooperative choice (that is, persist in the confrontation). Schelling argues that success in Chicken is enhanced when

---

3. Snyder and Diesing, *Conflict among Nations*, 489.

4. James G. Blight, *The Shattered Crystal Ball: Fear and Learning in the Cuban Missile Crisis* (Savage, Md.: Rowman and Littlefield Publishers, 1990), 7–8, and McGeorge Bundy, *Danger and Survival: Choices about the Bomb in the First Fifty Years* (New York: Random House, 1988), 426.

one can show a commitment to the confrontational course of action.[5] The side that can convince the other that it will persist is more likely to win because the other will act to avoid the worst outcome and settle for the second worst outcome (swerving). As Schelling notes, the side that can effectively "throw away the steering wheel" is the side that will be able to convince the other to change. In much the same way, the state that can convince the other that it will persist with the noncooperative move in Chicken will win because the other will act to avoid the worst outcome (assuming that each driver sees death as the worst outcome).

When actors find themselves in a Prisoner's Dilemma, they will attempt to avoid mutual defection and at the same time attempt to avoid being exploited. One way to do this is to change the stakes of the contest by increasing the cost, or appearing to increase the cost, to the other side of mutual confrontation. In a sense, one actor is trying to convince the other that mutual confrontation is the worst outcome rather than mutual confrontation (mutual defection) being the second worst outcome. Thus, one would expect to see actions taken with the intent of convincing an opponent of just this, leading to a greater and more intensive search for alternative outcomes (other than mutual confrontation) when crises are seen as Chicken than when they are seen as Prisoner's Dilemmas. An expected corollary to this would be "Crises seen as Chicken will bring about a greater search for alternative outcomes than those perceived as Prisoner's Dilemmas." The reason for this follows from the earlier discussion. Mutual confrontation under Chicken brings about the worst outcome and is thus to be actively avoided, while mutual confrontation under a Prisoner's Dilemma does not bring about the worst outcome. Thus, parties will be more likely to persist in confrontational behavior in the structure of a Prisoner's Dilemma rather than Chicken.

An actor facing what is perceived as a Prisoner's Dilemma is going to attempt to do two things: first, try to make the situation look like Chicken to the other side, and second, attempt to convince the opponent that the confrontational stance will be pursued at all costs. The hope will be that the opponent will see the actor as being committed to the confrontational path in a game of Chicken, forcing the opponent to avoid the confrontation. In most of the cases considered here, this was done by making it appear that military force was likely to be used in any mutual confrontation. In some of the cases considered here, it was the threat of a nuclear confrontation that was used to shift the apparent stakes of mutual confrontation.[6] The explicitly threatened use of

---

5. Thomas C. Schelling, *Arms and Influence* (New Haven: Yale University Press, 1966), 116–25. See also Snyder and Diesing, *Conflict among Nations*, 198–201, for a discussion of a variety of tactics that can be used in crises, with historical examples.

6. This points to a possible mitigating factor in considering Proposition Five. It might be that states with nuclear weapons will have an edge in attempting to increase the stakes of mutual

military force, while always possible in any confrontation, seems to have served as the most common technique to raise the stakes of a confrontation.

Let us now turn to a discussion of the crises. The discussion will depart from a chronological account to consider those crises that provide the strongest support for Proposition Five and move to those that are weaker in their support. The discussion will begin with the Berlin blockade.

Berlin Blockade

The key element of Proposition Five is the impact that changes in perceptions about the costs of certain outcomes will have on the behavior of the parties to a crisis. The Berlin blockade provides ample opportunity to examine such changes and their impact on the crisis outcome. Perceptions about the cost of continued conflict (not yielding to Soviet demands) played an important role in determining the actions and intensity of effort put into solving the crisis on the part of the American leaders. The perception of danger varied from leader to leader, and these leaders' perceptions varied across time. Nevertheless, there are some general statements that can be made about this crisis and the role that the perceptions of the stakes involved played.

As discussed previously, the decisions of 22 July (which regularized the airlift and made final the decision not to directly challenge the blockade) marked an important turning point in the way American leaders viewed and responded to the crisis. The most important change was in the tension felt by those leaders and the urgency they felt about finding a resolution to the crisis. As Shlaim notes:

> The airlift strategy maximized the chances of preserving intact the three basic values underlying American foreign policy: maintaining the Western position in Berlin, avoiding war, and continuing with the political reconstruction of Germany. The belief that the expanded airlift would work obviated the need to sacrifice any of these values and thereby contributed to a reduction of the motivational stress under which the American decision-makers had been laboring.[7]

With respect to Proposition Five, what occurred was a change in perceptions about the cost of conflict and the consequences of continuing to resist Soviet

---

confrontation in hopes of getting the opponent to back away from that confrontation. On the other hand, wars fought by Korea, Vietnam, Afghanistan, and Iraq suggest that smaller powers will indeed take on nuclear-armed foes. This possible exception to the generality of Proposition Five will be considered more fully in chap. 8.

7. Avi Shlaim, *The United States and the Berlin Blockade, 1948–1949: A Study in Crisis Decision-Making* (Berkeley: University of California Press, 1983), 269.

demands. The American leaders' perception of the relative costs of continuing the confrontation versus the costs of giving in to the Soviet demands went from seeing the cost of confrontation as the worst outcome to seeing the cost of giving in as the worst outcome. Put in the game theory terms of Proposition Five, the American leaders' perception of the situation facing them went from Chicken to a Prisoner's Dilemma.

While discussing the views of American leaders in the first days of the crisis, the distinction between the views of those in Berlin and in Washington must again be made. In Berlin, Clay had been warning for quite some time about the pressures that the Soviets were attempting to put on the Western position and the pressures that they were likely to continue to exert. Clay reported these pressures without giving them much chance for success, and his main aim seems to have been to bolster Washington's support for a continued presence in Berlin.

Clay caused quite a flurry in Washington with a cable that he sent in March warning of a change in the way the Soviets had been acting:

> For many months, based on logical analysis, I have felt and held that war was unlikely for at least ten years. Within the last few weeks, I have felt a subtle change in Soviet attitude which I cannot define but which now gives me a feeling that it may come with dramatic suddenness. I cannot support this change in my own thinking with any data or outward evidence in relationships other than to describe it as a feeling of a new tenseness in every Soviet individual with whom we have official relations. I am unable to submit any official report in the absence of supporting data but my feeling is real.[8]

The baby blockade followed very shortly after this cable, and it seems that the two events made decision makers in Washington particularly concerned about the possibility of war with the Soviet Union over Berlin. Clay felt that the blockade was simply the culmination of a series of steps that had been made over a long period of time and, as such, was no real change in Soviet behavior. As a result, the change in attitude that General Clay seems to have undergone from 24 June to 22 July was less severe than the change experienced by those in Washington. Clay had always believed that the worst thing

---

8. Cable from General Clay to Lt. General Stephen J. Chamberlin, director of Intelligence, Army General Staff. Jean Edward Smith, ed., *The Papers of General Lucius D. Clay: Germany 1945–1949*, vol. 2 (Bloomington: Indiana University Press, 1974), 568–69. (Hereafter *Clay Papers*.) Smith notes that Clay later admitted that this cable, submitted following the visit of General Chamberlin, was intended to be used to support the army's appropriations bill that was pending before Congress. Whatever its intentions, it did have a strong impact on leaders in Washington.

that could happen was for the United States (and the other Western powers) to give in to Soviet demands because that would reduce the American role in Germany and decrease the American ability to stand up to the Soviets.[9]

Seen from Washington, the situation was not as clear-cut. There was considerable domestic political debate about the wisdom of continuing the American presence in Berlin, particularly if it increased the risk of conflict with the Soviet Union. As mentioned previously, the image of the strength of the Red Army was very strong, and the chances of defeating it in a conflict were seen as very small. The argument being made here is that during the initial phases of the crisis, decision makers in Washington were afraid that continuing the confrontation with the Soviet Union (by resisting its demands and attempting to maintain the American position in Berlin) was the most dangerous course because it ran the risk of bringing about the worst outcome—war with the Soviet Union. The perceptions of the risks of conflict on the part of those in Washington changed over time as it became clear that the Soviets were not going to escalate the conflict. As outlined in the discussion of Proposition Four, there was little more that the Soviets could do to increase their pressure on Berlin without seriously escalating the conflict into military action. As this became clear to Western leaders, the high levels of tension that had been felt diminished.

With respect to the crisis dynamic that is suggested by Proposition Five, the character of the decision making at the time is that of great anxiety and tension as leaders feared that continuing to hold out in Berlin could bring about war with the Soviets. As that fear became less salient, the primary concern became the American position in Europe and images that others had of the fight against communism. As the perceived risk of war with the Soviets decreased, American leaders became more willing to push for the Western stake in Berlin, believing that giving up their position was the worst thing that could occur. When the leaders began to see that continuing the confrontation would not bring about their worst outcome (increased risk of war), the intensity of their search for a solution to the problem lessened. The change in their perceptions of the cost of the confrontation allowed them to act with less concern about the consequences.

Cuban Missile Crisis

The next strongest case to consider in support of Proposition Five is the Cuban Missile Crisis. Recall that the main difference (for our purposes) between a situation seen as Chicken and a situation seen as a Prisoner's Dilemma is the

---

9. Recall the teleconference discussion with Bradley noted in chap. 4. Smith, *Clay Papers*, vol. 2, 622–23.

relative cost of mutual conflict (both sides resist the demands of the other) and exploitation (one side gives in to the demands of the other). One of the ways out of a condition of mutual conflict in a Prisoner's Dilemma (without giving in to the opponent's demands) is to convince the opponent that mutual conflict is now the opponent's worst outcome and that the confrontational stance will persist. That is what happened in this crisis.

From the point of view of those in the American government, the worst thing that could happen to the United States was for the Soviet Union to install missiles in Cuba and have the United States do nothing about them. As Robert Kennedy and others have noted, the "do nothing" option was discarded very quickly during the ExComm discussions in favor of doing something to get those missiles out. Once it had been decided that the missiles would have to be removed from Cuba, the question became one of deciding what was the best way to do that. As noted in chapter 6, the initial decision that the missiles would have to be removed or withdrawn was made in the first forty-eight hours.[10] The two options were the quarantine and preparations for an air strike. These two options constituted a combination of a threat and incentive. The threat was that inaction on the Soviet's side ran the risk of bringing about an American air strike on those missile sites, while the incentive was that if the missiles were removed the United States would agree not to invade Cuba. In the final hours of the crisis, an additional possible incentive emerged in U.S. deliberations: the United States would ensure that the missiles in Turkey would be removed once the crisis was resolved. The problem for the United States was to convince the Soviet government that continued confrontation, with the possibility of a military attack on Cuba and the Soviet missiles, was the Soviet Union's worst outcome. In other words, the United States had to make the Soviets see the crisis as one of Chicken rather than a Prisoner's Dilemma. In the context of this discussion, what the Americans did was attempt to increase the stakes of the confrontation so that the Soviets would prefer backing down to continuing the confrontation.

The American military preparations were the mechanism by which the stakes in this confrontation were increased. There remains, however, little credible evidence from the Soviet side on this issue.[11] The consistent Soviet line has been that the crisis ended because of their diplomatic skill and desire to maintain peace.[12] In his analysis of the domestic forces operating on

---

10. Bundy, *Danger and Survival*, 397.

11. Ronald R. Pope, ed., *Soviet Views on the Cuban Missile Crisis: Myth and Reality in Foreign Policy Analysis* (Washington, D.C.: University Press of America, 1982), 1–3.

12. Pope, *Soviet Views on the Cuban Missile Crisis*, 234–37. In spite of the new openness of the Soviet Union during its period of glasnost, there has been very little concrete and credible evidence to support the argument that the Soviet actions were taken to protect Cuba. Contrary to what is reported in James G. Blight and David A. Welch, *On the Brink: Americans and Soviets Reexamine the Cuban Missile Crisis* (New York: Hill and Wang, 1989), the officials from the

Khrushchev, Tatu argues that it was the realization that military confrontation was a frighteningly real possibility that forced the Kremlin to find a way to end the crisis.[13] As Khrushchev noted in his address to the Supreme Soviet on 12 December:

> However, the government of the United States of America continued to exacerbate the atmosphere. The U.S. military forces pushed the development of events so as to carry out an attack on Cuba. We received information from Cuban comrades and from other sources on the morning of October 27 directly stating that this attack would be carried out in the next two or three days. We interpreted these cables as an extremely alarming warning signal. And the alarm was justified. Immediate action was necessary to prevent an attack on Cuba and to preserve peace.[14]

Tatu's argument is that the Soviets began to feel the pressure of the American military buildup by the 25th and that by the 28th, when Khrushchev agreed to remove the missiles, forces within the Kremlin had concluded that a confrontation not only was likely but was the worst outcome that could arise. Thus, it seems that the United States had managed, through its rhetoric and actions (the military preparations), to increase the stakes of the confrontation as seen by the Soviets. As mentioned in chapter 6, this interpretation is consistent with the argument made by Blight about nuclear inadvertence.[15] His argument is that the U.S. and Soviet leaders approached the crisis initially as a situation in which they were willing to risk the possibility that either side might be willing to risk nuclear war over Cuba but this perspective changed radically in the last two days (26–28 October) to a situation where they began to fear nuclear war might occur despite the wishes of either side. The cost of backing down or finding a way out that involved some sort of compromise began to appear more appealing than the inadvertence that might have come from a continued confrontation. While Blight's argument is not directly in line with the perspective taken here, it is suggestive of the dynamics being described.

In the process of raising the stakes of the confrontation, the United States

---

Soviet side of the crisis were not directly involved in the crisis and could not produce solid evidence to buttress their claims that this was done to protect Castro. Such claims support the Soviet argument that it was their diplomatic skill and forbearance that prevented World War III, but for now the evidence is not convincing. For a further elaboration of this debate, see Ray S. Cline, "The Cuban Missile Crisis," *Foreign Affairs* 68, no. 4 (Fall 1989): 190–96, and Mark Kramer, "Remembering the Cuban Missile Crisis: Should We Swallow Oral History?" *International Security* 15, no. 1 (Summer 1990): 212–18.

13. Michel Tatu, *Power in the Kremlin* (New York: Viking Press, 1969), 267–73.

14. *Pravda*, 13 December 1962, reprinted in *Current Digest of the Soviet Press* 14, no. 51 (1962): 5.

15. Blight, *The Shattered Crystal Ball*, 5–10.

also managed to increase the pace of the confrontation and the search for an outcome. Tatu notes that the realization on the 25th that this was turning into a dangerous confrontation caused the Soviets to send a number of different messages with regard to an acceptable compromise solution.[16] The search for a compromise increased as the initial response of the Kennedy administration to Khrushchev's proposals was negative, leading Khrushchev to propose withdrawal of the missiles in Cuba in return for a noninvasion pledge from the United States.

On the American side, it is harder to detect a change in the pace of events. Standard accounts do not provide evidence to suggest a change in pace coming from a change in perceptions about the stakes. There was certainly a change in the way that American leaders felt about the crisis as it went from phase two to phase three (from a situation in which the American knowledge of Soviet actions was kept secret to the situation in which President Kennedy broadcast American knowledge of Soviet behavior), when it became an open confrontation with the Soviet Union. But with respect to phase three (the open confrontation with the Soviet Union), there was little apparent change in the way that American decision makers viewed the stakes of the confrontation. The pace of the American efforts to bring the crisis to an end was dictated more by the speed with which the Soviets were installing the missiles in Cuba than any change in perceptions about the stakes of the crisis. The dynamics of the crisis seem to have been driven (on the American side) more by the course of events rather than any real change in perceptions of the crisis. As Soviet ships approached the quarantine line, there appears to have been an increase in concern, as well as an increase in tension after Major Rudolf Anderson, Jr.'s U-2 was shot down over Cuba. But it seems that events affected the level of concern, not a change in the assessment of risks.

Blight's analysis can be used here as well to understand Proposition Five. If we consider the fear of nuclear inadvertence as being analogous to the mutual confrontation phase of Chicken (collision), then the proposition seems to be well supported. In Blight's analysis, there was a change in activity as American leaders began to fear on 27 October that events were getting out of hand, with this activity being directed to finding—in a short period of time— a mutually satisfactory way out of the confrontation. This change in perception of the stakes, from seeing the worst outcome coming from capitulation to seeing the worst outcome coming from continuing confrontation and the resulting chance of inadvertent nuclear war, is consistent with the dynamics outlined in Proposition Five.

---

16. Tatu, *Power in the Kremlin*, 265–73. For a useful review of the potential for loss of control, see Jonathan M. Roberts, *Decision-Making during International Crises* (New York: St. Martin's Press, 1988), 280–84.

The final assessment of Proposition Five and the Cuban Missile Crisis is that both Soviet and American actions seem to support the hypothesis. The initial Soviet response to Kennedy's speech was unyielding, but as time went on and the military preparations of the United States became more obvious, the need to arrive at a solution to the crisis grew. When it became clear to the Soviets that the stakes had increased to the point where mutual conflict was likely to bring about their worst outcome, their search for a way out quickened. On the American side, the initial American unwillingness to accept the presence of Soviet missiles never changed, while the willingness of President Kennedy to consider communicating an assurance to the Soviets that the missiles in Turkey would be removed suggests that there was a change in the willingness of the American leaders to carry through on their unyielding stance on the missiles.[17] What seems clear is that there was a shift in perceptions about the cost of conflict, and this shift in perceptions had an effect on American behavior.

October 1973 Middle East War

The crisis that faced the United States in the October 1973 War provides similar strong support for Proposition Five. Kissinger appears to have seen aspects of both Chicken and the Prisoner's Dilemma in this confrontation. He refers to the series of communications and threats as a game of Chicken, and he notes that after receiving the letter from Brezhnev suggesting joint action and threatening unilateral action, "Both of us were now caught in the rhythm of confrontation, which has its own logic. One side or the other would have to veer away from collision."[18] At the same time, however, it seems that his ranking of preferences would suggest that the confrontation also contained elements of a Prisoner's Dilemma. If one considers the sending of troops as a "defection" and the withholding of troops as "cooperation," it seems that Kissinger's ranking of the four combinations suggests a Prisoner's Dilemma, where mutual defection (both sides sending troops) is preferred to exploitation (unilateral Soviet intervention). It is difficult to rank Kissinger's preferences for the other two options, mutual nonintervention of troops and unilateral American intervention. It is hard to say if Kissinger would have preferred sending American troops unilaterally over both sides sending none at all. He probably would have preferred mutual cooperation over having the United States exploit Soviet restraint, which would not create a true Prisoner's Di-

---

17. For a detailed discussion of the revelations about Kennedy's willingness to consider a trade for the missiles in Turkey, see Blight and Welch, *On the Brink*, 83–84, 113–15, and Bundy, *Danger and Survival*, 430–36.

18. Henry Kissinger, *Years of Upheaval* (Boston: Little, Brown and Company, 1982), 585, 589.

lemma. The question is somewhat moot because there is little evidence to show that the United States was willing to send its troops unilaterally.[19] As suggested in the previous chapter in the discussion of Proposition Four, whether or not Kissinger was actually willing to carry through on a military confrontation with the Soviets in the Middle East is unknown, but the American actions certainly created that possibility. Soviet behavior suggests that they viewed the crisis as Chicken, and when the cost of exploitation was seen to be less than the cost of confrontation, they were willing to back down.

The dynamics of the relationship between the United States and the Soviet Union during the war suggest that the situation went from one of being a mutual Prisoner's Dilemma to one of Chicken as the perceptions on both sides were made more complete with additional information. The apparent Soviet defection in the eyes of the United States (intervening with troops for unilateral advantage), leading to the exploitative outcome, was countered by an American move toward mutual defection, that is, mutual troop intervention. What kept the two countries out of that situation is that the American move also changed the stakes. The American nuclear alert, and the implied nuclear confrontation, altered the relative balance in Soviet eyes of the cost of defection, that is, the cost of sending troops. In terms of the conventional balance between the United States and the Soviet Union in the region, and the Soviet ability to introduce troops on its own, John Scherer argues that the Soviets were in a strong position. Scherer argues that when the United States shifted the "terms of discussion" to a nuclear level, the Soviets were without an appropriate response and had to back down.[20] The game shifted from one of a Prisoner's Dilemma to one of Chicken when the threatened American response shifted the worst outcome for the Soviets to that involving an American-Soviet confrontation, rather than seeing Egyptian forces destroyed in the Sinai.

When it appeared to the Americans that the Soviet Union was trying to opt out of the relatively cooperative (at least not openly confrontational) stance that had existed between the two throughout the war, the United States saw a strong threat to its interests and acted rapidly to counter it. In the language of game theory the United States saw a "defection" coming and

---

19. Raymond L. Garthoff, quoting an unnamed "senior NSC official" notes that the United States did have contingency plans for the introduction of American troops. These troops were not "to resist by force" the introduction of Soviet troops, but rather they were to show matching U.S. determination and create the basis for quid pro quo withdrawals once the cease-fire had been reached. *Detente and Confrontation: American-Soviet Relations from Nixon to Reagan* (Washington, D.C.: Brookings, 1985), 376 n. 64.

20. John L. Scherer, "Soviet and American Behavior during the Yom Kippur War," *World Affairs* 141, no. 1 (Summer 1978): 17. Scherer suggests that Kissinger was fully aware that the Soviets had no "appropriate response to a nuclear alert" and therefore considered the American alert a safe gesture.

moved rapidly to head it off by increasing the cost of that defection. When the Soviets saw that the cost of a defection had increased, they chose not to defect. In terms of Proposition Five, when the nature of the confrontation changed from one of a Prisoner's Dilemma to one of Chicken, the crisis came to a resolution quickly.

The evidence also supports the corollary suggested for Proposition Five. Recall that it was suggested that when a situation is perceived as being one of Chicken, there will be a more intensive search for an alternative to mutual confrontation than if it had been seen as a Prisoner's Dilemma. When the American nuclear alert raised the stakes to a situation where continued mutual confrontation would lead to the worst outcome for the Soviet Union, all indications suggesting an airlift disappeared. The American attempt to raise the stakes, and make it appear that they were willing to "play" for those stakes, seems to have convinced the Soviets, and they backed down from their threat to send troops.

Berlin Wall Crisis

In order to assess the accuracy of Proposition Five, it will be helpful to outline the various outcomes that American leaders feared in Berlin. Unlike the discussion of the previous propositions, it makes little difference to the analysis if the crisis is broken up into the two different phases that have been used so far (4 June–13 August and 13 August–18 August). One of the reasons for this is that the construction of the Berlin Wall evoked no appreciable increase in the degree of concern felt by many of the most important decision makers in Washington. This has been mentioned previously, but it is now appropriate to go further into this matter.

As noted earlier, one of the most serious criticisms made of the handling of the Berlin Wall crisis by the Kennedy administration was that there was an insufficiently vigorous response to the wall. Many have commented that the Kennedy administration had in effect decided that it would not challenge the Soviets if they chose to move on East Berlin, and the initial State Department announcement about the crisis, with its emphasis on Western access to East Berlin, not the reverse, seems to suggest that there is some truth to this statement.[21] As discussed in chapter 3 in the consideration of Proposition One, the position put forth by the Kennedy administration after the two ultimatums on Germany (the letters to Konrad Adenauer in February and the

---

21. Honore M. Catudal, *Kennedy and the Berlin Wall Crisis: A Case Study in U.S. Decision Making* (Berlin: Berlin-Verlag, 1980), 251, arrives at this conclusion, as do Jean Edward Smith, *The Defense of Berlin* (Baltimore: Johns Hopkins University Press, 1963), 293–98, and Eleanor Lansing Dulles, *Berlin: The Wall Is Not Forever* (Chapel Hill: University of North Carolina Press, 1967), 61–65, who are much more critical than Catudal.

threats at the Vienna Summit) made clear that the United States was interested in protecting the status of West Berlin. This concern for the rights of West Berlin has been noted by those who are sympathetic to Kennedy. As Sorensen puts it:

> The President's first and most basic decision [following the clash at the Vienna Summit over Berlin] was that the preservation of Western rights in West Berlin was an objective for which the United States was required to incur any cost, including the risk of nuclear war.[22]

What is unclear is whether or not those in the Kennedy administration knew that they were in effect dooming East Berlin to Soviet control. Unlike the Truman administration eleven years before in its statement about the U.S. "defense perimeter" and Korea, the Kennedy administration did not respond strongly to a challenge in an area that they had seemed to say they would not defend.

The result of this ambiguity about how seriously the Kennedy administration viewed this crisis is that it becomes difficult to assess the accuracy of Proposition Five. It seems clear that the Kennedy administration felt that the worst outcome for the United States would be confrontation with the Soviets (possibly including nuclear war) over Berlin. This concern appears to have been felt by all those involved. What differed was their assessments of how likely it was that this outcome would be reached and what courses of action would increase that likelihood. The defense buildup measures that Kennedy had outlined in his 25 July speech were substantial and were aimed at showing the Soviets that the United States would not back down from its commitment to Germany and Berlin.[23] There was strong public support for this move as well as the announced intention to defend Western rights in Berlin. The *New York Times* opined in an editorial that it was "confident that the American people and free men everywhere will support" President Kennedy.[24] A series of Gallup Polls taken before and after the president's speech found strong support for defending Western rights in Berlin, even if it meant going to war. In a poll taken prior to President Kennedy's speech (23–28 June) over 76 percent of those who had heard of the dispute in Berlin (80 percent of those questioned had heard of the crisis) agreed that the United States should keep its troops in Berlin, along with the French and British, even at the risk of war.

---

22. Theodore C. Sorensen, *Kennedy* (New York: Harper and Row, 1965), 586.

23. Kennedy announced an additional $3.2 billion for defense expenditures in 1961 as well as an increase in the total number of armed forces by more than two hundred thousand men (bringing the total to one million). John F. Kennedy, *Public Papers of the Presidents of the United States: John F. Kennedy, 1961* (Washington, D.C.: GPO), 535–36.

24. *New York Times*, 26 July 1961.

A poll taken immediately before President Kennedy's speech (13–18 July) found over 70 percent supporting the suggestion that the United States and its allies should "try to fight their way into Berlin" if "Communist East Germany closes all roads to Berlin." The same question asked following the construction of the Berlin Wall found almost 65 percent agreeing that the United States should fight its way to Berlin![25]

At a general level, the greatest fear of American leaders was that a confrontation with the Soviets could lead to war, yet they were willing to argue that they would run that risk to protect Western rights in Berlin. This poses some problems, as the public position of the Kennedy administration suggests that the situation with respect to the general crisis over Berlin was seen as one of a Prisoner's Dilemma if the choices are defined as "defend Western rights in Berlin" or "sign a peace treaty with East Germany." When the same analysis is applied to the specific crisis over the wall, the perspective seems to change to that of Chicken. While the administration seemed willing to run large risks over Berlin in general, this same willingness did not apply to the construction of the wall. If the choices facing decision makers are defined as "accept the wall" or "challenge the wall," the perspective is that of Chicken because leaders felt that challenging the wall might lead to serious military conflict with the Soviets, something they did not want to do.

Thus, there is general support for Proposition Five although it is difficult to be definitive. The problem of separating the decision makers' concerns about the threat to Berlin in general from those about the threat to East Germany in particular limits our ability to be specific about Proposition Five. The discussion now turns to the final crisis to be considered.

Iranian Crisis of 1946

This crisis does not afford much of an opportunity to test Proposition Five. One of the key elements in this is that this crisis differs from the others considered here in that there was very little chance or opportunity for American and Soviet military forces to confront each other in or near Iran during this crisis. All American military forces had been removed from Iran, and there was no immediate capability for challenging the continued Soviet occupation of Iran. The reason for mentioning this is that much of the driving force behind Proposition Five is the difference in perceived costs of confrontation and exploitation. In most of the crises considered so far in this chapter, the costs of mutual confrontations are seen as military conflicts between the two sides, and those costs include the risk of nuclear war. As discussed, the

---

25. All polling data are from George H. Gallup, *The Gallup Poll: Public Opinion 1935– 1971*, vol. 3, 1959–1971 (New York: Random House, 1972), 1729, 1735.

military option did not exist in Iran, and this element seems to have been of little concern to American decision makers. While there were other areas that the United States could have chosen as arenas in which to confront the Soviet Union (Eastern Europe, the Far East), military conflict was not considered as an option. The costs of mutual confrontation were seen more in terms of American credibility with respect to pledges to smaller countries and the integrity of the new United Nations than in potential military confrontation. The main point here is that there did not appear to be any sense that this situation was becoming one of Chicken, that is, one in which continued confrontation would bring about the worst outcome. This crisis seems to have been one that can be seen as a Prisoner's Dilemma, where the worst thing that could happen would be to back down in the face of a challenge. The belief in Washington was that the worst things that could happen were for the United States not to push for the responsibility of the great powers to live up to agreements made with smaller powers and for the United Nations to be unable to resolve the first important issue to come before it. Thus, it is difficult to test Proposition Five because there was no apparent change in perceptions on the part of decision makers in Washington about the relative costs of confrontation and capitulation. In the other cases, there were changes in the perceptions of the relative balance between confrontation and capitulation, and these provided a more fertile ground for testing this proposition.

Conclusion

Proposition Five assumes that the choice facing decision makers in a crisis can be framed as a rather narrow one: resist the demands of an opponent or give in to that opponent's demands. This proposition takes note of the fact that under some circumstances the costs of resisting the challenge (assuming that the opponent does not cease the challenge) are greater than the costs of giving in while in others the situation is reversed. Proposition Five simply suggests that when decision makers see the costs of challenging the opponent as greater than the costs of giving in, there will be a more significant effort made to end the crisis than when the costs of giving in are greater.

Turning to the cases, there was generally strong support for Proposition Five. Three of the cases (the Berlin blockade, Cuban Missile Crisis, and October 1973 Middle East War) gave strong support to Proposition Five while the Berlin Wall crisis gave limited support and the Iranian crisis was difficult to test. The lack of support in the Iranian crisis raises some interesting questions that are worth considering. In Chicken, mutual conflict is the worst outcome. In a Prisoner's Dilemma, giving in (exploitation) is the worst outcome. In the Iranian case, it does not appear that American leaders ever saw mutual confrontation as being the worst outcome. It seems that the crisis was seen as a Prisoner's Dilemma, where the worst thing that could happen was not to challenge the Soviet moves. In the four crises that provide (in varying degrees) support for Proposition Five, American decision makers at one point or another saw mutual conflict as being the worst outcome. Why? The reason appears to be the risk of military conflict. When American leaders felt that there was a risk of military conflict with the Soviet Union during one of these crises, they appeared to feel a greater sense of urgency and seemed to work harder to avoid that outcome. This raises an interesting question: does Proposition Five apply in situations where there is no serious potential for significant military conflict? One is left to wonder if the situations in which the costs of mutual conflict are seen to be greater than the costs of having to give in to an opponent require the potential for significant conflict. In looking at the United States and the Soviet Union in these post–World War II crises, it was only those crises with the potential for nuclear conflict, or outright conventional conflict, in which the type of behavior expected in Proposition Five was seen. This suggests that a possible limitation of this proposition is that it only applies to situations where an adversary is of similar military strength or possesses nuclear weapons. This issue will be taken up in greater detail in the concluding chapter.

CHAPTER 8

Conclusions

This study started out with a rather simple question: What happens when parties to a dispute see the world in different ways? Surrounding that particular question were a number of related ones. Would having different views make disputes more or less likely to occur? Would having different views make disputes easier to resolve or more difficult to resolve? What would it take for the parties to a dispute to come to look at the world in the same way? What were the mechanisms of change in the views of those involved in the dispute? All of these questions are related on a number of different dimensions, and answering them will help further our understanding of crisis behavior. As noted in chapter 1, the literature on crises is extensive, and one should be wary of adding even more. The strength of this study is its explicit consideration of different types of misperception and the impact that these different types of misperception can have on crises. The concepts of *situational* and *dispositional misperceptions* have been developed and connected to a model of crisis decision making. This model was applied to five case studies of U.S.-Soviet crises in the post–World War II era, and general support was found, although there are clearly instances where the theory and the model need to be adjusted.

Before looking specifically at the propositions and the case studies to see how well they fared, a few general comments are appropriate. In reviewing the progress of this study, there are three significant findings. Two of these findings are of theoretical importance, and the third is of substantive importance to the policy process. The first of the theoretical results is that there are important gains that can be made in our understanding of foreign policy decision making that come from differentiating between types of misperception based on the sources of the misperception. The second finding of theoretical interest is an affirmation of the important role that perceptions do play in crisis behavior. There is a strong crisis dynamic that is fueled by perceptions and changes in those perceptions. The source of change is new information that is provided to decision makers. This finding is of interest because it suggests that even removing all barriers to understanding the nature and actions of an opponent will be insufficient to prevent crises, for factors such as conflict of interests or conflict of goals will still lead to crises.

The finding with implications for the policy process is that it does make a difference when decision makers continue to be provided with new information about the situation at hand. Previous studies suggest that making extra efforts to provide decision makers with additional information about an opponent would be unlikely to change the leader's mind because misperceptions, once held, are hard to change. What has been shown here is that this need not be the case. Misperceptions can be changed, and one of the ways in which they can be changed is for more information to be made available to the decision maker. The most important element here is that this change is more likely to occur if the misperceptions are situational misperceptions rather than dispositional misperceptions.

This conclusion will do four things: review the five propositions advanced in chapters 3 through 7, review the evidence found to support them, draw some conclusions about what has, and has not, been learned from this analysis, and discuss some of the theoretical and methodological difficulties encountered. In this way, this conclusion will serve substantive ends, by reviewing what has been learned from this effort, and heuristic ends, by reviewing the way these lessons were learned and what might be done in the future to further our understanding of misperception and crisis. Let us now turn to a review of the propositions and the evidence to support them.

Propositions and Evidence

Table 1 shows how the propositions fared against the evidence from the five case studies. In general, the evidence supported the propositions, but there are some exceptions that should be discussed.

> *Proposition One*: Actors will tend to assume that their opponent(s) see the world in the same way as they themselves see it, and see their acts, motives, and preferences as they intend them to be seen.

This proposition has an intuitive appeal as it seems to capture an element of interstate relations. It is similar to one of Jervis's hypotheses on misperception that deals with the way decision makers will see others.[1] Jervis's hypothesis reads "[W]hen actors have intentions that they do not try to conceal from others they tend to assume that others accurately perceive those intentions." Interestingly enough, it turned out to be very difficult to find direct proof in the case studies to support Proposition One. There were very few instances of decision makers claiming that an opponent had misunderstood them or claim-

---

1. Robert Jervis, "Hypotheses on Misperception," *World Politics* 20, no. 3 (April 1968): 476.

TABLE 1. Propositions and Evidence

| | Evidence | | | | |
Proposition	Iran	Blockade	Berlin Wall	Cuban Missile	Oct. 1973 War
One	No support	Limited support	Limited support	Supported	Supported
Two	Limited support	Supported	Limited support	Supported	Supported
Three	Limited support	Limited support	Limited support	Limited support	Limited support
Four	Supported	Supported	Supported	Supported	Supported
Five	No support	Supported	Limited support	Supported	Supported

Proposition One: Actors will tend to assume that their opponent(s) see the world in the same way as they themselves see it, and see their acts, motives, and preferences as they intend them to be seen.

Proposition Two: Decision makers will tend to see crises as the result of deliberate actions by their opponents in pursuit of outcomes beneficial to the opponent and detrimental to themselves.

Proposition Three: Crises that are unintended by either side will be found to be the result of misperceptions, which will frequently be situational.

Proposition Four: A crisis will continue until perceptions on both sides of the dispute match.

Proposition Five: Crises perceived as Prisoner's Dilemmas will tend to be of longer duration than those perceived as Chicken.

ing that there should have been no misunderstanding because things were so clear. The best example of when this did occur was during the Cuban Missile Crisis. Many have reported that the decision makers felt that they had been absolutely clear that the introduction of offensive weapons into Cuba would be unacceptable. In this case, all were shocked when the Soviet Union did just that, as they were convinced that they had made their position quite clear. One reason for this is that it seems that the assumption attributed to decision makers in Proposition One is true. States appear to be able to communicate their interests, intentions, and actions to their opponents clearly and on a regular basis. One of the implicit assumptions of Proposition One that probably needs to be revised is that there is a great deal of misunderstanding and confusion in the making and carrying out of foreign policy. Contrary to this assumption, it seems that states are able to be clear and convey what they wish to convey more often than some might imagine.

In retrospect, this result should not be seen as so surprising. States are always going to find themselves in conflict with others, despite the best efforts of leaders to avoid crises. There will simply be circumstances in which leaders will not be able to overcome their differences—even when they understand each other perfectly. In retrospect, one is struck by the almost absurd lengths to which the United States and its coalition partners went to communicate to Saddam Hussein their desire that Iraqi forces leave Kuwait. It was almost as if these leaders thought that "if we tell him just one more time" he would finally understand and leave Kuwait. As Iraqi Foreign Minister Aziz made clear after the last-minute meeting between him and U.S. Secretary of State Baker a week before the start of the air campaign, the Iraqis understood full well what the Americans and others were telling them, but they still were not going to leave Kuwait.

What accounts for the poor performance of Proposition One is the lack of emphasis given in chapter 3 to the basic fact that states will continue to find themselves in conflict—in spite of the best interests of leaders to communicate with each other. This was particularly true in the Iranian crisis and the Berlin Wall crisis, where the Soviets apparently felt that they had interests that needed to be protected and they acted to protect them, probably knowing that a confrontation with the United States was likely.

A second element that is reinforced by the case studies is that crises do not come about just because of misperceptions or clashing interests. They can also come about because one state feels that there is something to be gained by provoking a crisis. Deliberate crises, such as the Berlin blockade, the Cuban Missile Crisis, and possibly the October 1973 War are all examples of a state (in these cases, the Soviet Union) hoping to take advantage of a particular situation, knowing that a crisis is likely to ensue. This is consistent with the discussion of Lebow's spinoff crises that was presented in chapter 1. Finally, there were brinkmanship crises. These crises will come about because of a perceived difference in power that one state feels that it can exploit. In each of these situations, a crisis can come about with or without misperceptions.

Returning to the discussion of those cases to which Proposition One applies, the two clearest instances are the Cuban Missile Crisis and the October 1973 Middle East War. In both of these cases, American leaders believed that they had been clear about what would and would not be tolerated, and they believed that the Soviets had understood them. As noted in the discussion of the Cuban Missile Crisis, President Kennedy expressed puzzlement and outrage over Soviet behavior because he felt that he had been very clear about the intolerable nature of missiles in Cuba. During the October 1973 War, Kissinger believed quite strongly that the United States had made it very clear that it would not tolerate the introduction of Soviet troops into the Middle East. In none of the other cases were there such clearly stated beliefs that the Soviets must have understood what the United States was saying or doing.

Because of the lack of direct evidence in the other crises, one is almost left with having to argue that decision makers in these crises acted "as if" Proposition One were true. That type of argument would be that decision makers act under the assumption that what they are doing is clear and that their actions will be perceived in the way they wish them to be perceived. Considering how few crises there seem to be in the world, there is perhaps some truth to this suggestion.

There was very little evidence to suggest that leaders made it a practice to ask what type of impression their moves might be conveying. Rarely did decision makers argue that what they were doing was likely to be ambiguous or unclear and that, as a result, additional measures should be taken to ensure clarity. The only evidence of this type of behavior came during periods of high tension where there was a (perceived) risk of military confrontation. During the Berlin blockade, there were efforts made to ensure that the Soviets did not get an incorrect impression of American intentions. Previous practices, such as allowing Soviet representatives to walk through west-bound trains, were allowed to continue, and no significant departures from established routines were allowed. The concern was that the Soviet Union would see any departures from past behavior as being indicative of new attitudes or intentions. During the Cuban Missile Crisis, there were efforts to try to see events from the perspective of the Soviet Union and make sure that American actions were seen in the manner in which they were intended to be seen (such as the sending of SAC messages in the clear). Other than these few incidents, there was no evidence that would suggest that decision makers did not assume their messages were clear.

There is another possible explanation for this lack of evidence: it just might be the case that the measures used here were insufficient for the task. It might be the case that decision makers are so sure that what they are doing is clear to the other side that they do not even think in those terms. As a result, in trying to understand what others are doing, they do not think that a possible explanation might be a lack of clarity in their actions. Because clarity of intentions is such an influential part of decision makers' views of the world, they might not be inclined to look to this as a possible explanation of events. Admittedly, this is just speculation that would be very difficult to prove, but it does suggest a possible explanation for the lack of evidence for Proposition One.

One hypothesis that suggests itself from the evidence of these case studies as they relate to Proposition One is:

> The higher the perceived stakes attached to a particular set of actions or events, the more likely it is that decision makers will feel that there is a chance that the opponent will misinterpret actions and motives.

During times when there were fears of conflict, American leaders seem to have been concerned about the possibility that what they thought would be clear to the other side would not be clear. One of the frequent reasons given for rejecting General Clay's proposals to use military forces (not necessarily military force) to challenge the Berlin blockade was the fear that such a move would be misunderstood by the Soviet Union as being the first step in a military conflict. In his account of the Cuban Missile Crisis, Robert Kennedy notes that the question of how acts would appear to the other side was given a great deal of attention, particularly when the first intercepts of ships crossing the blockade line were made. Finally, efforts made to cross the barrier set up by the East Germans in Berlin were always carefully considered, with an eye toward how the Soviets would view events.[2] These actions were not explicitly covered in chapter 2.

> *Proposition Two*: Decision makers will tend to see crises as the result of deliberate actions by their opponents in pursuit of outcomes beneficial to the opponent and detrimental to themselves.

The evidence provided by these case studies for Proposition Two is more supportive than that found for Proposition One. The general assumption on the part of American leaders seems to have been that if an action was causing them problems and the other side was doing it, then the opponent must be doing it for just that reason.[3] In general, U.S. decision makers seemed to believe that opponents knew that their actions were going to cause problems for the United States and that was the reason for their actions. This sentiment was particularly clear in the Berlin blockade, Cuban Missile Crisis, and the October 1973 Middle East War. American leaders were very firm in their beliefs about Soviet culpability and deliberateness in these crises. There almost seems to have been a reverse application of Proposition One: decision makers assumed that the Soviets knew what they (the Soviets) were doing and, if what they were doing was detrimental to American interests, then it must have been because that is what the Soviets wanted. This suggestion is similar to one of Jervis's hypotheses, which is "[A]ctors tend to see the behavior of others as more centralized, disciplined, and coordinated than it is."[4] This type of behavior seemed to occur frequently in the cases studied here.

There were two partial exceptions to Proposition Two found in these case studies. The first was in the Iranian Crisis of 1946. One of the uncertainties that contributed to the feeling of crisis on the part of American leaders concerned Soviet motives: Why were the Soviets taking these actions and how far did they intend to go? Were Soviet actions aimed at gaining influence at the

---

2. General Albert Watson (Berlin Garrison commander) and General Clay (Kennedy's personal emissary to Berlin) each ordered that a number of actions be taken to emphasize the point that the Soviets and East Germans could not restrict the access of Western military personnel to East Berlin. These included sending armed military convoys through various checkpoints and armed military escorts for civilian officials with the right to enter East Berlin. See Jean Edward Smith, *The Defense of Berlin* (Baltimore: Johns Hopkins University Press, 1963), 309–24. See also Norman Gelb, *The Berlin Wall* (New York: New York Times–Quadrangle, 1986), 232–44.

3. This is true with respect to the Soviets as well, but with much less information available about their deliberations in these crises, one cannot be as definitive in making such claims.

4. Jervis, "Hypotheses on Misperception," 474.

expense of Western interests, or were the Soviets simply acting to protect what they felt were their own interests? The long history of Soviet involvement in the region had been noted frequently in the State Department's reviews of events, and there were many in and out of the government who argued that, for this reason, the United States should not get involved. In addition, many suggested that the problems in Iran were part of a dispute between the United Kingdom and the Soviet Union in an area of traditional rivalry and that the United States should not get involved in this great power rivalry. A final point made by some who argued that the United States need not get involved was that the Soviet Union did have legitimate concerns about the security of its southern regions along the Iranian border. These factors served to keep some from immediately concluding that Soviet moves were designed to hurt the United States.

This same confusion about what constituted legitimate concerns (or at least understandable concerns) was also found in the Berlin Wall crisis. There were those who recognized that the mass exodus of refugees from East Germany to West Berlin was placing a tremendous political and economic burden on the East German regime and, indirectly, on the Soviet Union. The political burden was the embarrassment faced by the regime at having so many of its citizens want to flee the country, while the economic burden was the impact on the economy of having so many skilled people out of the work force. Many in the administration fully expected the Soviet Union (through East Germany) to take some sort of action to limit the flow of the refugees. The result of this was that many were not willing to believe that the Soviet actions on the refugee issue were designed to create problems for the United States or that the crisis was a deliberate creation by the Soviets. On the question of the Soviet demands for a peace treaty with East Germany, there was total agreement that the Soviet Union was attempting to create problems for the United States and the other Western powers that would benefit the Soviet Union. There was strong support to resist Soviet efforts to put pressure on the United States and West Germany on the issue of a peace treaty, but this support did not always carry over to resisting the construction of the wall.

These examples fit Lebow's description of spinoff crises that was discussed in chapter 5. They also suggest a possible limitation on the application of Proposition Two: Proposition Two might be less useful in describing behavior during spinoff crises. It is certainly true that American officials felt the Iranian and Berlin Wall situations were crises, but as compared with their views toward the other crises considered here, they were not as eager to assume that they were the result of deliberate actions on the part of the Soviet Union vis-à-vis the United States.

Proposition Three: Crises that are unintended by either side will be found to be the result of misperceptions, which will frequently be situational.

It is worth repeating the definition of situational and dispositional misperceptions presented in chapter 1. Situational misperceptions involve situations where an actor's perception of reality is plausible based on the information available, yet that perception about reality turns out to be incorrect. The implicit assumption here is that other actors in the same situation, faced with the same information, would be very likely to come to the same (incorrect) conclusion. It is the information available that drives the actor toward a particular conclusion, and changes in the information will lead to changes in the conclusions. Only when more information about the nature of what is being observed is provided can the individual conclude with confidence that what is being interpreted is not correct.

Dispositional misperceptions come from an actor's internal predisposition to see the world in a certain way or process certain types of information in a particular way. Here the assumption is that other actors, viewing the same information, would be less likely to arrive at the same conclusions. In cases involving this type of misperception, more information is unlikely to affect the actor's view of what is happening.

A complicating factor in attempting to assess Proposition Three was that most of the crises, expected or unexpected, that the United States found itself in were the result, on the American side, of dispositional elements. The argument laid out in chapter 5 suggesting that dispositional misperceptions would be unlikely to lead to a crisis was simply wrong. Dispositional misperceptions, like situational misperceptions, were found to be likely to contribute to crises. Clearly, some rethinking needs to be done of the relative contributions of dispositional and situational misperceptions to crises.

On the Soviet side it appears that these crises were frequently the result of situational elements. The discussion of Proposition Three in chapter 5 envisioned situations in which states would find themselves in crises that neither side intended because of misperceptions or misunderstandings. Ambiguous or conflicting information about the actions of an opponent would contribute to a sense of crisis that would end when information became available that suggested that there was no need for concern. The expectation was that the misperceptions involved would be situational because of the impact of ambiguous or misleading information. Things turned out not to have been that simple.

From the American side, all of these crises were unintended, and with the partial exception of the Berlin Wall crisis and the October 1973 War, they were also unexpected.[5] The problem here is that these crises were not unin-

---

5. Recall that American leaders expected the Soviets to do something about the refugee crisis; they just were not sure what. Kissinger fully expected trouble from the Soviets if the cease-fire did not hold; he was just unsure what form it would take.

tended in the way this term was discussed in chapter 1: none of these crises involved actions taken by the United States that it felt would be uncontroversial, only to find itself in a crisis. Rather, all of these crises involved actions taken by the Soviet Union that eventually caused American leaders to feel that they were in a crisis situation. American leaders did not expect the Soviets to act in certain ways in certain situations. In this sense these crises were unexpected. In each of these crises, on the American side, dispositional factors seem to have played a large role. In Iran, many in the United States did not want to believe that the cooperation and harmony that existed during World War II was over nor that the Soviet Union was actually acting in a manner detrimental to the United States. In the Berlin blockade crisis, many of those in Washington did not feel that the Soviets were going to take action against Berlin. As noted, the Berlin Wall crisis was not a surprise but the wall was. During the Cuban Missile Crisis, the evidence strongly suggests that many simply chose not to believe that the Soviets would put missiles into Cuba—a clear case of dispositional factors playing a significant role. Finally, during the October 1973 War, American leaders felt that they had been very clear with respect to the undesirability of the Soviets sending troops to the Middle East and were surprised when it appeared that the Soviets were doing just that.

There is also evidence that situational factors played significant roles in these cases. Situational factors clearly played a role during the Iranian crisis and the October 1973 Middle East War. In both of these cases military moves on the part of the Soviet Union were ambiguous enough to cause concern in the United States. The evidence in both suggested strong military actions that the United States would be opposed to, and until information became available that suggested that there was no threat, the crises went on.

Looking at these crises from the perspective of the Soviet Union, the picture is more complicated and harder to assess. Strong arguments can be made in favor of both situational and dispositional elements in explaining Soviet behavior. The Iranian crisis, the Berlin Wall, and the October 1973 Middle East War were all spinoff crises as far as the United States was concerned (that is, the crises resulted from Soviet actions that were not aimed directly at American interests). From the Soviet perspective it seems that for many of these crises, the Soviets underestimated the strength of an American response. Strong arguments can be made that the Soviets interpreted American statements prior to the Berlin blockade and the Berlin Wall as meaning that there were certain types of actions that the United States would not oppose. In the Berlin blockade, the lack of any strong American response to the many restrictions imposed by the Soviets in the months leading up to the complete blockade might have suggested that the Americans would not respond to further steps. The emphasis prior to the Berlin Wall on the protection of Western rights in West Berlin and the emphasis on Western access to Berlin might have suggested to the Soviets that they could avoid a crisis if they acted carefully and did not infringe on any of these rights. The problem with this line of argument, as will be discussed further, is that it is hard to know exactly what the Soviets were thinking.

Thus, the assessment of Proposition Three is generally favorable, but there are some issues that would need to be addressed before taking it any further. These issues concern the nature of an unexpected crisis as compared with an unintended crisis, as well as the operational differences between situational and dispositional misperceptions.

> *Proposition Four*: A crisis will continue until perceptions on both sides of the dispute match.

Proposition Four, while the most simply stated of the five propositions, is the most complex. Simply put, the concept behind Proposition Four is this: disputes generally end when both sides agree on a given outcome. The agreement need not be the result of discussions or negotiations; it may simply be that both sides act in a manner that would be expected if there was such an agreement. This argument is similar to that made by Blainey, discussed in chapter 6, who argues that wars end when there is agreement about the distribution of power between two disputants. In other words, both parties agree on who is the stronger party and who is the weaker party, and the war is over. This does not mean that there is any objective truth to the matter—only that the beliefs allow for an end to the war. The same image can be used to understand the end of crises. A crisis will end when both parties agree on who will back down or when one party is able to convince the other that there is no reason to believe there is a crisis. The crisis that opened our discussion in chapter 1 (the Cuban "brigade" crisis) came to an end when American leaders who had believed there was a crisis concluded, on the basis of further information, that there was indeed no need to feel there was one. The agreement in this instance was between the Soviet assertion that those troops did not pose a threat and the eventual American belief of that claim. A few illustrations from the case studies will help to clarify this point.

During the October 1973 Middle East War, the crisis was caused (from the American point of view) by intelligence information that suggested the Soviet Union was about to send troops to the Middle East. When more information became available to suggest that the Soviets were not sending troops, the crisis came to an end. The agreement here was that the Soviets understood that the United States was indeed serious in its opposition to Soviet troops and that there was every reason to believe American statements that it would use force to keep those troops out of the Middle East. As a result of this understanding, the Soviets did not send troops, and when the Americans realized this, the crisis came to an end.

A second way for a crisis to end is for one side to convince the other that the costs of continuing the crisis are too high. It may be the initiator of the crisis who is able to convince the target that giving in to the initiator's demands will be less costly than resisting them, or it may be the target who is able to convince the initiator that the cost of getting concessions out of the target is too high. There were no direct examples of the first type of ending (the initiator having its demands met) found in these case studies. The closest example was in the Berlin Wall crisis, where the Soviets were able to carry out their moves (blocking exits from East Berlin and East Germany) in such a way that challenging them would have been very costly for the United States. As Bundy notes, no one was willing to argue that Berlin was worth nuclear war.[6] In essence, the cost of resistance for the United States was very high.

The Berlin blockade, the Cuban Missile Crisis, and the October 1973 War all fit into the second type of situation, where the target is able to put up a stiff enough resistance to convince the initiator (the Soviet Union) to back off. In each case, the American response (or threatened response) appears to have raised the cost of continuing the crisis too high for the Soviets to continue to push their demands. In the Berlin blockade, the American ability to supply Berlin without directly challenging the blockade forced the Soviets to choose between further escalation of the crisis or retreating. In the Cuban Missile Crisis and the October 1973 War, the threatened American military actions raised the cost to the Soviets of continuing their military actions.

Overall, each case had elements that supported the view of crisis termination suggested by Proposition Four. A crisis will end when there is some degree of convergence on the part of the perceptions of the parties. That convergence will be to a point where the resolution to the crisis can occur, whether it be the realization that there is no crisis at all or the realization that the crisis is becoming very dangerous very quickly.

Proposition Five: Crises perceived as Prisoner's Dilemmas will tend to be of longer duration than those perceived as Chicken.

Proposition Five rests on a simple assumption about behavior: the more costly a certain course of action is likely to be, the greater the effort will be to avoid that course of action or the greater the effort will be to reduce the cost. The reasoning behind Proposition Five was prompted by an observation about

---

6. McGeorge Bundy, *Danger and Survival: Choices about the Bomb in the First Fifty Years* (New York: Random House, 1988), 368–69.

interstate relations: most conflicts seem to contain some aspects of a Prisoner's Dilemma. The central element in a Prisoner's Dilemma is that both parties, acting in their own self-interest, will end up in a situation that is worse for them than if they had cooperated. The contrast between a Prisoner's Dilemma and Chicken is that the relative costs of continued confrontation and exploitation are seen to be different. In a Prisoner's Dilemma, exploitation is the worst outcome while in Chicken confrontation is seen as the worst outcome. Thus, if we think of a crisis as being mutual confrontation or noncooperation, then the expectation is that a state will work harder to end the crisis when mutual confrontation is the worst outcome than when exploitation (giving in to or not opposing the other's demands) is the worst outcome.

Turning to the cases, there was generally strong support for Proposition Five. Three of the cases (the Berlin blockade, Cuban Missile Crisis, and October 1973 Middle East War) gave strong support to Proposition Five while the Berlin Wall crisis gave limited support and the Iranian crisis was difficult to test. The lack of support in the Iranian crisis raises some interesting questions that are worth considering. In Chicken, mutual conflict is the worst outcome. In a Prisoner's Dilemma, giving in (exploitation) is the worst outcome. In the Iranian case, it does not appear that American leaders ever saw mutual confrontation as being the worst outcome. It seems that the crisis was seen as a Prisoner's Dilemma, where the worst thing that could happen was not to challenge the Soviet moves. In the four crises that provide (in varying degrees) support for Proposition Five, American decision makers at one point or another saw mutual conflict as being the worst outcome. Why? The reason appears to be the risk of military conflict. When American leaders felt that there was a risk of military conflict with the Soviet Union during one of these crises, they appeared to feel a greater sense of urgency and seemed to work harder to avoid that outcome.

There is one interesting aspect of this discussion: during the October 1973 Middle East War, the United States tried to create a situation of Chicken for the Soviets by raising the stakes of mutual conflict from diplomatic squabbling over influence in the Middle East to the possibility of nuclear war. The nuclear alert ordered by Nixon and Kissinger seemed to convince the Soviets of the seriousness of the American response and, at the same time, raise the stakes of the confrontation to a more serious level. This was a clear attempt to alter the payoffs in the crisis so that the opponent would alter its course of action. This type of behavior was also seen in the Cuban Missile Crisis when American military preparations significantly raised the potential cost to the Soviets of not removing their missiles from Cuba. Again there was an attempt to alter the opponent's perception of the relative values of the payoffs. In both of these examples, nuclear weapons and the fear of nuclear war were the driving forces behind these changes in perceived costs.

One way to think about these cases, with an eye to further understanding of crises, is to consider the nuclear dimension. For three of the five crises studied here (the Berlin Wall, Cuban Missile Crisis, and October 1973 War) the United States and the Soviet Union were in a position of being able to threaten each other with massive destruction if the crises got out of hand. The discussion of Proposition Five suggested that the fear of nuclear war acted to bring crises to a rapid resolution because of the tremendous costs that would be incurred if the crises got out of hand. It would be instructive to ask if there was a difference when this fear did not exist. An argument that is frequently made is that nuclear weapons have made a qualitative difference in the ways that states must think about, and interact with, each other. It is much more difficult to pose a threat to national survival without nuclear weapons than with them, and it would be interesting to know if nuclear crises are different than nonnuclear crises.

This discussion points to an important problem that arose in the course of this research—assessing the perceptions of decision makers. This was both an empirical and theoretical problem, and it is to a discussion of this we now turn.

Problems

There were three important problems encountered in the course of the re-search for this study, two theoretical and one empirical. Let us discuss the empirical problem first because it affects the theoretical problems as well.

The most difficult task encountered in doing this research was getting sufficient data to test the propositions. The particular type of data that was difficult to find was that which would have allowed an accurate assessment or characterization of the perceptions of decision makers. It was frequently difficult to locate data that would show how decision makers perceived events and valued various outcomes. Even though for some cases very detailed information was available (e.g., the Berlin blockade and particularly the Cuban Missile Crisis), it was nevertheless difficult at times to characterize the views of decision makers.

The solution to this problem is not obvious. Some of the secondary sources used for these case studies made use of extensive archival research, transcripts of meetings, and personal interviews with the participants. These types of sources are about as close as one can get to actually being there, and yet there were still gaps that could not be filled. While the difficulties of "getting into the decision maker's head" are great, it is still necessary to make the attempt, for it is in "their heads" that crises do truly occur, and it is their perceptions that we must understand.

The first of the two theoretical problems encountered is related to the empirical problems just discussed: how to determine if a misperception is situational or dispositional. The theoretical underpinnings of the two concepts are strong, and the research undertaken here has not suggested the need to modify the conceptual basis of the theory. The empirical efforts to verify the existence and operation of these two concepts did run into problems. The type of data needed to determine situational or dispositional misperceptions is clear, but getting it was another problem.

The second theoretical problem encountered related to the concept of unintended crises. As mentioned above in the review of Proposition Three, the idea of an unintended crisis was to capture those types of situations in which a state takes actions that it believes to be unobjectionable, only to find that another state takes great exception to them, thus provoking a crisis. The crisis is unexpected from the first state's point of view, but it comes about because of something that state did. Interestingly enough, none of the evidence from the cases suggests that the United States found itself in these crises because of this type of behavior. It seems that the Soviets found themselves in crises of this type but not the United States. The United States did find itself in crises that were unintended, in the sense of being unexpected, but they were not the result of actions that the United States took. What frequently happened was that American leaders (for various reasons) believed that the Soviets would not do something, only to find out that they were wrong.

One possible objection to these findings is that the Soviets appear to take the blame for these crises while the United States is seen as simply reacting to Soviet actions. There are two answers to this criticism. The first is that a very strong argument can be made that in these crises the United States was responding to Soviet moves, some of which were deliberately designed to create a crisis (the Berlin blockade, the Cuban Missile Crisis, and possibly the October 1973 War) while others were moves that the Soviets took for reasons of their own and not solely to provoke a crisis (the Iranian and Berlin Wall crises). Soviet claims that their moves in the Berlin Wall crisis and the Cuban Missile Crisis were defensive moves against Western or American aggression lack credibility.

The second answer is that it is very difficult to tell when the Soviets feel they are in a crisis or when they feel that American moves are threatening to them. As mentioned in chapter 7, there is no evidence that the Soviet Union has ever put its nuclear forces on alert while the United States did so in two of these crises. Another factor is that Soviet government officials are not in the habit of writing memoirs recounting their views of American actions nor is the Soviet press active in reporting governmental deliberations. One can only hope that the openness of glasnost will continue into the post-Soviet Union era, allowing scholars further access to historical materials from the Soviet era.

What Has Been Learned

The theoretical core of this study rests on two related notions: first, the idea that perceptions of events or actions do change as information about these factors changes and, second, that the degree of change is affected by the source of the perception (or misperception). These two ideas underlie the development and refinement of the five propositions considered here. The propositions advanced relate to those factors that give rise to misperceptions and the impact that these misperceptions can have on the course of a crisis. The testing of these propositions against the case studies suggested some ways in which the two core ideas can be modified, as well as areas in which the suggested propositions do not accurately capture reality.

As discussed, there were three important theoretical findings here. The first was that there are gains in our understanding that can come from modifying the concept of misperception to take into account the source of the misperception. The major thrust behind this concept was the belief that there are indeed different kinds of misperceptions. Previous work on misperceptions had done little to make any sort of distinction between different types of misperceptions, and it was to this end that a large part of the theoretical development of this study was devoted. It seemed logical that misperceptions that were derived from incoming information would be likely to change when that information changed. It also seemed likely that misperceptions that were driven by an actor's particular way of viewing events or actors would only be likely to change when those attitudes changed, not when information about those events or actors changed. This conception of misperception has important implications for the ways scholars look at failures in foreign policy and their arguments about the ways the foreign policy process should be altered to work better.

Situational misperceptions can cause foreign policy and intelligence failures even when the decision makers involved are free of the types of biases and distortions that would lead to dispositional misperceptions. If the information reaching decision makers is fragmentary, or even wrong, the process can still result in failure even if the decision makers involved are free of bias. In this sense, the system can still fail the decision makers. A finding that situational misperceptions contributed to a crisis or foreign policy failure suggests that one needs to look more closely at the process generating the information that failed the decision maker.

Dispositional misperceptions can also cause problems in foreign policy, but the root of those problems will be found within the decision maker. A finding that dispositional misperceptions have contributed to a crisis or foreign policy failure suggests that one needs to look at the actors involved and assess the ways in which they handled the information available. The system and people that generate information for decision makers can work perfectly, but if there are dispositional factors at work, there can still be problems. In such cases, the decision makers fail the system by misusing accurate information that they are given. There is more that can be developed from this first theoretical contribution. Being aware of the difference between situational and dispositional misperceptions can help scholars and analysts refine their explanations of foreign policy behavior and events.

The second finding of theoretical interest was that there is indeed a dynamic to crises that can be traced to, among other things, changes in information flows. The course of crises, and the ways in which decision makers think about crises, will be affected by the ways in which information moves through the decision-making process. It was possible to see in the records of these cases the ways in which perceptions changed when the information available changed. This suggests that one has to consider not just what states do, but when that information becomes available to the other parties. It is interesting to speculate on what impact the increase in speed of information flows, coming from improvements in information technology, will have on foreign policy and crisis behavior. In figure 2, chapter 6, the diagram of information flows and perception change, one wonders what the impact will be of having the outputs of one state's decision-making process (e.g., actions or statements in response to those of another state) becoming inputs into the other state's decision-making process at an ever-faster rate. It could be the case that crises might accelerate or decelerate at a more rapid pace because of the speed at which information moves through the foreign policy decision-making system.

The third finding of theoretical interest was that there can be crises even when there is full information and no misperceptions. This is not to say that no one has ever recognized this possibility before. Rather, it is to say that the importance of misperception in crisis behavior should not be overemphasized. Crisis prevention should not focus solely on removing obstacles to information flows and accurate perceptions: it should also pay attention to the underlying interests and goals of the states involved. Focus should not simply be on the process elements of crises but also on "condition." Stripping away all of the rhetoric and propaganda between the Bush administration and the Iraqi government was unlikely to prevent the Persian Gulf War. Both parties had goals and interests that inevitably brought them into conflict. All of this suggests that there might need to be a shift away from focusing on misperception as the cause of crises and a move toward a greater focus on the underlying goals and interests of states.

There is room to expand on the research presented so far. There is no reason to think that the results would not be similarly productive and useful, providing further validation of the concepts of situational and dispositional misperception. This book has shown the usefulness of combining insights from both the political and psychological literatures. Strong support was found for the model of information flow and perception change that was outlined in chapter 1. This discussion ends on a positive and cautious note. The information presented herein suggests that certain misperceptions can be corrected within the decision-making process by the provision of more information about the actions and intentions of an opponent. This implies that misperceptions are not an insoluble problem in interstate relations. The note of caution is that misperceptions are not the only cause of problems. The findings presented here also point to the importance of considering the role of conflicts of interest in interstate relations when trying to account for interstate crises. Simply providing for obstacle- and value-free flows of information will be insufficient to prevent crises. A heightened awareness of the interests of other states, and the ways in which a state's interest might conflict with them, will also be necessary.

Bibliography

Abel, Elie. *The Missile Crisis*. New York: Bantam, 1968.

Acheson, Dean. *Present at the Creation: My Years in the State Department*. New York: W. W. Norton, 1969.

———. "Dean Acheson's Version of Robert Kennedy's Version of the Cuban Missile Affair." *Esquire* 71 (February 1969). Reprinted in *The Cuban Missile Crisis*, ed. Robert A. Divine, 196–207. Chicago: Quadrangle, 1971.

Allison, Graham T. *Essence of Decision: Explaining the Cuban Missile Crisis*. Boston: Little, Brown and Company, 1971.

AlRoy, Gil Carl. *The Kissinger Experience: American Policy in the Middle East*. New York: Horizon Press, 1975.

Anderson, John R. *Cognitive Psychology and Its Implications*. San Francisco: W. H. Freeman, 1980.

Anderson, Terry H. *The United States, Great Britain, and the Cold War, 1944–1947*. Columbia: University of Missouri Press, 1981.

Aruri, Naseer H., ed. *Middle East Crucible: Studies on the Arab-Israeli War of October 1973*. Wilmette, Ill.: Medina University Press, 1975.

Ashley, Richard K. "Bayesian Decision Analysis in International Relations Forecasting: The Analysis of Subjective Processes." In *Forecasting in International Relations: Theory, Methods, Problems, Prospects*, ed. Nazli Choucri and Thomas W. Robinson, 149–71. San Francisco: W. H. Freeman, 1978.

Axelrod, Robert. *Conflict of Interest: A Theory of Divergent Goals with Applications to Politics*. Chicago: Markham, 1970.

———. "Schema Theory: An Information Processing Model of Perception and Cognition." *American Political Science Review* 67, no. 4 (December 1973): 1248–66.

———. "The Rational Timing of Surprise." *World Politics* 31, no. 2 (January 1979): 228–46.

———, ed. *Structure of Decision: The Cognitive Maps of Political Elites*. Princeton: Princeton University Press, 1976.

Ballard, Jack Stokes. *The Shock of Peace: Military and Economic Demobilization after World War II*. Washington, D.C.: University Press of America, 1983.

Bell, Coral. "The October Middle East War: A Case Study in Crisis Management during Detente." *International Affairs* (London) 50, no. 4 (October 1974): 531–43.

Benn, S. I. "Rationality and Political Behavior." In *Rationality and the Social Sciences: Contributions to the Philosophy and Methodology of the Social Sciences*, ed. S. I. Benn and G. W. Mortimore, 246–67. London: Routledge and Kegan Paul, 1976.

Blainey, Geoffrey. *The Causes of War*. London: Macmillan, 1973.

Blair, Bruce G. "Alerting in Crisis and Conventional War." In *Managing Nuclear Operations*, ed. Ashton B. Carter, John D. Steinbruner, and Charles A. Zraket, 75–120. Washington, D.C.: Brookings, 1987.

Blechman, Barry M., and Douglas M. Hart. "The Political Utility of Nuclear Weapons: The 1973 Middle East Crisis." *International Security* 7, no. 1 (Summer 1982): 132–56.

Blechman, Barry M., and Stephen S. Kaplan. *Force without War: U.S. Armed Forces as a Political Instrument*. Washington, D.C.: Brookings, 1978.

Blight, James G. *The Shattered Crystal Ball: Fear and Learning in the Cuban Missile Crisis*. Savage, Md.: Rowman and Littlefield Publishers, 1990.

Blight, James G., and David A. Welch. *On the Brink: Americans and Soviets Reexamine the Cuban Missile Crisis*. New York: Hill and Wang, 1989.

Blight, James G., Joseph S. Nye, Jr., and David A. Welch. "The Cuban Missile Crisis Revisited." *Foreign Affairs* 66, no. 1 (Fall 1987): 170–88.

Brams, Steven J. *Game Theory and Politics*. New York: Free Press, 1975.

———. *Paradoxes in Politics: An Introduction to the Nonobvious in Political Science*. New York: Free Press, 1976.

———. *Superpower Games: Applying Game Theory to Superpower Conflict*. New Haven: Yale University Press, 1985.

Brecher, Michael, ed. *Studies in Crisis Behavior*. New Brunswick, N.J.: Transaction, 1979.

Brecher, Michael, and Patrick James. *Crisis and Change in World Politics*. Boulder, Colo.: Westview Press, 1986.

Brecher, Michael, and Jonathan Wilkenfeld. *Crisis, Conflict, and Instability*. Oxford: Pergamon, 1989.

Brown, G. M. "The Consequences of Yom Kippur: Some Preliminary Notes." *Australian Outlook* 28, no. 2 (August 1974): 196–204.

Brune, Lester H. *The Missile Crisis of October 1962: A Review of Issues and References*. Claremont, Calif.: Regina Books, 1985.

Bueno de Mesquita, Bruce. *The War Trap*. New Haven: Yale University Press, 1981.

Bundy, McGeorge. *Danger and Survival: Choices about the Bomb in the First Fifty Years*. New York: Random House, 1988.

Bundy, McGeorge, and James G. Blight. "October 27, 1962: Transcripts of the Meeting of the ExComm." *International Security* 12, no. 3 (Winter 1987–88): 30–92.

Burchett, Wilfred. "The Superpower Show That Flopped." *Far Eastern Economic Review* 82, no. 44 (5 November 1973): 29–30.

Byrnes, James F. *Speaking Frankly*. New York: Harper and Brothers, 1947.

Caldwell, Dan. "A Research Note on the Quarantine of Cuba, October 1962." *International Studies Quarterly* 22, no. 4 (December 1978): 625–33.

———. *American-Soviet Relations: From 1947 to the Nixon-Kissinger Grand Design*. Westport, Conn.: Greenwood Press, 1981.

———, ed. "Department of Defense Operations during the Cuban Crisis: A Report by

Adam Yarmolinsky, 13 February 1963." *Naval War College Review* 32, no. 4 (June–July 1979): 83–99.

Calvert, Randall L. "The Value of Biased Information: A Rational Choice Model of Political Advice." *Journal of Politics* 47, no. 2 (May 1985): 530–55.

Campbell, John C. *The United States in World Affairs, 1945–1947.* New York: Harper and Brothers, for the Council on Foreign Relations, 1947.

Carroll, John S., and John W. Payne, eds. *Cognition and Social Behavior.* 11th Symposium on Cognition, Carnegie-Mellon University, 1975. Hillsdale, N.J.: Lawrence Erlbaum Associates, 1976.

Carter, Ashton B., John D. Steinbruner, and Charles A. Zraket, eds. *Managing Nuclear Operations.* Washington, D.C.: Brookings, 1987.

Carter, Jimmy. *Public Papers of the Presidents of the United States: Jimmy Carter, 1979.* Washington, D.C.: GPO, 1979.

———. *Keeping Faith.* New York: Bantam, 1982.

Cate, Curtis. *The Ides of August: The Berlin Wall Crisis, 1961.* New York: M. Evans, and Company 1978.

Catudal, Honore M. *Kennedy and the Berlin Wall Crisis: A Case Study in U.S. Decision Making.* Berlin: Berlin-Verlag, 1980.

Charles, Max. *Berlin Blockade.* London: Allan Wingate, 1959.

Chayes, Abram. *The Cuban Missile Crisis: International Crises and the Role of Law.* Oxford: Oxford University Press, 1974.

Choucri, Nazli, and Thomas W. Robinson, eds. *Forecasting in International Relations: Theory, Methods, Problems, Prospects.* San Francisco: W. H. Freeman, 1978.

Clay, Lucius D. *Decision in Germany.* Westport, Conn.: Greenwood Press, 1950.

———. "Berlin." *Foreign Affairs* 41, no. 1 (October 1962): 47–58.

Cline, Ray S. "The Cuban Missile Crisis." *Foreign Affairs* 68, no. 4 (Fall 1989): 190–96.

Cohen, Raymond. *Threat Perception in International Crisis.* Madison: University of Wisconsin Press, 1979.

Cottam, Martha L. *Foreign Policy Decision Making: The Influence of Cognition.* Boulder, Colo.: Westview Press, 1986.

Cross, John G. *The Economics of Bargaining.* New York: Basic Books, 1969.

Dallin, Alexander. *The Soviet Union at the United Nations: An Inquiry into Soviet Motives and Objectives.* New York: Praeger, 1962.

———, ed. *Diversity in International Communism: A Documentary Record, 1961–1963.* New York: Columbia University Press, 1963.

Davis, Morton D. *Game Theory: A Nontechnical Introduction.* Rev. ed. New York: Basic Books, 1983.

Davison, W. Phillips. *The Berlin Blockade: A Study In Cold War Politics.* Princeton. Princeton University Press, 1958.

Dawisha, Karen. "Soviet Decision Making in the Middle East: The 1973 October War and the 1980 Gulf War." *International Affairs* (London) 57 (Winter 1980–81): 43–59.

de Rivera, Joseph. *The Psychological Dimension of Foreign Policy.* Columbus, Ohio: Charles E. Merrill Publishing Company, 1968.

Divine, Robert A., ed. *The Cuban Missile Crisis*. Chicago: Quadrangle, 1971.

Donovan, Robert J. *Conflict and Crisis: The Presidency of Harry S. Truman, 1945–1948*. New York: W. W. Norton, 1977.

Dowty, Alan. "United States Decision-Making in Middle East Crises: 1958, 1970, 1973." *Middle East Review* 12, no. 3 (Spring 1980): 23–30.

———. *Middle East Crisis: U.S. Decision-Making in 1958, 1970, 1973*. Berkeley: University of California Press, 1984.

Druks, Herbert. *Harry S. Truman and the Russians, 1945–1953*. New York: Robert Speller and Sons, 1966.

Duffy, Gloria. "Crisis Mangling and the Cuban Brigade." *International Security* 8, no. 1 (Summer 1983): 67–87.

Dulles, Eleanor Lansing. *Berlin: The Wall Is Not Forever*. Chapel Hill: University of North Carolina Press, 1967.

Dunn, Lewis A., ed., with Amy E. Gordon. *Arms Control Verification and the New Role of On-Site Inspection*. Lexington, Mass.: Lexington Books, 1990.

Edmead, Frank. "Changes in Perception during the Course of Conflict." In *Cognitive Dynamics and International Politics*, ed. Christer Jönsson, 158–77. New York: St. Martin's Press, 1982.

Elster, Jon, ed. *Rational Choice*. Oxford: Basil Blackwell, 1986.

Etzold, Thomas H., and John Lewis Gaddis, eds. *Containment: Documents on American Policy and Strategy, 1945–1950*. New York: Columbia University Press, 1978.

Evangalista, Matthew A. "Stalin's PostWar Army Reappraised." *International Security* 7, no. 3 (Winter 1982–83): 110–38.

Falkowski, Lawrence S., "Introduction: Evaluating Psychological Models." In *Psychological Models in International Politics*, ed. Lawrence S. Falkowski, 1–14. Boulder, Colo.: Westview Press, 1979.

———, ed. *Psychological Models in International Politics*. Boulder, Colo.: Westview Press, 1979.

Freedman, Robert O. *Soviet Policy toward the Middle East since 1970*. 3d ed. New York: Praeger, 1982.

Frei, Daniel, ed. *International Crises and Crisis Management: An East-West Symposium*. Westmead, Farnborough, Hampshire, England: Saxon House, 1978.

———, ed. *Managing International Crises*. Beverly Hills, Calif.: Sage, 1982.

Gaddis, John Lewis. *The United States and the Origins of the Cold War, 1941–1947*. New York: Columbia University Press, 1972.

Galante, Pierre. *The Berlin Wall*. Garden City, N.Y.: Doubleday, 1965.

Gallup, George H. *The Gallup Poll: Public Opinion 1935–1971*. Vol. 1, *1935–1948*. New York: Random House, 1972.

———. *The Gallup Poll: Public Opinion 1935–1971*, Vol. 3, *1959–1971*. New York: Random House, 1972.

Garthoff, Raymond L. *Detente and Confrontation: American-Soviet Relations from Nixon to Reagan*. Washington, D.C.: Brookings, 1985.

———. *Reflections on the Cuban Missile Crisis*. Rev. ed. Washington, D.C.: Brookings, 1989.

Gelb, Norman. *The Berlin Wall*. New York: New York Times–Quadrangle, 1986.

George, Alexander L. "The Causal Nexus between Cognitive Beliefs and Decision-Making Behavior: The 'Operational Code'." In *Psychological Models in International Politics*, ed. Lawrence S. Falkowski, 95–124. Boulder, Colo.: Westview Press, 1979.

———. "U.S.-Soviet Global Rivalry: Norms of Competition." In *New Issues in International Crisis Management*, ed. Gilbert R. Winham, 67–89. Boulder, Colo.: Westview Press, 1988.

George, Alexander L., and Richard Smoke. *Deterrence in American Foreign Policy: Theory and Practice*. New York: Columbia University Press, 1974.

Golan, Galia. "Soviet Decision Making in the Yom Kippur War, 1973." In *Soviet Decision-Making for National Security*, ed. Jiri Valenta and William Potter, 145–217. London: George Allen and Unwin, 1984.

Goodrich, Leland M., and Anne P. Simons. *The United Nations and the Maintenance of International Peace and Security*. Washington, D.C.: Brookings, 1955.

Gromyko, Anatolii A. "The Caribbean Crisis 1: The U.S. Government's Preparation of the Caribbean Crisis" and "The Caribbean Crisis 2: Diplomatic Efforts of the USSR to Eliminate the Crisis." *Voprosy istorii*. nos. 7–8 (1971). Reprinted in *Soviet Law and Government* 11, no. 1 (Summer 1972): 3–53.

———. *Through Russian Eyes: President Kennedy's 1036 Days*. Washington, D.C.: International Library, 1973.

Gurwitz, Sharon B., and Lawrence Panciera. "Attribution of Freedom by Actors and Observers." *Journal of Personality and Social Psychology* 32, no. 3 (September 1975): 531–39.

Hamburger, Henry. *Games as Models of Social Phenomena*. San Francisco: W. H. Freeman, 1979.

Hampson, Fen Osler. "The Divided Decision-Maker: American Domestic Politics and the Cuban Crises." *International Security* 9, no. 3 (Winter 1984–85): 130–65.

Hastings, Max, and Simon Jenkins. *The Battle for the Falklands*. New York: W. W. Norton, 1983.

Heidelmeyer, Wolfgang, and Guenther Hindrichs. *Documents on Berlin, 1946–1963*. Munich: R. Oldenbourg Verlag, 1963.

Heikal, Mohamed. *The Road to Ramadan*. London: Colling; New York: Quadrangle, 1975.

Hermann, Charles F. "International Crisis as a Situational Variable." In *International Politics and Foreign Policy: A Reader in Research and Theory*, rev. ed., ed. James N. Rosenau, 402–21. New York: Free Press, 1969.

———, ed. *International Crises: Insights from Behavioral Research*. New York: Free Press, 1972.

Herrmann, Richard K. "Perceptions and Foreign Policy Analysis." In *Foreign Policy Decision Making: Perception, Cognition, and Artificial Intelligence*, ed. Donald A. Sylvan and Steve Chan, 25–52. New York: Praeger, 1984.

Hess, Gary R. "The Iranian Crisis of 1945–46 and the Cold War." *Political Science Quarterly* 89, no. 1 (March 1974): 117–46.

Hilsman, Roger. *To Move a Nation: The Politics of Foreign Policy in the Administration of John F. Kennedy*. Garden City, N.Y.: Doubleday, 1967.

Hoagland, Steven W., and Stephen G. Walker. "Operational Codes and Crisis Outcomes." In *Psychological Models in International Politics*, ed. Lawrence S. Falkowski, 125–67. Boulder, Colo.: Westview Press, 1979.

Holsti, Ole R. "The Belief System and National Images: A Case Study." In *International Politics and Foreign Policy: A Reader in Research and Theory*, rev. ed., ed. James N. Rosenau, 543–50. New York: Free Press, 1969.

———. *Crisis, Escalation, War*. Montreal: McGill-Queen's University Press, 1972.

———. "Foreign Policy Decision Makers Viewed Psychologically: 'Cognitive Processes' Approaches." In *In Search of Global Patterns*, ed. James N. Rosenau, 120–44. New York: Free Press, 1976.

———. "Foreign Policy Formation Viewed Cognitively." In *Structure of Decision: The Cognitive Maps of Political Elites*, ed. Robert Axelrod, 18–54. Princeton: Princeton University Press, 1976.

Horelick, Arnold L. "The Cuban Missile Crisis: An Analysis of Soviet Calculations and Behavior." *World Politics* 16, no. 3 (April 1964): 363–89.

Horelick, Arnold L., and Myron Rush. *Strategic Power and Soviet Foreign Policy*. Chicago: University of Chicago Press, 1966.

Hybel, Alex Roberto. *The Logic of Surprise in International Conflict*. Lexington, Mass.: D. C. Heath and Company, 1986.

Jabber, Paul, and Roman Kolkowicz. "The Arab-Israeli Wars of 1967 and 1973." In *Diplomacy of Power: Soviet Armed Forces as a Political Instrument*, ed. Stephen S. Kaplan, 412–67. Washington, D.C.: Brookings, 1981.

Janis, Irving L. *Victims of Groupthink: A Psychological Study of Foreign-Policy Decisions and Fiascoes*. Boston: Houghton Mifflin Company, 1972.

———. "International Crisis Management in the Nuclear Age." In *Psychology and the Prevention of Nuclear War: A Book of Readings*, ed. Ralph K. White, 381–96. New York: New York University Press, 1986.

Janis, Irving L., and Leon Mann. *Decision Making: A Psychological Analysis of Conflict, Choice, and Commitment*. New York: Free Press, 1977.

Jervis, Robert. "Hypotheses on Misperception." *World Politics* 20, no. 3 (April 1968): 454–79.

———. *Perception and Misperception in International Politics*. Princeton: Princeton University Press, 1976.

———. "Political Decison-Making: Some Recent Contributions." *Political Psychology* 2 (Summer 1980): 86–101.

———. *"Perception and Misperception*: An Updating of the Analysis." Paper presented at the annual meeting of the International Society of Political Psychology, Washington, D.C., 24–27 June 1982.

———. "A Critique of Early Psychological Approaches to International Misperception." In *Psychology and the Prevention of Nuclear War: A Book of Readings*, ed. Ralph K. White, 274–78. New York: New York University Press, 1986.

———. "Cognition and Political Behavior." In *Political Cognition*, ed. Richard R. Lau and David O. Sears, 319–36. Hillsdale, N.J.: Lawrence Erlbaum Associates, 1986.

Jones, Robert H. *The Roads to Russia: United States Lend-Lease to the Soviet Union*. Norman: University of Oklahoma Press, 1969.

Jönsson, Christer, ed. *Cognitive Dynamics and International Politics.* New York: St. Martin's Press, 1982.

Kahneman, Daniel, Paul Slovic, and Amos Tversky, eds. *Judgment under Uncertainty: Heuristics and Biases.* Cambridge: Cambridge University Press, 1982.

Kalb, Marvin, and Bernard Kalb. *Kissinger.* Boston: Little, Brown and Company, 1974.

Kaplan, Stephen S. *Diplomacy of Power: Soviet Armed Forces as a Political Instrument.* Washington, D.C.: Brookings, 1981.

Kass, Ilana. *Soviet Involvement in the Middle East: Policy Formulation, 1966–1973.* Boulder, Colo.: Westview Press, 1978.

Kelley, Harold H. "The Situational Origins of Human Tendencies: A Further Reason for the Formal Analysis of Structures." *Personality and Social Pscyhology Bulletin* 9, no. 1 (March 1983): 8–30.

Kennan, George F. *Russia and the West under Lenin and Stalin.* Boston: Little, Brown and Company, 1961.

———. *Memoirs: 1925–1950.* Boston: Little, Brown and Company, 1967.

Kennedy, John F. "Cuban Missile Crisis Meetings, October 16, 1962." *Presidential Recordings Transcripts.* Boston: John F. Kennedy Library.

———. "Cuban Missile Crisis Meetings, October 27, 1962." *Presidential Recordings Transcripts.* Boston: John F. Kennedy Library.

———. *Public Papers of the Presidents of the United States: John F. Kennedy, 1961–63.* Washington, D.C.: GPO, 1961–63.

Kennedy, Robert F. *Thirteen Days: A Memoir of the Cuban Missile Crisis.* New York: W. W. Norton, 1969.

Kern, Montague, Patricia W. Levering, and Ralph B. Levering. *The Kennedy Crises: The Press, the Presidency, and Foreign Policy.* Chapel Hill: University of North Carolina Press, 1983.

Khrushchev, Nikita. "Report to the Supreme Soviet of the USSR, December 12, 1962." *Pravda.* 13 December 1962, and "Speech at the VI Congress of the Socialist Unity Party of Germany, January 16, 1963." *Pravda.* 17 January 1963. Reprinted in Alexander Dallin, ed. *Diversity in International Communism: A Documentary Record, 1961–1963.* New York: Columbia University Press, 1963.

———. *Khrushchev Remembers.* Boston: Little, Brown and Company, 1970.

Kinder, Donald R., and Janet A. Weiss. "In Lieu of Rationality: Psychological Perspectives on Foreign Policy Decision Making." *Journal of Conflict Resolution* 22, no. 4 (December 1978): 707–35.

Kissinger, Henry. *The White House Years.* Boston: Little, Brown and Company, 1979.

———. *Years of Upheaval.* Boston: Little, Brown and Company, 1982.

———. "Kissinger News Conterence." *Department of State Bulletin,* 29 October 1973, 535–36.

Kolkowicz, Roman. *The Soviet Military and the Communist Party.* Princeton: Princeton University Press, 1967.

Kramer, Mark. "Remembering the Cuban Missile Crisis: Should We Swallow Oral History?" *International Security* 15, no. 1 (Summer 1990): 212–18.

Kuniholm, Bruce Robellet. *The Origins of the Cold War in the Near East: Great Power Conflict and Diplomacy in Iran, Turkey, and Greece*. Princeton: Princeton University Press, 1980.

LaFeber, Walter. *America, Russia, and the Cold War, 1945–1980*. 4th ed. New York: Wiley, 1980.

Laqueur, Walter. *A World of Secrets: The Uses and Limits of Intelligence*. New York: Basic Books, 1985.

Lebow, Richard Ned. *Between Peace and War: The Nature of International Crisis*. Baltimore: Johns Hopkins University Press, 1981.

———. "Decision Making in Crises." In *Psychology and the Prevention of Nuclear War: A Book of Readings*, ed. Ralph K. White, 397–410. New York: New York University Press, 1986.

———. "Clausewitz, Loss of Control, and Crisis Management." In *New Issues in International Crisis Management*, ed. Gilbert R. Winham, 37–64. Boulder, Colo.: Westview Press, 1988.

Leighton, Richard M. *The Cuban Missile Crisis of 1962: A Case Study in National Security Crisis Management*. Washington, D.C.: National Defense University, 1978.

Lenczowski, George. *Russia and the West in Iran, 1918–1948: A Study In Big-Power Rivalry*. New York: Greenwood Press, 1968.

Levering, Ralph B. *American Opinion and the Russian Alliance, 1939–1945*. Chapel Hill: University of North Carolina Press, 1976.

Lie, Trygve. *In the Cause of Peace: Seven Years with the United Nations*. New York: Macmillan, 1954.

McCalla, Robert B. "The Dynamics of Perception in U.S.-Soviet Crises." Ph.D. diss., University of Michigan, 1987.

McClelland, Charles A. "Access to Berlin: The Quantity and Variety of Events, 1948–1963." In *Quantitative International Politics: Insights and Evidence*, ed. J. David Singer, 159–86. New York: Free Press, 1968.

MacGillivray, Karen Patrick, and Gilbert R. Winham. "Arms Control Negotiations and the Stability of Crisis Management." In *New Issues in International Crisis Management*, ed. Gilbert R. Winham, 90–117. Boulder, Colo.: Westview Press, 1988.

Maghoori, Ray, and Stephen M. Gorman. *The Yom Kippur War: A Case Study in Crisis Decision Making in American Foreign Policy*. Washington, D.C.: University Press of America, 1981.

Mandel, Robert. *Irrationality in International Confrontation*. New York: Greenwood Press, 1987.

Millis, Walter, ed. *The Forrestal Diaries*. New York: Viking Press, 1951.

Minix, Dean A. *Small Groups and Foreign Policy Decision-Making*. Washington, D.C.: University Press of America, 1982.

Morrow, James D. "A Limited Information Model of Crisis Bargaining." Paper presented at 1987 annual meeting of the International Studies Association, Washington, D.C., April 1987.

Motter, T. H. Vail. *The Persian Corridor and Aid to Russia*. Washington D.C.: Office of the Chief of Military History, Department of the Army, 1952.

Murphy, Robert. *Diplomat among Warriors*. Garden City, N.Y.: Doubleday, 1964.

Nelson, Daniel J. *Wartime Origins of the Berlin Dilemma*. University, Ala.: University of Alabama Press, 1978.

Neustadt, Richard E., and Ernest R. May. *Thinking in Time: The Uses of History for Decision-Makers*. New York: Free Press, 1986.

Nisbett, Richard, and Lee Ross. *Human Inference: Strategies and Shortcomings of Social Judgment*. Englewood Cliffs, N.J.: Prentice-Hall, 1980.

Nixon, Richard M. "Press Conference of 26 October 1973." *Department of State Bulletin*, 12 November 1973, 583.

———. *RN: The Memoirs of Richard Nixon*. New York: Grosset and Dunlap, 1978.

Nogee, Joseph L., and Robert H. Donaldson. *Soviet Foreign Policy since World War II*. New York: Pergamon, 1981.

O'Donnell, Kenneth P., and David F. Powers. *"Johnny, We Hardly Knew Ye": Memories of John Fitzgerald Kennedy*. Boston: Little, Brown and Company, 1970.

Oneal, John R. *Foreign Policy Making in Times of Crisis*. Columbus: Ohio State University Press, 1982.

Paige, Glenn D. *The Korean Decision: June 24–30, 1950*. New York: Free Press, 1968.

Paterson, Thomas G. *Soviet-American Confrontation: Postwar Reconstruction and the Origins of the Cold War*. Baltimore: Johns Hopkins University Press, 1973.

Plous, S. "Perceptual Illusions and Military Realities: The Nuclear Arms Race." *Journal of Conflict Resolution* 29, no. 3 (September 1985): 363–89.

Pope, Ronald R., ed. *Soviet Views on the Cuban Missile Crisis: Myth and Reality in Foreign Policy Analysis*. Washington, D.C.: University Press of America, 1982.

Quandt, William B. *Soviet Policy in the October 1973 War*. Report prepared for the Office of the Assistant Secretary of Defense, International Security Affairs. R-1864-ISA. Santa Monica: RAND Corporation, May 1976.

———. *Decade of Decision: American Policy toward the Arab-Israeli Conflict, 1967–1976*. Berkeley: University of California Press, 1977.

———. "Soviet Policy in the October Middle East War II." *International Affairs* (London) 53 (October 1977): 587–603.

Rapoport, Anatol, and Albert M. Chammah. *Prisoner's Dilemma: A Study in Conflict and Cooperation*. Ann Arbor: University of Michigan Press, 1965.

Rapoport, Anatol, Melvin J. Guyer, and David B. Gordon. *The 2x2 Game*. Ann Arbor: University of Michigan Press, 1976.

Rezun, Miron. *The Soviet Union and Iran: Soviet Policy in Iran from the Beginnings of the Pahlavi Dynasty until the Soviet Invasion in 1941*. Geneva: Sijthoff and Noordhoff International Publishers, 1981.

Richardson, James L. "Crisis Management: A Critical Appraisal." In *New Issues in International Crisis Management*, ed. Gilbert R. Winham, 13 36. Boulder, Colo.: Westview Press, 1988.

Roberts, Jonathan M. *Decision-Making during International Crises*. New York: St. Martin's Press, 1988.

Rock, Irvin. *The Logic of Perception*. Cambridge, Mass.: MIT Press, 1983.

Rosenau, James N., ed. *International Politics and Foreign Policy: A Reader in Research and Theory*. Rev. ed. New York: Free Press, 1969.

————, ed. *In Search of Global Patterns*. New York: Free Press, 1976.

Rosenberg, David Alan. "U.S. Nuclear Stockpile, 1945 to 1950." *Bulletin of the Atomic Scientist* 38, no. 5 (May 1982): 25–30.

Royal Institute of International Affairs. *British Interests in the Mediterranean and Middle East: A Report by a Chatham House Study Group*. London: Oxford International Press, 1958.

Rubinstein, Alvin Z. *Soviet Policy toward Turkey, Iran, and Afghanistan: The Dynamics of Influence*. New York: Praeger, 1982.

————, ed. *The Foreign Policy of the Soviet Union*. New York: Random House, 1960.

Rusten, Lynn, and Paul C. Stern. *Crisis Management in the Nuclear Age*. Washington, D.C.: National Academy Press, 1987.

Sadat, Anwar. *In Search of Identity: An Autobiography*. New York: Harper and Row, 1978.

Sagan, Scott D. "Nuclear Alerts and Crisis Management." *International Security* 9, no. 4 (Spring 1985): 99–139.

Sampson, Anthony. *The Seven Sisters*. New York: Bantam, 1975.

Schelling, Thomas C. *Arms and Influence*. New Haven: Yale University Press, 1966.

————. *Strategy of Conflict*. Cambridge: Harvard University Press, 1980.

Scherer, John L. "Soviet and American Behavior during the Yom Kippur War." *World Affairs* 141, no. 1 (Summer 1978): 3–23.

————. "Reinterpreting Soviet Behavior during the Cuban Missile Crisis." *World Affairs* (London) 144, no. 2 (Fall 1981): 110–25.

Schick, Jack M. *The Berlin Crisis, 1958–1962*. Philadelphia: University of Pennsylvania Press, 1971.

Schlesinger, Arthur M., Jr. *A Thousand Days: John F. Kennedy in the White House*. Boston: Houghton Mifflin Company, 1965.

Schmid, Alex P. *Soviet Military Interventions since 1945*. New Brunswick, N.J.: Transaction, 1985.

Schwartz, Morton. *The Foreign Policy of the USSR: Domestic Factors*. Encino, Calif.: Dickenson Publishing Company, 1975.

Schweitzer, Nicholas. "Bayesian Analysis: Estimating the Probability of Middle East Conflict." In *Quantitative Approaches to Political Intelligence: The CIA Experience*, ed. Richard J. Heuer, Jr., 11–30. Boulder, Colo.: Westview Press, 1978.

Sen, Amartya. "Behavior and the Concept of Preference." In *Rational Choice*, ed. Jon Elster, 60–81. London: Basil Blackwell, 1986.

Shapiro, Michael J., and G. Matthew Bonham. "Cognitive Process and Foreign Policy Decison-Making." *International Studies Quarterly* 17, no. 2 (June 1973): 147–74.

Shapiro, Michael J., and G. Matthew Bonham. "A Cognitive Process Approach to Collective Decision Making." In *Cognitive Dynamics and International Politics*, ed. Christer Jönsson, 19–36. New York: St. Martin's Press, 1982.

Shaver, Kelly G. *Principles of Social Psychology*. 2d ed. Cambridge, Mass.: Winthrop Publishers, 1981.

Shlaim, Avi. *The United States and the Berlin Blockade, 1948–1949: A Study in Crisis Decision-Making*. Berkeley: University of California Press, 1983.

Shulman, Marshall D. *Stalin's Foreign Policy Reappraised*. Cambridge: Harvard University Press, 1963.

Singer, J. David, ed. *Quantitative International Politics: Insights and Evidence*. New York: Free Press, 1968.

Slominski, Martin J. "The Soviet Military Press and the October War." *Military Review* 54, no. 5 (May 1974): 39–47.

Slusser, Robert M. *The Berlin Crisis of 1961: Soviet-American Relations and the Struggle for Power in the Kremlin, June–November 1961*. Baltimore: Johns Hopkins University Press, 1973.

Smith, Jean Edward. *The Defense of Berlin*. Baltimore: Johns Hopkins University Press, 1963.

———, ed. *The Papers of General Lucius D. Clay: Germany 1945–1949*. Vol. 2. Bloomington: Indiana University Press, 1974.

Smith, Walter Bedell. *My Three Years in Moscow*. Philadelphia: J. B. Lippincott Company, 1950.

Snyder, Glenn H. "'Prisoner's Dilemma' and 'Chicken' Models in International Politics." *International Studies Quarterly* 15, no. 1 (March 1971): 66–103.

Snyder, Glenn H., and Paul Diesing. *Conflict among Nations: Bargaining, Decision Making, and System Structure in International Crises*. Princeton: Princeton University Press, 1977.

Snyder, Richard C., H. W. Bruck, and Burton Sapin, eds. *Foreign Policy Decision Making: An Approach to the Study of International Politics*. Glencoe, Ill.: Free Press, 1962.

Sorensen, Theodore C. *Kennedy*. New York: Harper and Row, 1965.

Sprout, Harold, and Margaret Sprout. "Environmental Factors in the Study of International Politics." In *International Politics and Foreign Policy: A Reader in Research and Theory*, rev. ed., ed. James N. Rosenau, 41–56. New York: Free Press, 1969.

Starn, Ralph. "Historians and Crisis." *Past and Present* no. 52 (August 1971): 3–22.

Steinbruner, John D. *The Cybernetic Theory of Decision: New Dimensions of Political Analysis*. Princeton: Princeton University Press, 1974.

Suedfeld, Peter, and Philip E. Tetlock. "Integrative Complexity of Communications in International Crises." *Journal of Conflict Resolution* 21, no. 1 (March 1977): 169–84.

Sunday Times Insight Team. *Insight on the Middle East War*. New York: Doubleday, 1974.

Sylvan, Donald A., and Steve Chan, eds. *Foreign Policy Decision Making: Perception, Cognition, and Artificial Intelligence*. New York: Praeger, 1984.

Tagiuri, Renato, and Luigi Petrullo, eds. *Person Perception and Interpersonal Behavior*. Stanford: Stanford University Press, 1958.

Tanter, Raymond. *Modelling and Managing International Conflicts: The Berlin Crises*. Beverly Hills: Sage, 1974.

Tatu, Michel. *Power in the Kremlin*. New York: Viking Press, 1969.

Taubman, William. *Stalin's American Policy: From Entente to Detente to Cold War*. New York: W. W. Norton, 1982.

Tetlock, Philip E. "Integrative Complexity of American and Soviet Foreign Policy Rhetoric." *Journal of Personality and Social Psychology* 49, no. 6 (1985): 1565–85.

Tetlock, Philip E., and Charles B. McGuire, Jr. "Cognitive Perspectives on Foreign Policy." In *Psychology and the Prevention of Nuclear War: A Book of Readings*, ed. Ralph K. White, 255–73. New York: New York University Press, 1986.

Thomas, Lewis V., and Richard N. Frye. *The United States and Turkey and Iran.* Cambridge: Harvard University Press, 1951.

Trachtenberg, Marc. "The Influence of Nuclear Weapons in the Cuban Missile Crisis." *International Security* 10, no. 1 (Summer 1985): 137–63.

Truman, Harry S. *Public Papers of the Presidents of the United States: Harry S. Truman, 1952–53.* Washington, D.C.: GPO, 1952–53.

———. *Mr. Citizen.* New York: Bernard Geis Associates, 1953.

———. *Memoirs, Volume II: Years of Trial and Hope, 1946–1952.* Garden City, N.Y.: Doubleday, 1956.

Tversky, Amos, and Daniel Kahneman. "The Framing of Decisions and the Psychology of Choice." In *Rational Choice*, ed. Jon Elster, 123–41. London: Basil Blackwell, 1986.

Ulam, Adam B. *Expansion and Coexistence: Soviet Foreign Policy, 1917–1973.* 2d ed. New York: Praeger, 1974.

Ury, William L., and Richard Smoke. *Beyond the Hotline: Controlling a Nuclear Crisis.* A report of the United States Arms Control and Disarmament Agency. Cambridge: Harvard University Law School, Nuclear Negotiation Project, 1984.

U.S. Congress, House of Representatives, Committee on Appropriations, Subcommittee on Department of Defense Appropriations for 1964. *Hearings.* 88th Cong., 1st sess., 1963.

U.S. Department of State. *Foreign Relations of the United States*, 1943–1948. Washington, D.C.: GPO, 1961–1974.

———. *Foreign Relations of the United States, The Conferences at Cairo and Tehran, 1943.* Washington D.C.: GPO, 1961.

———. *Foreign Relations of the United States, The Conference of Berlin*, 1945, Vols. 1 and 2. Washington, D.C.: GPO, 1960.

———. *Foreign Relations of the United States, The Conferences at Malta and Yalta, 1945.* Washington, D.C.: GPO, 1955.

———. *Documents on Germany, 1944–1985*, no. 9446, Washington, D.C.: Office of the Historian, Bureau of Public Affairs, n.d.

———. "Messages Exchanged by President Kennedy and Chairman Khrushchev during the Cuban Missile Crisis of October 1962." *Department of State Bulletin*, 19 November 1973, 635–55.

Valenta, Jiri, and William Potter, eds. *Soviet Decision-Making for National Security.* London: George Allen and Unwin, 1984.

Vick, Alan J. "Building Confidence during Peace and War." *Defense Analysis* 5, no. 2 (1989): 97–113.

Welch, David A., and James G. Blight. "The Eleventh Hour of the Cuban Missile Crisis." *International Security* 12, no. 3 (Winter 1987–88): 5–29.

Whaley, Barton. *Codeword BARBAROSSA.* Cambridge: MIT Press, 1973.

Whetten, Lawrence L. *The Canal War: Four-Power Conflict in the Middle East.* Cambridge: MIT Press, 1974.

White, Ralph K. "Motivated Misperceptions." In *Psychology and the Prevention of Nuclear War: A Book of Readings*, ed. Ralph K. White, 279–301. New York: New York University Press, 1986.

————, ed. *Psychology and the Prevention of Nuclear War: A Book of Readings.* New York: New York University Press, 1986.

Whiting, Allen S. *China Crosses the Yalu: The Decision to Enter the Korean War.* New York: Macmillan, 1960.

Wiegele, Thomas C. "The Psychophysiology of Elite Stress in Five International Crises." *International Studies Quarterly* 22, no. 4 (December 1978): 467–511.

Williams, Phil. *Crisis Management: Confrontation and Diplomacy in the Nuclear Age.* New York: Wiley, 1972.

Williams, William Appleman. *The Tragedy of American Diplomacy.* 2d rev. ed. New York: Dell, 1972.

Winham, Gilbert R., ed. *New Issues in International Crisis Management.* Boulder, Colo.: Westview Press, 1988.

Winter, Sidney G., Jr. "Concepts of Rationality in Behavior Theory." Discussion paper no. 7, August 1969, Institute of Public Policy Studies, University of Michigan.

Wohlstetter, Roberta. "Cuba and Pearl Harbor: Hindsight and Foresight." *Foreign Affairs* 43, no. 4 (July 1965): 691–707.

Wright, George. *Behavioural Decision Theory: An Introduction.* Harmondsworth, Middlesex, England: Penguin Books, 1984.

Yergin, Daniel. *Shattered Peace: The Origins of the Cold War and the National Security State.* London: Andre Deutsch, 1977.

Young, Oran. *The Politics of Force: Bargaining during International Crises.* Princeton: Princeton University Press, 1968.

Zimmerman, William. *Soviet Perspectives on International Relations, 1956–1967.* Princeton: Princeton University Press, 1969.

Zumwalt, Elmo R., Jr. *On Watch: A Memoir.* New York: Quadrangle–New York Times Book Company, 1976.

Index

Accidental crises, 112. *See also* Unintended crises
Accidental wars, 111–12
Acheson, Dean, 33, 48, 55, 101, 105
Aide-memoire crisis, 47–48, 49, 105
Allison, Graham T., 19, 129
Axelrod, Robert, 148
Aziz, Tariq, 70, 191

Baker, James A., 70, 191
Balance of belief, 70
Bargaining, 71, 112, 145–46; during Cuban Missile Crisis, 59, 72; "salami tactics," 122; in Prisoner's Dilemma and Chicken, 172
Bayesian analysis, 149
Bell, Coral, 138
Berlin Blockade Crisis, 40–45, 71; and international crises, 11; and role of Four Power control of Berlin, 40–42; and "baby blockade and airlift," 42; decision makers' views on origin of, 77–79; and role of Marshall Plan, 94–95, 119; deliberate nature of, 94–99; unintended nature of, 118–22; as unintended crisis for United States, 118–19; as unintended crisis for Soviet Union, 119–22; termination of, 156–58; duration of, 175–77; as Prisoner's Dilemma, 173; role of domestic politics in, 177; escalation concerns about, 193
Berlin Wall Crisis, 45–51; U.S. response to, 45; legal rights in, 45, 50, 81; and refugee problems, 46–47,

49–50, 109; relation of, to aide-memoire crisis, 47–49; and Vienna Summit (1961), 48–49; decision maker's views on origin of, 79–80; deliberate nature of, 104–8; unintended nature of, 122–24; termination of, 158–60; duration of, 183–85; and public opinion, 184–85; U.S. views on Soviet interests in, 195
Blainey, Geoffrey, 111, 145, 153, 168, 198
Blight, James G., 74, 162, 173, 179–80
Bohlen, Charles, 120
Bradley, Omar, 97
Brams, Steven J., 153
Brezhnev, Leonid, 77; and October 1973 War ceasefire, 12; and "ultimatum letter," 64, 92, 134, 165, 181; and U.S. overreaction during October 1973 War, 93, 138–39
Brinksmanship crises, 14, 114, 192
Bundy, McGeorge, 126, 199; and clarity of U.S. messages to Soviets about Cuba, 72; and missiles in Turkey, 90; and Berlin Wall Crisis, 124, 132, 158–59, 199; and Cuban Missile Crisis, 161–62, 165
Byrnes, James F., 36–37, 99, 103

Carroll, Joseph, 18
Carter, Jimmy, 3–4, 6
Castro, Fidel, 3, 57–58, 74–75, 90, 164
Catudal, Honore M., 107

"Chicken" games, 171–75; contrasted with Prisoner's Dilemma, 171–74; in Cuban Missile Crisis, 173; and crisis duration, 173–74; and nuclear weapons, 174; and October 1973 Middle East War, 181–82

Church, Frank, 3–4

CIA, 61, 74, 135

Clay, Lucius D., 42–44; and "baby blockade," 43; views of, on Soviet Union, 79, 94, 96–98, 157; and changes in Soviet intentions, 176–77; on termination of Berlin blockade, 193

Cognitive factors, 23–24, 70, 149

Cognitive dissonance, 22, 70, 149

Cold War, 28; origins of, 28, 35–37, 101; and Iranian Crisis (1946), 99

Crises: U.S.-Soviet, 7–8; definitions of, 8–11; international, 10–11; foreign policy, 11; intended, 11–15; unintended, 12–13, 112–15; brinksmanship, 14, 114, 192; as deliberate acts, 85–89, 192; justification of hostility, 114; spinoff, 114, 192. See also Crisis

Crisis: definition of, 8–11; international, 10–11; foreign policy, 11; termination of, 67, 95, 145–47, 169, 198–99; and perception change, 154–55, 169–70; duration of, 171–75; and loss of control, 179–80; role of nuclear weapons in, 187; role of conflict of interest in, 192. See also Crises

Crisis behavior: and shifting perceptions 6–8; role of individual in, 23–24; role of perceptions in, 23–26; information processing and, 147–51; and impact of increased stakes, 193–94

Cuban Brigade Crisis (1979), 2–5, 9, 29, 168

Cuban Missile Crisis, 51–59; revisionist accounts of, 14–15; influence of domestic politics on, 14–15, 57, 132– 33; role of subjective assessments in, 17–20; and "glasnost revelations," 51–53, 51n.59, 53n.61, 54n.62, 131; role of nuclear weapons in, 52, 165; and U.S. nuclear alert, 52–58; and OAS, 57; stages of, 58–59; decision makers' views on origin of, 71–76, 192; as deliberate crisis, 89–90; deliberate nature of, 89–91; legal aspects of, 90, 164n.42; unintended nature of, 125–133; and dispositional misperceptions, 126–27, 129–32; and situational misperceptions, 127–28; termination of, 160–65; as "Chicken," 177; duration of, 177–81; and perception change, 180–81

Decision makers: importance of views of, 19–20; views of, on origins of crisis, 67–71, 190–94; views of, on deliberate nature of crisis, 86–89, 194–95; and unintended crises, 112– 15, 195–98; and views in termination of crisis, 146–55, 198–99; role of views of, in duration of crisis, 171– 75, 199–201; impact of changing information on, 189–90

Decision making during crises, 24–26

Détente, 3, 28, 60, 91, 140

Diesing, Paul, 9, 68, 113, 146, 171–73

Dispositional misperceptions, 142–44, 196–98; definition of, 12, 23; and unintended crises, 12–13; role of new information in, 26–27; in Iranian Crisis, 115; in Cuban Missile Crisis, 126–27, 129–32; and information processing, 149–50, 198

Divine, Robert A., 52

Dobrynin, Anatolii, 58, 64, 91–92, 138, 163

Domestic politics: in Cuban Missile Crisis, 14–15, 57, 132–33; in Berlin Blockade, 177

Douglas, William O., 101

Dowty, Alan, 91

Dulles, Eleanor Lansing, 106
Dulles, John Foster, 27, 88

Ford, Gerald R., 17–18
Foreign policy crisis, 11
Forrestal, James F., 101, 102
Freedman, Robert O., 140
Fulbright, William, 50
Fundamental attribution error, 86

Game theory, 68–69, 152, 171–75
Garthoff, Raymond L., 20, 136
George, Alexander L., 128, 130, 132
Gilpatric, Roswell, 125
"Glasnost revelations," 51n.59, 53n.61, 54, 55n.66, 56, 131
Golan, Galia, 93
Gromyko, Anatolii, 56
Gromyko, Andrei, 90

Harriman, Averell, 103
Hermann, Charles F., 8, 11
Hilsman, Roger, 18, 128–29, 131
Hitler, Adolf, 21
Holsti, Ole R., 24, 25, 85
Horelick, Arnold L., 56, 131
"Hypotheses on Misperception," 83, 151, 190

Information processing, 6, 24, 25, 147–51; and dispositional misperceptions, 149–50; model of, 150; and situational misperceptions, 151–52
Intended crises, 11–15; and October 1973 Middle East War, 135–39
International crises, 10–11
Iranian Crisis of 1946, 31–40; and U.S. interests in Iran, 33–35; and Cold War origins, 35–37; role of United Nations in, 37–40; U.S. armed forces in, 39–40; decision makers' views on origin of, 81–83; deliberate nature of, 99–104; Soviet interests in, 100–103, 109, 195; impact of "Long Telegram" in, 101; revisionist views of,
104; role of dispositional misperceptions in, 115; role of situational misperceptions in, 115–16; unintended nature of, 115–18; as spinoff crisis, 117; termination of, 155–56; duration of, 185–86
Iraq, 31, 70, 81

Jabber, Paul, 138
Jackson, Henry, 3
Janis, Irving L., 22, 25
Jervis, Robert: on perceptions and crises, 17, 190, 194; and definition of misperception, 21; on perception change and new information, 26–27, 151; on actor's view of events, 67–68, 70, 83; and hostility of opponents, 85, 87; and views of opponent, 108, 194
Johnson, Lyndon B., 46, 81, 114

Kalb, Bernard, 64
Kalb, Marvin, 64
Kennan, George F., 101
Kennedy, John F.: and domestic politics and Cuban Missile Crisis, 14–15, 89; and "quarantine" and Cuban Missile Crisis, 19–20; and Berlin Wall Crisis, 46, 48–51, 158–59, 183–85; and Vienna Summit, 46, 48–49; and Cuban Missile Crisis, 54–58, 90, 163–65, 168, 180; on clarity of messages to Khrushchev, 73, 192–93; and "defensive weapons" in Cuba, 76; on Soviet role in Berlin Wall Crisis, 80–81, 104–8; on Soviet role in Cuban Missile Crisis, 87, 126; on U.S. interests in West Berlin, 104–8, 124; Soviet views of, 130–33; on missiles in Turkey, 181
Kennedy, Robert F., 73, 178, 193
Khrushchev, Nikita: and Berlin Wall Crisis, 46–49, 80, 160; on dangers of misperception, 53; and Cuban Missile Crisis, 55–58, 154, 165, 173; on

Khrushchev, Nikita (*continued*)
"defensive weapons" in Cuba, 76,
126; on U.S. overreaction to Cuba,
90, 179–80; views of President Kennedy, 130–31
Kimmel, Husband E., 21–23
Kissinger, Henry A., 12, 192, 200; and
October 1973 War cease-fire, 62–65,
133–34; on Soviet views of U.S., 71;
and U.S. response to Soviet moves,
76–77, 91–92; and relations with Israel, 136; and crisis warnings to Soviet Union, 138; and views of Soviet
actions, 140–41, 167, 181–82
Kolkowicz, Roman, 56, 138
Korean War, 13–14
Kosygin, Aleksei, 62, 93
Kuniholm, Bruce Robellet, 101
Kuwait, 70–71, 81, 191–92

LaFeber, Walter, 103
Lebow, Richard Ned: crisis definition
of, 9; and spinoff crises, 12, 109,
117, 192, 195; and brinksmanship
crises, 14; and definition of misperception, 21; and types of crises, 114;
and perception change in crises, 146
LeMay, Curtis E., 42
Lenczowski, George, 102, 156
Lie, Trygve, 37–38
London Times *Insight Team*, 61

McCone, John, 126
Macmillan, Harold, 48
McNamara, Robert, 14, 15, 17, 18, 132
Mann, Leon, 22, 25
Marshall, George, 44, 94–96, 119
Marshall Plan, 94–95, 119
May, Ernest, 6
Minshall, William E., 17–18
Minor, Harold, 34
Molotov, Vyacheslav, 100, 103
Misperception: and Cuban Brigade Cri-
sis, 2–5, 6; dispositional, definition
of: 12, 23; situational, definition of:
12, 22–23; role of individual in, 15–

20; and claims of self-defense, 16;
subjective nature of, 17–18; definition of, 21–22; and unintended
crises, 114–15; testing for situational
and dispositional, 151–52; impact of,
on decision making, 189; as affected
by new information, 190. *See also*
Perception
Murphy, Robert, 44, 79, 98, 157

Nash equilibrium, 153
Neustadt, Richard E., 6
Nisbett, Richard, 150
Nixon, Richard M., 59, 65, 91–92, 200
Nuclear weapons: and Iranian Crisis,
39, 39n.24; and Cuban Missile Crisis, 52, 165; and October 1973 Middle East War, 60, 65, 141–42, 182–
83; and "Chicken," 174; impact of,
on crisis duration, 187

October 1973 Middle East War, 12, 27,
59–65, 89; role of nuclear weapons
in, 60, 65, 141–42, 182–83; and
U.S. airlift, 62; cease-fire in, 62–64;
and U.S. nuclear alert, 64–65, 77,
135–37, 139–41, 165; decision
makers' views on origins of, 76–77,
192; deliberate nature of, 91–93; unintended nature of, 133–42; and situational misperceptions, 135, 139–41;
as intended crisis, 135–39; as unintended crisis, 139–41, 166; termination of, 165–68, 200; as Prisoner's
Dilemma and Chicken, 181–82; duration of, 181–83
O'Donnell, Kenneth P., 106, 159
Oneal, John R., 36, 39
Organization of American States (OAS),
57, 131, 164

Perception, 5–8; role of, in crises, 1;
and changes in information, 5–6, 26–
27; and crisis termination, 145–47,
199; change in, and crisis duration,
173–74; change in, and Cuban Mis-

sile Crisis, 180–81; change in, and October 1973 War, 182–83. *See also* Misperception
Pope, Ronald R., 75
Powers, David F., 106, 159
Prisoner's Dilemma, 68–69, 171–75; and Berlin Blockade Crisis, 173; impact of, on crisis duration, 173–74; and October 1973 Middle East War, 181–82
Proposition Five ("duration of crises"), 171–75, 199–201; and Berlin Blockade Crisis, 175–77; and Cuban Missile Crisis, 177–81; and October 1973 Middle East War, 181–83; and Berlin Wall Crisis, 183–85; and Iranian Crisis, 185–86
Proposition Four ("termination of crises"), 146–55, 198–99; and Iranian Crisis, 155–56; and Berlin Blockade Crisis, 156–58; and Berlin Wall Crisis, 158–60; and Cuban Missile Crisis, 160–65; and October 1973 Middle East War, 165–68
Proposition One ("decision maker's views on origins of crisis"), 67–71, 190–94; and Cuban Missile Crisis, 72–76; and October 1973 Middle East War, 76–77; and Berlin Blockade Crisis, 77–79; and Berlin Wall Crisis, 80–81; and Iranian Crisis, 81–83
Proposition Three ("unintended nature of crises"), 112–15, 195–98; and Iranian Crisis, 115–18; and Berlin Blockade Crisis, 118–22; and Berlin Wall Crisis, 122–24; and Cuban Missile Crisis, 125–33; and October 1973 Middle East War, 139–41
Proposition Two ("deliberate nature of crises"), 86–89, 194–95; and Cuban Missile Crisis, 89–91; and October 1973 Middle East War, 91–93; and Berlin Blockade Crisis, 94–99; and Iranian Crisis, 103–4; and Berlin Wall Crisis, 104–8

Propositions, summary of, 190–201
Public opinion, 36, 104; and Soviet Union, 35–37; and origins of Cold War, 36–37; and Berlin Wall, 184–85

Qavam, Amhad, 103

Reagan, Ronald, 7
Refugee Crisis (Berlin): 46, 48–51, 106, 109, 122, 158, 195
Ross, Lee, 150
Rossow, Robert Jr., 102–3, 116
Rubinstein, Alvin Z., 120
Rush, Myron, 131
Rusk, Dean, 58, 163

Sadat, Anwar, 91, 134, 136–37; and October 1973 Middle East cease-fire, 62–63, 76, 91, 134, 136, 137
"Salami tactics," 122
Scali, John, 138, 141
Schelling, Thomas C., 10, 145, 173–74
Schema theory, 148–49
Scherer, John L., 141, 182
Schlesinger, Arthur M., Jr., 123
Shaver, Kelly G., 87
Shlaim, Avi, 96, 175
Situational misperception, 142–44, 196–98; definition of, 12, 22–23; and impact of new information on, 26–27; and Iranian Crisis, 115–16; and Berlin Wall Crisis, 124; and Cuban Missile Crisis, 127–29; and October 1973 Middle East War, 135, 139–41; and information processing, 151–52, 189
Slusser, Robert M., 81
Smith, Jean Edward, 106–7
Smoke, Richard, 128, 130, 132
Snyder, Glenn H., 9, 68, 113, 146, 171–73
Sorensen, Theodore C., 126, 158, 159, 184
Soviet Union: and Iranian Crisis of 1946, 34, 38; U.S. public opinion and, 35–37; and Berlin Blockade Cri-

Soviet Union (*continued*)
  sis, 41–43; and Berlin Wall Crisis,
  47–49, 123–24; and Cuban Missile
  Crisis, 57–59; and October 1973
  Middle East War, 62–65
Spinoff crises, 12, 109–10, 114, 144,
  192, 195; and Iranian Crisis, 117
Stalin, Joseph, 120; misperceptions of,
  about Germany, 21–22; and Iranian
  Crisis of 1946, 32, 37, 39, 103; and
  threats on Berlin, 47; and beginning
  of Cold War, 100–101
Strategic Air Command (SAC), 52, 74,
  193
Stress, decision making and, 17, 24–
  25, 85, 88, 175
Suedfeld, Peter, 25

Tatu, Michel, 56, 74, 163, 179, 180
Tetlock, Phillip E., 25
Thompson, Llewelyn, 48
Trachtenberg, Marc, 55
Truman Doctrine (1947), 35
Truman, Harry S., 35; on Soviet Union
  and Iran, 38; and Berlin Blockade
  Crisis, 41–42, 44, 94–95; and Ira-
  nian Crisis, 99, 103–4; and Korean
  War, 184

Ulam, Adam B., 118, 120–22
Unintended crises, 12–14, 202; definition of, 12; occurrence of, 12–13;
  magnitude of, 13–14; and misperceptions, 114–15; and Iranian Crisis,
  115–18; and Berlin Blockade Crisis,
  119–22; and Berlin Wall Crisis, 122–
  24; and Cuban Missile Crisis, 125–
  33; and October 1973 Middle East
  War, 139–41, 166
United Nations: and Korean War, 13;
  and Iranian Crisis, 33, 35–39, 83,
  100, 186; post–World War II hopes
  for, 36–37; and October 1973 Middle
  East War, 63, 92

Vance, Cyrus, 3

War, accidental, 111–12
Welch, David A., 74
West Germany, 49, 107, 109, 120, 160,
  195
Whiting, Allen S., 13
Wohlstetter, Roberta, 75, 129

Yergin, Daniel, 104, 120